CROWDS AND PARTY

CROWDS
AND
PARTY

JODI DEAN

VERSO
London • New York

First published by Verso 2016
© Jodi Dean 2016

1 3 5 7 9 10 8 6 4 2

Verso
UK: 6 Meard Street, London W1F 0EG
US: 20 Jay Street, Suite 1010, Brooklyn, NY 11201
versobooks.com

Verso is the imprint of New Left Books

ISBN-13: 978-1-78168-694-2
eISBN-13: 978-1-78168-672-0 (US)
eISBN-13: 978-1-78168-766-6 (UK)

British Library Cataloguing in Publication Data
A catalogue record for this book is available from the British Library

Library of Congress Cataloging-in-Publication Data
A catalog record for this book is available from the Library of Congress

Typeset in Fournier by MJ & N Gavan, Truro, Cornwall
Printed in the US by Maple Press

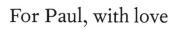

For Paul, with love

Contents

Acknowledgements

Writing is solitary. Thinking is collective. I am grateful to the many who extended the time, support, and critical energy that went into this book. Numerous comrades demonstrated solidarity with my project in multiple ways—alerting me to relevant texts, engaging my arguments in various media, providing new opportunities, pushing me to be clearer, bolder, disagreeing. These include but are not limited to Maria Aristodemou, Darin Barney, Tamara d'Auvergne, Donatella Della Ratta, Liza Featherstone, Jon Flanders, Doug Henwood, Bonnie Honig, Penelope Ironstone, Jason Jones, Andreas Kalyvas, Anna Kornbluh, Regina Kreide, Elena Loizidou, Davide Panagia, Korinna Patelis, Alexei Penzin, Artemy Magun, Joe Mink, Joe Ramsey, Kirsty M. Robertson, Corey Robin, John Seery, Joshua Sperber, Mina Suk, and Phillip Wegner.

I want to thank the Society for the Humanities at Cornell University for the Fellowship that enabled me to draft the book's early chapters. I appreciate the critical responses from the Society's 2013–2014 Fellows as well as the feedback from the Government Department's Political Theory Workshop. I am particularly indebted to Jason Frank, Anna-Marie Smith, Jason E. Smith, Becquer Seguin, and Avery Slater for their close readings of these chapters. The Society for the Humanities also provided generous support for the Fall 2013 conference, "Communist Currents," that I co-organized with Jason Smith and Bruno Bosteels. The conversations in and around this conference, as well as the resulting symposium published in *South Atlantic Quarterly*, were invaluable critical stimuli for *Crowds and Party*. Thanks go to Banu Bargu, Aaron Benanav, Bruno Bosteels, George Ciccariello-Maher, Joshua Clover, Susana Draper, James Martel, Sandro Mezzadra, Brett Neilson, Jordana Rosenberg, Alessandro Russo, Anna-Marie Smith, Jason Smith, Alberto Toscano, and Gavin Walker. Thanks as well to Michael Hardt for encouraging and publishing the symposium.

Additional opportunities to present chapter drafts helped me clarify my arguments. Thank you to the organizers, participants, and respondents at Johns Hopkins, Columbia, the University of Chicago, the Marxist Literary Group, the New School, and the CUNY Graduate Center and to fellow panelists and interlocutors at the 2015 Western Political Science Association Annual Meeting and American Political Science Annual Meeting. Thanks as well to comrades with Philly Socialists.

Special thanks go to Hannah Dickinson and Rob Maclean for their thoughtful commentaries and suggestions. I am also deeply indebted to James Martel, not just for his close reading of the entire manuscript but also for his ongoing enthusiastic—and critical—engagement with my project. Kian Kenyon-Dean and Sadie Kenyon-Dean continue to inspire and provoke. Finally, I am grateful to Paul A. Passavant for his careful readings, our ongoing discussions, and the form of life we make together.

Introduction

On October 15, 2011, a massive crowd filled New York's Times Square. Most were Occupiers, demonstrating in concert with anti-capitalist protests in nine hundred cities around the world. October 15 was also the five-month anniversary of Spain's movement to occupy the squares. Half a million people came out in Madrid. Riots broke out in Rome. In Times Square, nearly thirty thousand people blocked traffic as mounted police pushed them up against quickly set-up barricades. Tourists caught in the crush joined the Occupiers in chanting "We are the 99 percent."

I had been separated from my group at Sixth Avenue when police started blocking streets to prevent more people from joining up with the protest. I made my way through to a small traffic island at Broadway and Forty-Third. A couple of shoppers, crammed up against those of us with signs, excitedly asked whether we were going to occupy Times Square. They added that they supported Occupy Wall Street and were glad that someone was finally doing something. Together we booed the police when they dragged off protesters who ventured beyond the barricades.

That fall Occupy Wall Street was the most important thing in the world.[1] Occupations were rising up everywhere.[2] On the New York City subways, passengers read the *Occupy Gazette* and the *Occupied Wall Street Journal*. People praised the Occupiers and condemned the police. We all wondered how far we could go. Would it be, as *Adbusters* had urged in an initial call for the occupation of Wall Street, our Tahrir moment?

After the Times Square demonstration, many of us proceeded down to Washington Square Park for a general assembly (GA). The general assembly was a primary organizational form during the Occupy movement. Prominent in the Spanish demonstrations and indebted to the horizontalism and autonomy of movement practices in Argentina and Mexico, the GA structures discussion according to democratic egalitarian principles aiming toward consensus. By the time I arrived in Washington Square Park, what looked like a thousand people were sitting in a circle near the park's center. Multiple police vans lined the curb just outside the park's fence on lower Fifth Avenue. A few barricades were scattered near the Washington Square Arch. Twenty or thirty police stood around faux-casually. Over the next few hours, they would close in to form a line.

At the GA, people were debating whether we would "take the park." Some had brought tents and sleeping bags with an eye to spreading the occupation from Zuccotti to Washington Square. Zuccotti Park, renamed "Liberty Square" during the occupation, had rapidly become overcrowded. Although its proximity to Wall Street gave it enormous symbolic value, its location on the edge of New York's financial district was inconvenient. The local fast food restaurants had been accommodating, even welcoming, but the paucity of nearby toilet and shower facilities was taking its toll on the hundreds of Occupiers sleeping in the park. In contrast,

---

1   Naomi Klein, "Occupy Wall Street: The Most Important Thing in the World Now," *The Nation*, Oct. 6, 2011.

2   Paul Mason, *Why It's Kicking Off Everywhere: The New Global Revolutions*, London: Verso, 2012.

Washington Square Park is next to New York University, close to the New School and Cooper Union, easily reachable by subway, and, all in all, in a popular, visible, heavily trafficked part of the city.

We knew that Washington Square Park was closing at midnight. We felt the police tightening their line, starting to deny newcomers entry to the park. After the fifteen-minute or so breakout session where we talked with those around us about taking the park, we pulled back together as one assembly. Speaker after speaker, amplified by the People's Mic (where the crowd repeats the words of a speaker so that those who are farther away know what is being said), urged us to take the park. *We are many. We outnumber them. We can do it. We must do it.* Upraised hands twinkled approval in waves of support round and round the circle. Then, a tall, thin, young man with curly dark hair and a revolutionary look began to speak.

> We can take this park!
> *We can take this park!*
> We can take this park tonight!
> *We can take this park tonight!*
> We can also take this park another night.
> *We can also take this park another night.*
> Not everyone may be ready tonight.
> *Not everyone may be ready tonight.*
> Each person has to make their own autonomous decision.
> *Each person has to make their own autonomous decision.*
> No one can decide for you. You have to decide for yourself.
> *No one can decide for you. You have to decide for yourself.*
> Everyone is an autonomous individual.
> *Everyone is an autonomous individual.*

The mood was broken. The next few speakers also affirmed their individuality, describing some of the problems they would encounter if they had to deal with security from NYU or if they got arrested. We were no longer a "we," a collective. Asserting ourselves as individuals, we became individuated, concerned first with our own particular preoccupations. Collective strength devolved into the problem of individuals aggregating by choices and interests that may or may not converge. Reducing autonomy to individual decision, we destroyed the freedom of action we had as a crowd.

Crowds and Party comes out of this moment of collective de-subjectivation. Occupy Wall Street foundered against a contradiction at its core. The individualism of its democratic, anarchist, and horizontalist ideological currents undermined the collective power the movement was building. Making collective political action dependent on individual choice, the "theology of consensus" fragmented the provisional unity of the crowd back into disempowered singularities.[3] The movement's decline (which began well before Occupiers were evicted) exposes the impasse confronting the Left. The celebration of autonomous individuality prevents us from foregrounding our commonality and organizing ourselves politically.

At the same time and together with the global wave of popular unrest, the collective energy of Occupy at its height nevertheless points to an "idea whose time has come." People are moving together in growing opposition to the policies and practices of states organized in the interest of capital as a class. Crowds are forcing the Left to return again to questions of organization, endurance, and scale. Through what political forms might we advance? For many of us, the party is emerging as the site of an answer.

Against the presumption that the individual is the fundamental unit of politics, I focus on the crowd. Across the globe, crowds are pressing their opposition and rupturing the status quo, the actuality of their movement displacing the politics of identity. Bringing

---

3   L. A. Kaufman, "The Theology of Consensus," *Berkeley Journal of Sociology*, May 26, 2015.

together thinkers such as Elias Canetti and Alain Badiou, I highlight the "egalitarian discharge" of the crowd event as an intense experience of substantive collectivity. I make fidelity to this event the basis for a new theory of the communist party. Because global movements are themselves pushing us to consider the possibilities in and of the party form, we have to recommence imagining the party of communists.[4] Who might we be and become as an international revolutionary party again, *in our time*? To think clearly about these questions, we need to consider the party form unfettered by the false concreteness of specific parties in the contingency of their histories. Liberals and democrats are not the only political theorists who can reflect on their modes of association in the abstract. Communists must do this as well.

As a means of breaking out of the binaries of reform or revolution, mass or vanguard party that historically have inflected discussions of the party form, I approach the function and purpose of the communist party psycho-dynamically. I draw from Robert Michels and Jacques Lacan to think through the affects the party generates and the unconscious processes it mobilizes. The role of the party isn't to inject knowledge into the working class. Nor is it to represent the interests of the working class on the terrain of politics. Rather, the function of the party is to hold open a gap in our setting so as to enable a collective desire for collectivity.[5] "Through such a gap or moment," Daniel Bensaïd writes, "can arise the unaccomplished fact, which contradicts the fatality of the accomplished fact."[6] The crowd's breach of the predictable and

---

4 Compelling versions of this argument are made by Peter D. Thomas, "The Communist Hypothesis and the Question of Organization," Gavin Walker, "The Body of Politics: On the Concept of the Party," and Jason E. Smith, "Contemporary Struggles and the Question of the Party: A Reply to Gavin Walker," *Theory & Event* 16: 4, Winter 2013.

5 For an account of communist desire in terms of the collective desire for collectivity see my *The Communist Horizon*, London: Verso, 2012.

6 Daniel Bensaïd, "Leaps! Leaps! Leaps!" in *Lenin Reloaded*, eds.

given creates the possibility that a political subject might appear. The party steps into that breach and fights to keep it open for the people.

Canetti makes a point I return to throughout the book: crowds come together for the sake of an absolute equality felt most intensely in a moment he refers to as the "discharge." Akin to Lacan's notion of "enjoyment" ("*jouissance*," the only substance known to psychoanalysis), the discharge provides a material ground for the party. The party is a body that can carry the egalitarian discharge after the crowds disperse, channeling its divisive promise of justice into organized political struggle.

Crowds

In the opening decades of the twenty-first century, crowds have disrupted the settings given by capital and the state. Breaking with the suffocating reflexivity of contribution and critique in the mediated networks of communicative capitalism, insistent crowds impress themselves where they don't belong. Their very presence challenges the privatization of ostensibly public places from São Paulo, to Istanbul, to New York. Intense and temporary aggregations in multiple locations now appear as one struggle. We see Montreal connected to Athens connected to Tahrir Square connected to Madrid connected to Oakland. Instead of the incommunicable strikes of a multitude of singularities, crowds and riots in place after place communicate the collective movement of the people, pushing questions of similarity, meaning, and alliance: of what politics will the crowd have been the subject?

Some contemporary crowd observers claim the crowd for democracy. They see in the amassing of thousands a democratic insistence, a demand to be heard and included. In the context of

Sebastian Budgen, Stathis Kouvelakis, and Slavoj Žižek, Durham, NC: Duke University Press, 2007, 148–63, 158.

communicative capitalism, however, the crowd exceeds democracy. Communicative capitalism reconfigures the relation between crowds, democracy, capitalism, and class. On the one hand, the democratic reading of the crowd blocks these changes from view. It harnesses the crowd into the service of the very setting that the crowd disrupts. On the other hand, the democratic reading opens up a struggle over the subject of politics: the determination whether a crowd is the people or the mob.

In the nineteenth and twentieth centuries, the crowd posed questions of power and order. "The crowd—" Walter Benjamin writes, "no subject was more entitled to the attention of nineteenth century writers."[7] At the time, the crowd appears as a quintessential political expression of the people.[8] Inseparable from the rise of mass democracy, the crowd looms with the threat of the collective power of the masses, the force of the many against those who would exploit, control, and disperse them. Whether feared or embraced, the flood, intrusion, or crush of crowds thrusts the collective many into history.

Commentators wanting to keep the people in their place warn against "the extraordinary rebellion of the masses."[9] They depict crowds as brutal, primitive, even criminal, mobs. In contrast, commentators seeking the overthrow of the elites champion the crowd's political vitality. Workers, peasants, and commoners of

---

7   Walter Benjamin, "On Some Motifs in Baudelaire," in *Illuminations*, ed. Hannah Arendt, New York: Schocken Books, 1978, 166.

8   But not only in the nineteenth and twentieth centuries. There is a vibrant historical literature on pre-industrial and revolutionary crowds, some of the best of which comes from the British Marxist Historians group. See, for example, George Rudé, *Ideology and Popular Protest*, Chapel Hill, NC: University of North Carolina Press, 1995; and E. J. Hobsbawm, *Primitive Rebels*, New York: Norton, 1959. For a recent engagement with the post-revolutionary US American crowd, see Jason Frank, *Constituent Moments*, Durham, NC: Duke University Press, 2010.

9   José Ortega y Gasset, *The Revolt of the Masses*, New York: Norton, 1932. Original Spanish publication in 1930.

every sort are recognizing and asserting themselves as sovereign. Marx famously describes the crowds of the Paris Commune as the people "storming heaven." For nineteenth- and twentieth-century observers, then, crowds and popular democracy are intertwined. At issue is whether the sovereignty of the people can be anything other than mob rule.

A benefit of the democratic reading of the crowd is its revelation of a split: the mob or the people. The crowd forces the possibility of the intrusion of the people into politics. Whether the people is the subject of a crowd event is up for grabs. The crowd opens up a site of struggle over its subject. A crowd might have been a mob, not an event at all. It might have been a predictable, legitimate gathering, again, not an event but an affirmation of its setting. And it might have the people rising up in pursuit of justice.[10] Which a crowd event is, or, better, which it will have been, is an effect of the political process the crowd event activates. The crowd does not have a politics. It is the opportunity for politics. The determination whether a crowd was a mob or the people results from political struggle.

Resisting for a while the urge to classify crowds in terms of a pre-given political content enables us to consider crowds in terms of their dynamics. Crowds are more than large numbers of people concentrated in a location. They are effects of collectivity, the influence—whether conscious, affective, or unconscious—of others.[11] Contemporary social science analyzes these effects with terms like "band-wagoning," "bubbles," and "information cascades." Mainstream commentary continues to use terms from earlier crowd theory: "imitation," "suggestion," and "contagion."

The most influential early crowd theorist is Gustave Le Bon. His widely reprinted and translated book, *The Crowd: A Study of*

---

10   As I explain in *The Communist Horizon*, this is a divisive vision of the people as the rest of us.

11   See Teresa Brennan, *The Transmission of Affect*, Ithaca, NY: Cornell University Press, 2004.

the Popular Mind, laid the groundwork for twentieth-century the-
orization of crowds. I engage Sigmund Freud's take up of Le Bon
as Freud formulates a psychoanalytic theory of group psychology. Benito Mussolini also found Le Bon inspiring, particularly Le
Bon's discussion of the leader.[12] But we need not follow Mussolini
into such a narrow focus. The emphasis on the leader displaces our
attention from what is ingenious in Le Bon's notion of the crowd,
namely, his rendering of the crowd as a "provisional being formed
of heterogeneous elements."

Le Bon presents the crowd as a distinct form of collectivity.
The crowd is not a community. It doesn't rely on traditions. It
doesn't have a history. The crowd is not held together by unstated
norms or an obscene supplement that extends beyond its own
immediacy (although crowd images and symbols clearly shape the
reception and circulation of crowd events).[13] Rather, the crowd
is a temporary collective being. It holds itself together affectively via imitation, contagion, suggestion, and a sense of its own
invincibility. Because the crowd is a collective being, it cannot
be reduced to singularities. On the contrary, the primary characteristic of a crowd is its operation as a force of its own, like an
organism. The crowd is more than an aggregate of individuals. It
is individuals changed through the torsion of their aggregation,
the force aggregation exerts back on them to do together what is
impossible alone.

The democratic claim for the crowd was powerful in the
nineteenth and twentieth centuries. Democracy could name an
opposition. Even as communists registered the limits of bourgeois democracy in its use as an instrument of capitalist class rule,

---

12 Simonetta Falasca-Zamponi, *Fascist Spectacle*, Berkeley, CA: University of California Press, 1997, 21.

13 Christian Borch provides a history of sociology structured as a history
of "crowd semantics," that is, an analysis of the crowd as a theoretical concept
in sociology. See his *The Politics of Crowds: An Alternative History of Sociology*,
New York: Cambridge University Press, 2012.

democracy could still register a challenge to existing structures of power. In the twenty-first century, however, dominant nation-states exercise power as democracies. They bomb and invade as democracies for democracy's sake. International political bodies legitimize themselves as democratic, as do the contradictory entangled media practices of communicative capitalism.[14] When crowds amass in opposition, they poise themselves against democratic practices, systems, and bodies. To claim the crowd for democracy fails to register this change in the political setting of the crowd.

Democratic governments justify themselves as rule by the people. When crowds gather in opposition, they expose the limits of this justification. The will of the majority expressed in elections stops appearing as the will of the people. That not-all of the people support this government or those decisions becomes openly, physically, intensely manifest.[15] Disagreement and opposition start to do more than circulate as particular contributions to the production of nuggets of shareable outrage in the never-ending flow of clickbait in which we drown one another. They index collective power, the affective generativity that exceeds individual opinions. Many press back, using the strength of embodied number to install a gap in the dominant order. They make apparent its biases, compromises, and underlying investments in protecting the processes through which the capitalist class accumulates wealth. They

14   For a more detailed discussion of communicative capitalism see my *Publicity's Secret*, Ithaca, NY: Cornell University Press, 2002; *Democracy and Other Neoliberal Fantasies*, Durham, NC: Duke University Press, 2009; and *Blog Theory*, Cambridge, UK: Polity Press, 2010.

15   In his account of the idea and image of crowds in late nineteenth- and early twentieth-century Europe, Stefan Jonsson presents the mass as an effect of representation, more particularly of the problem of representing "socially significant passions" and the structuring of the social field via a distinction between representatives and the represented. See his *Crowds and Democracy: The Idea and Image of the Masses from Revolution to Fascism*, New York: Columbia University Press, 2013, 26.

expose the fragility of the separations and boxes upholding electoral politics. The crowd reclaims for the people the political field democracy would try to fragment and manage.

Under communicative capitalism, the democratic claim for the crowd reinforces and is reinforced by the hegemony of ideals of decentralization and self-organization. Early crowd theorists describe the crowd as primitive, violent, and suggestible. In our present context, these descriptions are often inverted as "smart mobs" and the "wisdom of crowds."[16] Such inversions appropriate the crowd, enlisting it in support of capitalism as they strip away its radical political potential.

Business writers like James Surowiecki, for example, talk about the crowd in terms of collective intelligence.[17] Surowiecki's primary interest is in how to harness this intelligence, which he treats as information compiled from diverse and independent sources. His claim is that a crowd of self-interested people working on the same problem separately in a decentralized way will come up with the best solution. Cognitive diversity is key, necessary for avoiding imitation and groupthink (necessary, in other words, for blocking the affective binding-together of a provisional collective being). Surowiecki's exemplary crowds are corporations, markets, and intelligence agencies. Their wisdom depends on mechanisms like prices and systems that are able "to generate lots of losers and then to recognize them as such and kill them off."[18] In actuality, Surowiecki's crowds are not so much crowds as they are data pools. He can treat the crowd as wise because he has condensed it into information, dispersed it into individual heads, and re-aggregated it under conditions that use the many to benefit the few. Aggregation, Surowiecki admits, is decentralization's paradoxical partner.

---

16   Howard Rheingold, *Smart Mobs*, New York: Basic Books, 2002.
17   James Surowiecki, *The Wisdom of Crowds*, New York: Doubleday, 2004.
18   Surowiecki, 29.

Eugene W. Holland commandeers Surowiecki's claims for the wisdom of crowds in his attempt to envision a free-market communism.[19] Holland wants to show the plausibility of horizontal, bottom-up, decentralized, and self-organized social organization. Jazz, soccer, the internet, and markets all demonstrate, Holland argues, how group members adapt themselves to one another in the absence of top-down coordination. There are limits to these examples as social models. When playing, musicians and soccer players know and accept that they are involved in a common endeavor.[20] A performance and a game necessarily restrict who and how many people can play. Jazz and soccer don't scale. Further, and more fundamentally, Holland ignores the unavoidable production of inequality on the internet and in markets. Concerned with avoiding anything that smacks of state power, he neglects the extreme division between the one and the many that arises immanently. Self-organization in complex networks doesn't guarantee horizontality. In fact, it produces hierarchy.

The clearest exposition of the constituent role of inequality in complex networks comes from Albert-László Barabási.[21] Complex networks are networks characterized by free choice, growth, and preferential attachment. Free markets and the internet are prime examples. Complex networks have a specific structure, a "power-law distribution" of the items in the network. The most popular node or item in the network generally has twice as many links as the second most popular, which has more than the third most popular, and so on, such that there is very little difference among the crowd of those at the bottom but massive differences between top and

19   Eugene W. Hollland, *Nomad Citizenship*, Minneapolis, MN: University of Minnesota Press, 2011.

20   Kian Kenyon-Dean uses high school band as a compelling counterexample. Unlike the jazz ensemble unified through the music, high school band is typically divided into at least three groups: band geeks that want to play, the resistant disrupters, and the indifferent. See "Social Force," *Graphite*, May 26, 2015.

21   Albert-László Barabási, *Linked*, Philadelphia, PA: Perseus, 2002.

bottom. This is the structure that produces blockbuster movies, best-selling novels, and giant internet hubs. The idea appears in popular media as the "80/20 rule," the winner-take-all or winner-take-most character of the economy and the "long tail."[22]

In these examples, the "one" in first place emerges through the generation of a common field. These commons can be generated in a variety of ways: in comments on a post (think of Reddit and the ways that readers vote posts up and down; Holland's examples are Slashdot and Kuro5hin), in web articles (think *Huffington Post* blogs or other sites offering lots of clickbait), on Twitter (via hashtags), and through competitions (think of contests for the best city tourism app), to use but a few examples. The contest generates a common field that will produce a winner. The more participation there is—the larger the field—the greater becomes the inequality, that is to say, the greater is the difference between the one and the many. Expanding the field produces the one.

Holland, like so many advocates of self-organization, ignores the structure that free choice, growth, and preferential attachment produce. Using Wikipedia to illustrate his point, Holland emphasizes the equality of Wikipedians.[23] Clay Shirky, however, notes that "the spontaneous division of labor driving Wikipedia wouldn't be possible if there were concern for reducing inequality. On the contrary, most large social experiments are engines for harnessing inequality rather than limiting it."[24] The so-called wisdom of crowds doesn't spontaneously generate a free and equitable order. And *contra* Holland, networked experiments in decentralized self-organization don't lead in the direction of de-hierarchicized social change but rather toward ever more extreme differentiation between the few and many. Networked commu-

---

22 The term "long tail" comes from Chris Anderson. For a longer discussion of power laws and the long tail, see my discussion in *The Communist Horizon*.

23 Holland, 88.

24 Clay Shirky, *Here Comes Everybody*, New York: Penguin, 2008, 125.

nication doesn't eliminate hierarchy. It entrenches hierarchy by using our own choices against us.

Although it may seem far removed from the brutal mob of the nineteenth century, the twenty-first century's wise crowd is similar in one crucial respect: both attempt to prevent the crowd from introducing a gap through which the people can appear. Depictions of primitive and atavistic crowds in the nineteenth century naturalize their disparagement and repression. Social order and mob rule are antithetical. These people don't belong in politics. They are not *the people* with a divisive claim to justice. Twenty-first century evocations of the wisdom of crowds like Surowiecki's and Holland's likewise efface the crowd gap, this time absorbing it into idealized market and networked processes. Militant, disruptive, political crowds become so many self-organizing units, the self-interests of which naturally converge. Nineteenth-century treatments of the crowd as a mob acknowledge antagonism, but try to prevent it from being linked to the people. Twenty-first century versions of smart mobs deny antagonism altogether, substituting the interactions of individuals and small groups for organized political struggle. Surowiecki and Holland try to ensure that these interactions don't coalesce into provisional heterogeneous beings but remain differentiated singularities. Each rejects imitation, a basic crowd dynamic, Surowiecki to avoid bubbles and riots, Holland to guarantee difference. They may use the term "crowds," but their crowds neither become collective beings nor force a gap. In the complex networks of communicative capitalism, the so-called "wisdom of crowds" isn't a matter of the intrusion of the many into politics. It's the generation and circulation of the many in order to produce the one.

Crowd Struggle Is Class Struggle

Not all crowds install a gap. The networks of communicative capitalism generate and rely on crowds, that is, massive pools of many.

State and capital try to keep them in check, to absorb them back into the state of things, into the incessant circulation of spectacles we collectively produce for the private accumulation of the few. For example, when the 2009 protests following Iran's presidential election were described as the "Twitter Revolution" and the 2011 overthrow of Egyptian president Hosni Mubarak was called the "Facebook Revolution," the disruptive acts of a revolutionary people were inscribed into a US-centric technophilic imaginary. The crowd opening was subsumed into communicative capitalism, proffered as more evidence of the liberatory character of the networked media practices that support and extend economic inequality. The question of the crowd's politics, what it was for or against, *what in fact was going on*, was subsumed under the story of masses using media. The story confirmed to those with smartphones and laptops that nothing different was happening here. It's all the same activity, just in a different place.

At the same time, the terms "Twitter Revolution" and "Facebook Revolution" mark these social media platforms as crowd fora. Twitter and Facebook are not just tools. They are manifestations of the affective intensities associated with crowds—cascade effects, enthusiasm, band-wagoning, contagion, and imitation. To describe revolutions in terms of their platforms is to imply that the networked crowd may incite an anti-capitalist, even communist, collective political subject, the revolt of the many against the few. Put in the vocabulary of dialectics, crowds can become "in and for themselves." Capitalists know this—and fear it. Consider the warning from a business writer advising companies how they can leverage the creative power of the crowd to cut costs. He admits that even though people will work for free, they "will want a sense of ownership over their contributions" and may "develop proprietary feelings over the company itself."[25] This business writer is expressing in capitalist terms the Marxist insight that people will

25 Jeff Howe, *Crowdsourcing*, New York: Crown Business, 2008, 181.

start to become conscious of the disconnect between their work and someone else's ownership of their work. At a moment when twenty-first-century capitalists are lauding the wisdom of crowds and celebrating crowd-sourcing as the future of business, to say "Twitter Revolution" and "Facebook Revolution" is to broach the possibility that the posting and sharing many could seize the means of communications.

Mainstream commentators on the last decade of protests have thus been right to link them to ubiquitous communication networks. But they are wrong when they imply that protests are occurring because people can easily coordinate with social media, that they are primarily struggles for democracy, or that they are indications of a push for freedom on the part of networked individuals.[26] The crowds and riots of the last decade—particularly those associated with the Occupy movement, Chilean student protests, Montreal debt protests, Brazilian transportation and FIFA protests, European anti-austerity protests, as well as the multiple ongoing and intermittent strikes of teachers, civil servants, and medical workers all over the world—are protests of the class of those proletarianized under communicative capitalism. These are not struggles of the multitude, struggles for democracy, or struggles specific to local contexts. Nor are they merely the defensive struggles of a middle class facing cuts to social services, wage stagnation, unemployment, foreclosure, and indebtedness. They are fronts in global communicative capitalism's class war, revolts of those whose communicative activities generate value that is expropriated from them.[27]

As Jaron Lanier notes, "We've decided not to pay most people for performing the new roles that are valuable in relation to the

---

26   This is Paul Mason's claim.

27   Nick Dyer-Witherford, *Cyber-Proletariat: Global Labour in the Digital Vortex*, London: Pluto Press, 2015. See also Christian Fuch's "Labor in informational capitalism and on the internet," *The Information Society* 26, 2010: 179–96.

latest technologies. Ordinary people 'share,' while elite network presences generate unprecedented fortunes."[28] This is the real face of the knowledge class, that is to say, the proletarianized people producing the information, services, relations, and networks at the core of communicative capitalism (what others sometimes refer to as the "knowledge economy" or "information society"). They make more and get less, intensifying inequality with every communicative contribution and its trace. A 2014 World Economic Forum report puts it bluntly: "the greater the role that data play in the global economy, the less the majority of individuals will be worth."[29]

Enda Brophy and Greig de Peuter demonstrate why, under communicative capitalism, paid, precarious, and unpaid labor should not be treated separately: these forms of labor constitute a "circuit of exploitation."[30] Brophy and de Peuter use the smartphone to draw out this labor circuit, making it legible in terms of work common to a "cybertariat." The "circuit of exploitation" around the smartphone links extraction, assembly, and design to mobile work, support work, and e-waste. We can fill out ideas of mobile and support work by adding in content provision and use, the data and metadata contributed to communication streams and then stored, mined, auctioned, and sold. The concept of "circuits of exploitation" lets us recognize communication networks as networks of exploitation linking communicative labor across the social field. Under communicative capitalism most of

28   Jaron Lanier, *Who Owns the Future*, New York: Simon & Schuster, 2013, 15.

29   Peter Haynes and M-H. Carolyn Nguyen, "Rebalancing Socio-Economic Asymmetry in a Data-Driven Economy," *The Global Information Technology Report 2014*, Geneva, Switzerland: World Economic Forum, 2014, 70, weforum.org.

30   Enda Brophy and Greig de Peuter, "Labors of Mobility: Communicative Capitalism and the Smartphone Cybertariat," *Theories of the Mobile Internet*, eds. Andrew Herman, Jan Hadlaw, and Thom Swiss, New York: Routledge, 2015.

us can't avoid producing for capitalism. Our basic communicative activities are enclosed in circuits as raw materials for capital accumulation.

Demographic data supports my claim that the last decade of revolts are the class struggle of those proletarianized under communicative capitalism. In an analysis of Occupy Wall Street, Ruth Milkman, Stephanie Luce, and Penny Lewis find that highly educated young people were overrepresented among OWS activists and supporters and that many were underemployed, indebted, or had recently lost their jobs.[31] A report based on data collected by Turkish security forces shows that over half the Gezi park protesters were in university or university graduates even as their incomes were in the bottom economic half.[32] Andre Singer, looking at the massive Brazilian protests of June 2013, likewise emphasizes the predominance of young, highly educated, and un- or underemployed adults.[33] More specifically, Singer notes that in protests in the eight state capitals, 43 percent of protesters had college degrees. In protests in São Paulo, nearly 80 percent had college degrees. These educational levels would suggest a middle-class revolt. But data on income and occupation point in the direction of the lower and lower-middle class, the bottom half of society where people are more likely to work as shop assistants, drivers, waiters, receptionists, and primary school teachers than as technicians or administrators. To make sense of the disparity between high education and low incomes, Singer posits a new proletariat or precariat taking to the streets, the exploited service and knowledge workers of communicative capitalism.

---

31   Ruth Milkman, Stephanie Luce, and Penny Lewis, "Changing the Subject: A Bottom-Up Account of Occupy Wall Street in New York City," City University of New York: The Murphy Institute, 2013, 4, sps.cuny.edu.

32   "78 percent of Gezi Park protest detainees were Alevis: Report," *Hurriyet Daily News*, Nov. 25, 2013.

33   Andre Singer, "Rebellion in Brazil," *New Left Review* 85, Jan.–Feb. 2014.

Looked at most broadly, the demographics of recent protests point to heavy involvement by those who are young, well educated, and un- or underemployed. Because of communicative capitalism's tight labor market, they encounter a decreasing return on their investment in education. In 2014, more than 80 percent of low-wage workers in the US had at least a high school degree; nearly 11 percent had bachelor's degrees.[34] As more people wind up in jobs for which they are overqualified, they end up pushing those without a college education out of the labor market entirely, thereby contributing indirectly to long-term unemployment.[35] In this regard, it should be noted that in 2013 the occupations employing the largest numbers of people in the US were all in the service sector: retail sales, cashiers, food service, office workers, nursing, and customer service.[36] The annual income of three of the top four occupations in the US (determined by percentage of the workforce)—retail, cashiers, and food service—is below the poverty line.[37]

Alongside the large-scale movements like 2011's Occupy, the movement of the squares in Spain and Greece, and the Arab spring, as well as 2013's protests in Turkey and Brazil, there has been a wide array of strikes and actions by others we might think of as proletarianized communicative laborers. In the US, the protests of civil service workers in Wisconsin in 2011 and the Chicago teachers' strike of 2012 stand out. Globally, the strikes

34 Cherrie Bucknor, "Low-wage Workers: Still Older, Smarter, and Underpaid," Center for Economic and Policy Research issue brief, May 2015, cepr.net.

35 Jordan Weissmann, "53% of Recent College Grads are Jobless or Unemployed—How?" *The Atlantic*, April 23, 2013; Katherine Peralta, "College Grads Taking Low-Wage Jobs Displace Less Educated," *Bloomberg Business*, March 12, 2014.

36 "Occupational Employment and Wages—May 2014," Bureau of Labor Statistics, US Department of Labor, March 25, 2015, bls.gov.

37 Brad Plumer, "How the recession turned middle-class jobs into low-wage jobs," *Washington Post*, Feb. 28, 2013.

are virtually innumerable. Consider just one month, March 2014.[38]
That month there were strikes of public sector and airport workers
in Germany, cleaners at the University of London, civil servants,
teachers, doctors, and pharmacists in Greece, teachers and education support workers in Western Australia, and non-teaching staff
and postal workers in India; there was a telecom strike in Ghana
and a sit-in at an airport in Sudan in protest over the contracting-
out of security jobs; seven thousand doctors in South Korea went
on strike in opposition to plans to introduce telemedicine and for-
profit hospital subsidiaries. And this is just a partial list for March.
Nonetheless, it points to the active, ongoing, but still disconnected
struggles in the workplaces of communicative laborers.

Given changes in the workplace associated with increased use
of technology, flexibilization, and precaritization, and linked to the
decline of unions, we should not expect class struggle in communicative capitalism to manifest primarily as workplace struggles.
Communicative production takes place throughout the social field.
That a struggle doesn't take the form of a classic workplace struggle, then, doesn't mean that it's not class struggle. Student, debt,
housing, and education protests need to be understood in terms
of the class politics of those encountering proletarianization, not
as separate and specific issue-based politics. On the flipside, that a
primary organizational feature of the recent protests has been the
general or mass assembly, often in parks or public squares, should
also not misdirect us away from class struggle. Incidentally, this is
one of the interesting features of the mainstream emphasis on the
fact that Occupiers were always on their phones uploading video
and tweeting and all the rest: for some contingent and mobile
workers, the park is a workplace. Phones are means of production.
When they occupy, communicating activists put these means of
production to a use of their own choosing, not capital's (although
capital can still expropriate their content and metadata).

38   The World Social Website provides comprehensive coverage of labor
struggles worldwide: wsws.org.

So what should we expect? Changes in communication and subjectivity under communicative capitalism, not to mention thirty years of resurgent capitalist class power, point to the real challenges for political organizing.[39] As I explore more fully in chapter one, intense attachments to unique individuality as people try to construct "personal brands" that can help them "stand out in a crowd" hinder solidarity. We should expect suspicion of those deemed threatening to that uniqueness. Likewise, because of the instability of meaning in communicative capitalism—what Slavoj Žižek terms the "decline of symbolic efficiency"—contemporary movements are less likely to rely on empty signifiers like "freedom" and "justice." We should thus expect greater reliance on common images, tactics, and names—the more generic, the greater the reach: umbrella, tent, mask, Occupy, hashtag.[40] Micro-politics, identity politics, anarchism, one-off demos, clicktivism, and ironic events seem more compelling (they would definitely be easier) than the sustained work of party building because they affirm the dominant ideology of singularity, newness, and now. At the same time, we should expect increasing emphasis on inequality as people cry out and push back against widespread debt, insecurity, and dispossession. And we should expect new, extended modes of coming together as the formerly fragmented experience first-hand the sense of invincibility accompanying collective power.

Reading the protests and revolts of the last decade as the class struggle of the people proletarianized under communicative capitalism, we can account for the ubiquity of personalized media, the demographics of the people protesting, the economic position of the protesters, *and* the political ambiguity of the protests. New proles often have a strong libertarian bent. They may present themselves as post-political, even anti-political (as in, for example, the Spanish movement of the squares). Their identities are so

---

39   For a detailed discussion of these changes see *Blog Theory*.

40   I owe this insight to conversations with the Brooklyn-based artist and activist collective Not An Alternative.

fluid that they can be channeled in different directions that they simultaneously always exceed. They have a hard time uniting as a class even as their actions are the expressions of a class.

A key characteristic of recent protests has been that they are out of doors. Unlike nineteenth- and early twentieth-century riots that could happen because people already interacted with one another in concentrated urban spaces, more recent ones require an extra effort of overcoming isolation, leaving home or work, remaining outside, and merging with crowds of strangers. People must self-consciously assemble themselves in settings not determined by capital and the state. It doesn't just happen. The surprise of their collectivity pushes against the expectations of disconnected consumption and screen-gazing that are so much a part of early twenty-first century sociality. The flash mob has been one of the forms experimenting with and drawing out this surprise-effect (although it has quickly been put to use in guerrilla marketing campaigns). Occupation has been even more effective, particularly as it has moved from inside to outside, enabling the occupying crowd to amplify its effect via visibility, noise, growth, and interaction with its setting. As isolated tactics, however, these forms have reached their limit. The challenge consists in changing political actions into political power.

We the Party

At the end of the nineteenth and for most of the twentieth century, parties organizing the working class held out the promise of consolidating mass power, whether into forms for its radical self-assertion or for its subordination and control. By the 1970s and '80s, however, wide swathes of the Left had become convinced that the party form was no longer adequate to left aspirations. This conviction had multiple sources: the stagnation and authoritarianism of the party-states of the former East; the complicity and betrayals of communist and socialist parties in the former West; the failure of class analysis to address and include the politics of identity, particularly with respect to sex and race, to mention but a few. The loss of confidence in the party as a form for left politics accompanied organized capital's attacks on unions, waged violently and directly through state power and policy as well as through corporate offshoring of factories and changes in the technical composition of labor. The political incapacity of socialist and communist parties in the face of this onslaught—an incapacity that manifested itself in Anglo-European contexts as adaptation to the individualist, consumerist, and market suppositions of the resurgent capitalist class and failure to defend working-class political achievements— seemed a final nail in the coffin of the politics of class and party that had defined the century. In the terms that came to define the theoretical debates of the time, there was nothing "essential" about class, class identity, class politics, or class struggle.[41] And, with no class politics, there was no need for a class party, that is, a party that takes as its goal the abolition of the conditions of capitalist exploitation that create classes. Instead, left politics would involve an ever-expanding array of issues and identities, the problematizing and pluralizing of sedimented practices and ideas throughout the terrain of the social, cultural, and increasingly, the personal.

All this would unfold against the background of a capitalism to which there was no alternative. Better put, any alternative (for those still interested in putting an end to capitalist exploitation— many radical democrats proceeded as if their goal were simply capitalism with a human face) would emerge not as a result of organized struggle or left strategy but immanently, organically, as a direct effect of capitalism's own development, spontaneism now refigured as autonomy.

Michael Hardt and Antonio Negri's *Empire* captured the political atmosphere on the dispersing Left at century's end. Hardt

---

41   See Ellen Meiksins Wood, *The Retreat from Class*, London: Verso, 1999.

and Negri offered a vision of innumerable local struggles across the globe, each striking at the heart of Empire.[42] These struggles may well be incommunicable, their cries and anger, goals and demands confined to their settings, but this incommunicability, *Empire* told us, is an advantage. Struggles are free to unfold on their own, unhindered by the discipline and constraint of larger organizations. Autonomous struggles don't reinforce state structures. They enhance the generative creativity of multiple modes of becoming, releasing the constituent power of the multitude from Empire's parasitic hold. Key to the appeal of the multitude concept, then, was its expression of weakness as strength. The absence of a common language—not to mention a program—didn't appear as an indication of the actual incapacity of the Left to cohere into a discernible politics and present a viable opposition to capitalist and right-wing forces. Instead it marked a liberation from the constraints of Marxist dogma, an opening for politicizations hroughout the social field.

Hardt and Negri turned left defeat into an opportunity to reimagine communist politics. This reimagining needs to go further. It can go further by highlighting division, antagonism, and political organization. Nearly forty years after the collapse of the Soviet Union, the wide array of politicized issues and identities enables a communism that, more fully than ever before, can take the side of the oppressed, indeed, that can make the multiple struggles of the oppressed into a side. It's imperative that multiplicity not replace class but be understood as a class characteristic. Let me explain.

The vision of a multitude of incommunicable struggles theorized by Hardt and Negri and held up in appeals to democracy replaces the antagonism of class struggle with pluralization, creativity, and becoming, thereby flattening out and immediatizing the terrain of struggle. Such a rendering of each strike as equivalent obliterates differences in resources, histories, and opportunities,

---

42   Michael Hardt and Antonio Negri, *Empire*, Cambridge, MA: Harvard University Press, 2000.

effacing the uneven development of capitalism. It obscures the dimension of time, as if struggles occurred in discreet bursts rather than building, unfolding, advancing, and retreating. And it disavows the tensions within struggles, as if histories of oppression left no trace on those who organize to dismantle the arrangements of power that continue them. In effect, the goal becomes, as in communicative capitalism itself, the production of the many, the multitude of singularities. The political effect is a failure to build a concentrated political force with the sustained capacity to confront and replace the capitalist mode of production. Instead, there are small battles, policy options, and cultural interventions, victories that can be absorbed and defeats that can be forgotten (when they aren't fetishized as yet another instance of inevitable left failure). To the extent that pluralization—and the moves to fragment and individuate that accompany it—is a left political priority, politics becomes passionately attached to the small and weak. This gives us the shape of the Left we have in the long tail of micro-initiatives.

The new cycle of struggles has demonstrated the political strength that comes from collectivity. Common names, tactics, and images are bringing the fragments together, making them legible as many fronts of one struggle against capitalism. Where the proliferation of issues and identities disperses and weakens us—inciting the snark that glorifies itself as critique even as it undermines solidarity—the crowd events of the last decade are forcing a new sense of collective power. They have pushed expectations of multiplicity into experiences of collectivity. The question that emerges from these experiences is how they might endure and extend, how the momentary discharge of equality that crowds unleash might become the basis for a new process of political composition.

The party suggests itself as a mode of association appropriate to such a process. It offers a political form that spans multiple levels and domains. Typically, parties scale across local, regional, national, and sometimes international levels. Rather than stuck in the local or confined to the abstractions of the global, the party is an organizational form operative on different scales; indeed, its success—electorally or otherwise—depends on this capacity. Further, parties are carriers of the knowledge that comes with political experience. Whether this knowledge is local—histories of relationships, of practices, of who knows whom, what, where, and how—or larger—knowledge of resource extraction and the structure of industry, of civil wars in far off places, of racial histories, of the challenges of social reproduction, of programming, database construction, and design—parties recognize the breadth and depth of knowledge important for political struggle and rule. Providing a body for a knowledge that exceeds what any one person can know, the party takes a position on that knowledge. It fits issues into a platform such that they are not so many contradictory and individual preferences but instead a broader vision for which it will fight. What is sometimes dismissed as party bureaucracy thus needs to be revalued as an institutional capacity necessary for political struggle and rule in a complex and uneven terrain.

The electoral success of Syriza, Greece's coalition of the radical Left, points to the new relevance of the party form. The Greek legacy of intense party politics is a unique feature of its political culture. Nevertheless, Syriza's initial victories stemmed in part from innovations in communist party organizing: commitment to social movements, respect for movements' autonomy, support of local solidarity networks, and enough involvement in institutions "to seem capable of transforming the balance of forces at the level of national political life."[43] For some Lefts, particularly in the US and UK, it is this last feature that has been conspicuously absent. Hence, our actions fail to gain momentum. Crowds amass, but they don't endure. In contrast, Syriza's initial achievements demonstrated a dynamic relation between crowd and party: the crowd that pushes the party to exceed expectations, the party that finds the courage of the people in the haste of the crowd.

---

43   Sebastian Budgen and Stathis Kouvelakis, "Greece: Phase One," *Jacobin*, Jan. 22, 2015.

Three additional aspects of Syriza's political opening contribute to rethinking the party today. The first concerns the limits of political victory confined to the level of the nation-state. The institutions not only of Europe but of global finance and governance restrict national governments' range of maneuver. This poses challenges to the Left internationally, suggesting, at a minimum, the necessity of strong left alliances and coordinated institutional strategies. More maximally it directs us toward the party as an infrastructure for such alliances and strategies. The second aspect involves defeat. No party will be everything to everyone. Just as individuals are internally divided and contradictory, split among conscious and unconscious desires, so is a party—like any institution—a body that is not self-identical. Political forms aren't pure. To expect perfection is to displace politics into an imaginary realm sheltered from difference and disappointment. Despite Syriza's inability to deliver on its promises (or, more strongly, despite its betrayal of the very supporters who mobilized in its behalf), it nevertheless shifted the terrain of the possible. Because of Syriza, the European, British, and North American Left have a sense of political possibility they previously lacked. Common sense has shifted, as is apparent in the political rise of Jeremy Corbyn in the UK and Bernie Sanders in the US. The third aspect of Syriza's political opening instructive for the Left concerns political will. Kouvelakis writes, "The Podemos experience in Spain as well as Syriza in Greece shows that if the radical Left makes suitable proposals, then it can arrive at an understanding with these movements and provide a credible political 'condensation' of their demands." The making of "suitable proposals" depends on political will, a Left able to put aside its differences, organize, and think strategically about the pursuit of political power. The problem posing itself today concerns less the details of party organization (membership requirements, centralization versus networked structure, mechanisms for accountable leadership) than it does solidary political will. Can the Left's wide array of associations come together in a way that will achieve a real political advance?

The supposition of *Crowds and Party* is that we have no choice but to answer "yes." To help us get to yes, to make a party of communists seem compelling to more of us again, I offer an approach to the party inspired by the crowd. Faithful to the egalitarian rupture of the crowd event, the communist party holds open the gap through which the people appear as the political subject. Readers anchored in the classics of revolutionary socialism might balk at what seems at first glance to be an abandonment of Marxist terms. They shouldn't. The "people" has a rich legacy in Marxism-Leninism-Maoism: the "people" are the revolutionary alliance of the oppressed (in contrast to the populist rendering of the people as an organic unity). Under conditions of communicative capitalism, crowds are the proletarianized many, those whose communicative engagements are expropriated from them in processes of accumulation and dispossession that benefit capital as a class. Readers inspired by radical democratic, anarchist, and post-Marxist theories might balk at a return to the party. They shouldn't. The party is a basic form of political struggle. If innovation is necessary for finding our way out of the current political impasse, then the party, too, can be a site for experimentation and change.

Typically, socialist and communist discussions of the party gel around the themes of reform or revolution, mass or vanguard, factory or state. These discussions are too limiting. Missing is the affective dimension of the party, the way that the perspective of the party operates through different organizational terrains. The party knots together unconscious processes across a differential field to enable a communist political subjectivity. To think through these processes as the effects of collectivity back upon itself, I draw out the psychodynamics of the party. Providing a strength and direction we would otherwise lack, the party generates the practical optimism through which struggles endure.

Many eschew the party as a form for political power, decision, and organization. They fall back into the affirmation of individual autonomy, reasserting capitalist ideology. Discarding the party form, they jettison the possibility of building collective power. I demonstrate how the power the party unleashes is the power we already have to change the world.

1

Nothing Personal

The era of communicative capitalism is an era of commanded individuality. The command circulates in varying modes. Each is told, repeatedly, that she is unique and encouraged to cultivate this uniqueness. We learn to insist on and enjoy our difference, intensifying processes of self-individuation. No one else is like us (like me). The "do-it-yourself" injunction is so unceasing that "taking care of oneself" appears as politically significant instead of as a symptom of collective failure—we let the social safety net unravel—and economic contraction—in a viciously competitive job market we have no choice but to work on ourselves, constantly, just to keep up. Required to find out, decide, and express it all ourselves, we construe political collectivity as nostalgia for the impossible solidarities of a different era. The second-wave feminist idea that the "personal is political" has become twisted into the presumption that the political is personal: how does this affect *me*?

Individualism has not always been so intense and unmitigated. As Jefferson Cowie details in his history of the United States in the 1970s, "reformed and diversified individualisms" undermined class-based approaches to economic rights over the course of the decade.[1] This chapter takes up this assault on collectivity. Looking

---

1 Jefferson Cowie, *Stayin' Alive*, New York: The New Press, 2010, 72.

at shifts in commanded individuality from the 1970s to the present, I highlight the enormous strains placed on the individual as it becomes the overburdened remainder of dismantled institutions and solidarities—the survivor. I revisit Christopher Lasch's *The Culture of Narcissism*, marking the ways capitalist processes simultaneously promote the individual as the primary unit of capitalism and unravel the institutions of solidaristic support on which this unit depends. Putting later sociologists in conversation with Lasch, I draw out the limits of Lasch's account. Even as Lasch's descriptions of celebrity culture, competition, and consumerism still resonate, individualism is today less an indication of narcissism than it is of psychosis. The chapter continues by considering a left example of the off-loading of responsibility onto the individual: the debate over the "new times" in *Marxism Today* that took place at the end of the 1980s. Against the background of the sociologists' conversation, the emphases on individual responsibility and identity in this debate appear as what they in fact were: the fragmentation of a collective perspective under the weight of reasserted capitalist class power. The last sections of the chapter begin an inversion that will be more fully developed in chapter two. They find possibilities of collectivity in the ruptures of the fragile individual form. With help from Elias Canetti's indispensable study of crowds, I introduce the power of the many and the relief it provides from the unbearable demand for individuality. My goal in the chapter is documenting an interlinked psychic and economic problem: the incapacity and contradictions of the individual form as a locus for creativity, difference, agency, and responsibility. Together with chapter two, this chapter aims to dislodge from left thinking the individualism that serves as an impasse to left politics.

Two commercials illustrate the celebration of personal uniqueness characteristic of communicative capitalism. Both are for soft

---

Throughout this chapter, I blur together individualism, individuality, and individuation, treating them as component aspects of capitalist society's requirement for and production of individuals.

drinks. Both, in different ways, engage the limits conditioning the very individuality that they command.

On January 9, 2012, Dr Pepper announced a new advertising campaign, "Always One of a Kind." The campaign's first commercial features hundreds of people in red t-shirts with white lettering converging in a crowd to march down streets and through a park. The t-shirts have slogans like "I'm One of a Kind," "I'm a Cougar," "I'm a Fighter," and "I'm a Pepper" (one of Dr Pepper's earlier slogans). The commercial's soundtrack is a cover of the 1968 Sammy Davis, Jr. hit, "I've Gotta Be Me." According to the press release accompanying the campaign's launch, the red t-shirt wearers are Dr Pepper fans "proudly showing off their own original expressions on t-shirts describing what makes them unique and different from the rest of the crowd."[2] In the optimistic words of the company's director of marketing, the campaign "should serve as a catalyst for expressing originality and being authentically you." Dr Pepper also offered fans the "opportunity to express their originality by ordering their own 'Always One of a Kind' t-shirts on DrPepper.com."

Putting aside the designation of customers as "fans," the targeted demographic appears to be people who want to express their uniqueness. The commercial hails them as individuals, inviting them to identify with particular slogans and identities. Within Dr Pepper's commercial imaginary, going to the streets isn't collective rage; it's individual self-expression, an opportunity to assert one's individuality and stand out. Crowds are that against which individuals define themselves. The Dr Pepper Brand, in this imaginary, is a natural continuation of primary urges to establish unique identities, a helpful, vital supplement for the crucial task of distinguishing oneself from others.

The commercial's presumption that people need support in

---

2 Product release: "Dr Pepper Celebrates Its Legacy Of Originality With The Launch Of The New 'Always One Of A Kind' Advertising Campaign," news.drpeppersnapplegroup.com, January 9, 2012.

expressing their originality—an authenticity catalyst of the kind
a t-shirt might provide—gives it an ironic inflection. Augmented
through the retro turn to Sammy Davis, Jr., the irony of expressing
one's authenticity via a branded soft drink invites another iden-
tificatory twist: are you like the crowd of those who *really* think
that Dr Pepper t-shirts make you unique, or does your capacity
to get the joke, to recognize that originality necessarily exceeds
any branded media image, make you different from, even superior
to, the rest of the crowd? The fact that some of the slogans are
reappropriations of offensive labels—"cougar" and "mamma's
boy," for instance—opens up this alternative. The wearers of
these shirts are unique in their strength, confident enough to assert
the labels, to *own* them. Thus, a further irony: their courage is
amplified by the crowd. The energy of the commercial, its *feel*,
comes less from what's written on the t-shirts (the majority of
which can't be read) than from the sea of red that carries people
along. The celebration of difference and creativity comes from the
enthusiasm of a crowd where people march shoulder to shoulder,
pumping their fists and taking confidence in their collectivity. Even
as collectivity as a trope is co-opted into the service of amplifying
individual courage, the fact of, the *need for*, this amplification cuts
through the individualist message as it acknowledges the power of
the crowd.

Coca-Cola's "Share a Coke" campaign likewise takes individuality as its theme, targeting a demographic the company presents
as preoccupied with the assertion of personal uniqueness.

"For teens and Millennials, personalization is not a fad, it's a
way of life," explains the press release announcing the campaign.
"It's about self-expression, individual storytelling and staying
connected with friends."[3] Launched in Australia in 2011 and
expanded into some fifty additional countries, the campaign alters
the Coke iconography by replacing the Coke logo with personal

3   Jay Moye, "Summer of Sharing: 'Share a Coke' Campaign Rolls Out in
the U.S.," coca-colacompany.com, June 10, 2014.

names. It encourages young consumers to finds cans and bottles with the names of themselves and their friends, photograph them, and share them online.

In the campaign, personal names take the place of the brand. Consumers aren't called on to show their individuality by wearing the brand. The brand comes to them, taking on their individual identities, letting individuals see themselves in it. The icon becomes abstract enough to carry individual identities while nonetheless transcending them. The appeal of the campaign arises not just from the personal name but from the personal name in the place of the known and popular. The social media dimension of the campaign testifies to the continuation of the place of the brand. The Coke icon is still there, now riding on and circulating through individual uploads of personal self-expression, less viral marketing than free product placement in the intimate moments of everyday life.

When the Left echoes injunctions to individuality, when we emphasize unique perspectives and personal experiences, we function as vehicles for communicative capitalist ideology. "Left" becomes nothing but a name on a bottle, the shape of which is determined for us and which relies on us for its circulation. Making individual difference the basis of our politics, we fail to distinguish between communicative capitalism and emancipatory egalitarian politics. Even worse, we strengthen the ideology that impedes the cultivation of politically powerful collectivities. To call on people to ground their politics in the personal experiences that differentiate them from others is to reinforce capitalist dynamics of individuation. Offering the fantasy of customizable politics, such a call says: look at yourself from the specific position and interests given to you by capitalism and do what you want. In so doing, it pushes away from the collectivity on which left politics depends.

Individualism without Individuals

The injunction to individuality is so ubiquitous that it's easy to forget its histories and modulations.[4] The research of sociologists such as Christopher Lasch, Richard Sennett, Jennifer M. Silva, and Carrie M. Lane treads a path through this history as it attends to the pathologies accompanying capitalist processes of individuation. As I detail below, key sites along this path—rugged individual, corporate gamesman, flexible temp worker, and sole survivor— open up the ways economic turmoil, changes in the structure of authority, and the loss of self-sufficiency give a tenuous quality to personal identity. The shifts from one site to another dem- onstrate moreover how the competitive pressures of capitalist processes become increasingly displaced onto and concentrated in the individual. The forces enjoining individuation undermine it. The more the individual, that fictitious subject of capitalism, is glorified, the more strained and impossible it becomes.

Lasch's influential book *The Culture of Narcissism: American Life in An Age of Diminishing Expectations* presents an individualism that has self-destructed. Appearing in 1979, the book highlights the rise of a therapeutic sensibility. The economic man of the nineteenth century "has given way to the psychological man of our

---

4   Jerrold Seigel provides a comprehensive history of the individual in his *The Idea of the Self: Thought and Experience in Western Europe Since the Seventeenth Century*, New York: Cambridge University Press, 2005. See also Jeremy Gilbert's critical overview of competitive individualism, *Common Ground: Democracy and Collectivity in an Age of Individualism*, London: Pluto Press, 2014, esp. 30–42. Although the individualism of the US American present tends to be projected into the past as if it had always accompanied US capitalism, in the decades following the Civil War, US industrialists pushed for monopoly capitalism. In the words of John D. Rockefeller, "The day of combination is here to stay. Individualism has gone, never to return," in Rob Chernow, *Titan: The Life of John D. Rockefeller, Sr.*, New York: Vintage, 2007, 148. Thanks to Corey Robin for drawing this to my attention.

times—the final product of bourgeois individualism."[5] For Lasch, the preoccupations with self, authenticity, and personal growth that became prevalent over the course of the 1970s are symptomatic of an individualism collapsing in on itself as commanded individuality struggles to realize the ever-increasing expectations coming to burden it.

Lasch describes his critique of the therapeutic individual as "radical," even as he shares conservative concerns with the weakening of the family and the rise of dependency. This overlap is worth noting. Not only does it point toward an increasing convergence among critics of the basic institutions of the welfare state, but it also indexes the common object of their concern: the fragile individual. The difference between Lasch's analysis and the conservative critique of welfare liberalism consists in their targets. Where conservatives attack the bureaucracy of the welfare state, Lasch attacks the bureaucracy of the corporation. He expands this attack into a full assault on the broader impact of corporate culture on American life. Lasch's innovation stems from his diagnosis of the "me decade's" preoccupation with psychic health as a symptom of the more fundamental intellectual and political bankruptcy of welfare state capitalism's liberal paternalism. The end of the individual in narcissistic hedonism and aggression is the outgrowth of capitalism, inclusive of and exacerbated by the liberal welfare state. Capitalism's own injunctions to individuality overburden and undermine the individual form.

Locating changes in the individual in the context of political and economic change, Lasch contrasts the narcissistic personality of the twentieth century with the rugged individual of the nineteenth century. His vision of the nineteenth-century American psyche (clearly an ideological figure or organizing motif) comes from the settler colonialism of the frontier. The pioneer fights to tame the West, to subdue nature, and eliminate the native threat. This fight

5 Christopher Lasch, *The Culture of Narcissism*, New York: Norton, 1979, xvi.

requires an attendant internal battle: domination over more immediate appetites and impulses. Lasch writes,

> Through compulsive industry and relentless sexual repression, nine-
> teenth-century US Americans achieved a fragile triumph over the
> id. The violence they turned against the Indians and against nature
> originated not in unrestrained impulse but in the white Anglo-Saxon
> superego, which feared the wildness of the West because it objecti-
> fied the wildness within each individual.[6]

He continues, "Capital accumulation in its own right sublimated
appetite and subordinated the pursuit of self-interest to the service
of future generations." The frontier American is egoistic and
brutal, this brutality tied to a self-constraint on behalf of civilized community. Violence is channeled, put to internal as well as
external use.

Lasch positions the corporation as the twentieth-century parallel to the frontier. In contrast to the fierce and rugged pioneers
fighting for survival, seventies Americans are stuck in a boring,
ordered, and banal society. Because the struggle for success has
replaced the struggle to survive, they have lost the capacity to
desire. Nonetheless US Americans in the seventies seethe with an
inner rage that bureaucratic society and its injunction to cheerful
getting along prevents them from expressing, the violent forces of
the id now lacking an outlet.

Lasch uses the "executive" as a figure for twentieth-century
narcissism. Unlike the "organization man" associated with mid-
century American anxiety about conformism, Lasch's executive is
the bureaucratic "gamesman." Seeking competitive advantage, the
gamesman wants to get ahead of everyone else. He values quick-
ness and mobility. He construes power in terms of momentum.
He replaces craftsmanship with socials skills that involve seduc-
ing, humiliating, and manipulating others. The gamesman doesn't

6   Ibid., 10.

interiorize rules as socially valid norms; he experiences both work and personal relations as power struggles. Bureaucratic emphases on rules and cooperation couple with personal exceptionalism—*rules don't apply to me.* The gamesman thus looks for ways to exploit conventions for his own benefit. "Activities ostensibly undertaken purely for enjoyment often have the real object of doing others in."[7] A friendly demeanor, an air of compassion, and an open, participatory approach to decision-making all conceal a power game that the majority will lose.

The sense that a game is being played extends beyond the corporation. The lower orders, Lasch writes,

> internalize a grandiose idea of the opportunities open to all, together with an inflated opinion of their own capacities. If the lowly man resents those more highly placed, it is only because he suspects them of grandly violating the regulations of the game, as he would like to do himself if he dared. It never occurs to him to insist on a new set of rules.[8]

The "lowly man" acquiesces uneasily to expectations of friendly cooperation, suppressing dissatisfaction into a growing emptiness.

Lasch's psychoanalytic explanation for the rise of the narcissistic personality highlights changes in the paternal function. Unlike the materially self-sufficient frontier family, the family in the second half of the twentieth century depends on help and advice from experts. Whether as medical and therapeutic child-rearing guidance or educational and juridical intervention in the domestic sphere, expertise dislodges symbolic patriarchal authority. This dislodging continues broader patterns associated with industrial development, more specifically with the separation of production and reproduction, the distancing of children from labor, and the diminution of opportunities for fathers to teach the technical skills

7   Ibid., 66.
8   Ibid., 186.

associated with their work directly to their children. The father's absence "encourages the development of a harsh and punitive superego based largely on archaic images of the parents, fused with grandiose self-images."[9] The child doesn't identify with parents; it introjects them, holding itself up to idealized standards and punishing itself for failing to achieve them. Put in Lacanian terms, the change in the paternal function is a decline in authority such that the symbolic law can no longer provide a site of relief from superegoic demands.[10] The poor ego is preoccupied with itself because it's always under attack.

The decline of symbolic authority in liberal therapeutic society induces a broader cultural narcissism. As corporate games take the place of frontier survival, welfare capitalism's bureaucratic rationality replaces the previous era's hierarchy with administrators, technicians, and experts. Rather than having symbolic authority, experts and administrators have knowledge. This knowledge is generally contestable and provisional: experts disagree; what a bureaucrat knows may not be useful. The culture of technocratic expertise and management absolves individuals of responsibility, making everyone a victim of sickness or circumstance. Narcissistic culture infantilizes by promoting dependence on the paternalist bureaucracies of welfare liberalism (corporation and state) and at the same time encouraging the pursuit of pleasure. The narcissistic person admires the strong and rich—celebrities—for their independence, their capacity to do and have whatever they want. Mass media encourages the fascination with celebrity, amplifying the narcissist's tendency to divide society into two groups: winners and losers, the great and the crowd. Self-fulfillment and hedonism are celebrated, yet unsatisfying and, increasingly, unattainable. In the absence of symbolic authority, people absorb themselves in a search for authenticity, their skepticism toward the falsity of mass culture's manufactured illusions manifesting as an ironic

---

9   Ibid., 178.
10   See Slavoj Žižek, *The Ticklish Subject*, London: Verso, 1999, 322–34.

detachment that further distances them from meaningful connections with others.

What Lasch diagnoses as pathological or secondary narcissism is a reactive individuality that accompanies changes in capitalist society associated with mass production and consumption. When consumption is a way of life, work need not be meaningful, fair, or morally necessary (as a previous generation held). Instead, the purpose of work is acquisition. Consumption solves all problems, fills all needs. Rather than postponing pleasure, consumerism enjoins gratification now. The concomitant growth in management and proliferation of technicians, experts, and knowledge professionals presents "new forms of capitalist control, which established themselves first in the factory and then spread throughout society."[11] Having lost its role in production, the family is stripped of its role in reproduction as its social tasks either become matters in need of expert intervention or reducible to problems solved by the right commodities. The effect of these developments is a realization of the logic of capitalism such that "the pursuit of self-interest, formerly identified with the rational pursuit of gain and the accumulation of wealth, has become a search for pleasure and psychic survival."[12] The result, which Lasch says was already foreseen by the Marquis de Sade, is the reduction of people to objects. Each person is to be used for the enjoyment of another: "pure individualism thus issues in the most radical repudiation of individuality."[13] The culture of narcissism erodes the individual it ostensibly celebrates.

In sum, Lasch links changes in the individual form to changes in capitalism. The shift from the rugged individual of the frontier to the gamesman of the corporation is economic and psychic. As the struggle to survive becomes a drive to consume, the self-reliance of the frontier morphs into dependence on corporate and state

11 Lasch, *The Culture of Narcisim*, 235.
12 Ibid., 69.
13 Ibid., 70.

bureaucracy. Frustrated individuals narcissistically strain against their traps, identifying with celebrities and searching for authenticity. They want to be unique, exceptional. The rules don't apply to them, so they need not abide by them. They can focus on themselves, their own well-being, using others as means to achieve it.

A quarter of a century later, Richard Sennett suggests that deepening inequality and economic insecurity have further changed the contemporary individual. Where Lasch highlights the bureaucratic corporation for its cultivation of gamesmanship and dependency, Sennett considers the so-called "new economy" of temporary workers, technology workers, and entrepreneurs (before and after the bursting of the dot-com bubble).[14] These workers aren't dependent on bureaucracy. They aren't locked into the banal security of the corporation and its internal machinations. Their lives and work are unstable, without guarantees, precarious. They lack a narrative for adulthood. Many work on short-term contracts. Companies want to be flexible—and to avoid providing health insurance and pensions. The critique of dependency has become itself an interiorized norm. Whether a firm employs the winner-take-all dynamic of internal markets, relies on subcontractors and temporary labor, or uses consultants and a revolving door of executives, primary business values are autonomy and self-direction. Workers worry about keeping their skills up-to-date, having the potential to learn new tasks quickly and cultivating easily transferable capacities such as "problem-solving."

Surprising, though, is the resonance of Sennett's account with Lasch's. One might expect the enforced self-reliance of the new economy to induce a sense of purpose and direction along the lines of the rugged individualism of the frontier. Instead, Sennett's sociological investigations into late capitalism suggest a self oriented toward the short term, focused on potential, and capable of jettisoning the past. This echoes Lasch's highlighting of

14   Richard Sennett, *The Culture of the New Capitalism*, New Haven, CT: Yale University Press, 2006.

immediacy, flexibility, and a break with historical continuity. Like Lasch, Sennett emphasizes the separation of power from authority, the diminution of trust, and the growth of anxiety. But where Lasch presents the pressure confronting the individual as an effect of a corporate culture that breeds gamesmanship and dependence, Sennett attributes the problem to the *loss* of corporate culture and the unmooring of individuals from the intelligible patterns of everyday life that results. The corporation no longer provides a stabilizing point of reference for the narrative of working life. Sennett writes,

> A shortened framework of institutional time lies at the heart of this social degradation; the cutting edge has capitalized on superficial human relations. This same shortened time framework has disoriented individuals in efforts to plan their life course strategically and dimmed the disciplinary power of the old work ethic based on delayed gratification.[15]

Lasch of course observes that the Protestant work ethic eroded decades ago. Sennett, however, links its disciplinary effects to the corporate structuring of life patterns (even for those working outside the corporation).

On the one hand, insofar as he attends to a certain loss, Sennett signals the decline of the symbolic that subtends Lasch's analysis of the change in paternal authority. With the vantage of two more decades, Sennett detects that this change is a loss. He analyzes this loss in terms of meaning and language: the absence of a place from which to narrate one's life. On the other hand, because Sennett concretizes this loss as a loss of narrative rather than of symbolic authority, he overlooks the real changes to the individual form that Lasch already diagnosed. Sennett wants to shore up the individual. Lasch recognizes the form's obsolescence. By emphasizing the

---

15   Ibid., 181.

missing narrative of adulthood, Sennett thus covers over the more fundamental disruption at the level of the symbolic.

For Sennett, the new economy has an upside. It allows for the emergence of new personal qualities such as "repudiation of dependence, development of one's potential ability, the capacity to transcend possessiveness."[16]Accentuating the bright side of the post–welfare state technologized economy, Sennett tries to redeem the project of the New Left, making its critique of bureaucracy, cult of individuality, and celebration of emotional authenticity into not simply vanishing mediators of communicative capitalism but real achievements to be continued. He packages his recommendations for this continuation as the cultural values that individual workers require to sustain themselves in the fast-paced and volatile economy: narrative, usefulness, and craftsmanship.[17]

Sennett's advocacy of a "cultural anchor" for an economy he recognizes as productive of extreme inequality and social instability puts Lasch's critique of monopoly capitalism in stark relief: Lasch's rejection of capitalism really is radical. More to the point, with his emphases on life narratives, usefulness, and craftsmanship Sennett increases the burden on the individual form. Instead of building up the collectivity and solidarity that might relieve some of the demands placed on individuals, his suggestions continue the turn in and on the individual, as if the cultural anchor were nothing more than the fetish to be held onto as we nevertheless acknowledge the impossibility of the command to individuate.

Jennifer M. Silva draws out an alternative to Sennett's emphasis on a missing narrative of adulthood. The narrative isn't missing. The narrative has changed, morphing into a more extreme version of the therapeutic self Lasch already identified in the collapse of its material and symbolic supports. What matters in the twenty-first century is individuation itself. "In a time when suffering is plentiful and work and family unreliable," Silva writes, competent

16   Ibid., 182.
17   Ibid., 185.

adulthood is defined "not in terms of traditional markers like financial independence, a career, or a marriage, but rather in terms of psychic development: achieving sobriety, overcoming addiction, fighting a mental illness, or simply not becoming one's parents."[18] Silva's alternative account of the pressures on contemporary adults draws from her ethnographic study of working-class adults in Massachusetts and Virginia. Her interviewees emphasize self-reliance, making it on their own. They can't rely on experts or institutions. Other people are likely to fail or betray them. Individualism preserves and protects their own best thing, the only thing they can rely on, themselves. Their repudiation of dependence is a reaction to the loss of dependable others. Rather than an achievement, independence is a fetish barely holding together the fragile individual form.

Silva's account of a transition to adulthood marked not by "entry *into* social groups and institutions but rather the explicit rejection *of* them" provides a poignant rejoinder to Sennett.[19] One man tells Silva that "the hardest part about being an adult is finding a real fucking job."[20] People aren't lacking *a narrative* for adulthood. Capitalism presents adulthood as an individual project. For the young working people Silva interviewed, individualism equals dignity. They tell heroic tales of self-sufficiency, turning inward as they manage feelings of betrayal, accept flexibility and flux, and buttress their sense of being utterly alone. Although the dependencies of the welfare state and corporate bureaucracy that Lasch associates with the therapeutic sensibility have been dismantled and replaced by a harsher, more competitive capitalism, therapeutic language remains the vocabulary through which to account for individual success and failure.

Instead of the jettisoning of the past that Lasch and Sennett

---

18   Jennifer M. Silva, *Coming Up Short: Working-Class Adulthood in an Age of Uncertainty*, New York: Oxford University Press, 2013, 125.

19   Ibid., 84.

20   Ibid., 98.

observe, Silva's subjects embrace the past as they narrate the challenges they have had to overcome in order to realize their authentic selves. Understood in terms of familial and personal experiences, the past provides an open field of explanations for hardship, failure, and the diminution of what they see as success. Unlike Lasch's empty narcissists, Silva's young adults have lives of inner purpose—surviving on their own in a context where the odds are against them. They struggle with illness and battle with addiction. They overcome dysfunctional families and past relationships. The fight to survive is the key feature of an identity imagined as dignified and heroic because it has to produce itself by itself.

Silva's young adults point to an imaginary identity beyond the rugged individualist and the narcissistic gamesman: the survivor. Unlike the symbolic identity of institutions (the place from which one sees oneself as acting), imaginary identity is the image one adopts of oneself. Since so many of Silva's informants feel they have had to do it all by themselves, in contexts of poverty and diminishing opportunity, they take the fact of their survival as the morally significant fact: making it on one's own is what bestows dignity. Some of the white survivors Silva interviews resent "socialists" like US President Barack Obama for trying to take away their last best thing, the special something that is all they have left, namely, the dignity they have because they are completely self-reliant. The black survivors, too, narrate their experiences in individual rather than collective terms. They, too, seek to hold on to the only person they can count on—themselves. Betrayed by schools, the labor market, and the government, Silva's working-class informants in general feel "completely alone, responsible for their own fates and dependent on outside help at their peril." For them, surviving means internalizing the painful lesson that "being an adult means trusting no one by yourself."[21]

---

21   Ibid., 9.

What Sennett lauded as a repudiation of dependence appears in Silva's account as a deep skepticism of solidarity. Reliance on other people requires acknowledging one's insufficiency as an individual, one's inability to survive alone. The hostility to the needy expressed by some of Silva informants suggests a defense against their own need. Hostility lets them displace their need onto others and thereby shore up a fragile and impossible individuality. Having learned that they can't rely on anyone, these young working-class adults try to numb their sense of betrayal by affirming the worst cultural scripts of individualism, personal responsibility, and self-reliance, hardening themselves to the world around them. Their hostility to various forms of government intervention, particularly affirmative action, makes them ideal supports for neoliberal capitalism. Incidentally, those of us who write and circulate critical exposés—stories of governmental corruption, university failure, and corporate malfeasance—may not be helping our cause. We may be affirming what some in the working class already know to be true: they are being betrayed.

Likewise countering Sennett's happy rendering of the repudiation of dependence, Carrie M. Lane's research on white-collar technology workers in Dallas situates the emphasis on individual responsibility in the context of wide-scale layoffs and unemployment.[22] Insecurity is a primary feature of the lives of these tech workers. Most alternate through contract positions of varying duration, unemployment, and self-employment.[23] Lane notes how the technology workers she interviewed embrace a "career management" ideology that casts "insecurity as an empowering

---

22 Carrie M. Lane, *A Company of One*, Ithaca, NY: Cornell University Press, 2011.

23 Lane's subjects were men and women, in their twenties through sixties, from different racial and ethnic backgrounds—African American, Asian American, Latino, Indian, Pakistani, Chinese, and Japanese. Most, however, were white men between the ages of thirty and fifty.

alternative to dependence on a single employer."[24] They construe loyalty as a thing of the past: since everyone is a victim of economic forces beyond their control, neither companies nor employees owe each other anything. Owners and workers both want to make money however they can. No one should expect a company to provide employment security or opportunities for professional development. Such an expectation indicates a childish attitude of dependence. According to one executive, "To give my employees job security would be to disempower them and relieve them of the responsibility that they need to feel for their own success."[25] Laid-off and job-seeking tech workers adopt the corresponding individualist mindset: success comes from doing "whatever it takes" to get by, get through, get that next job.

The survivor is a compelling identity under conditions of extreme competition and inequality. It validates surviving by any means necessary. Survival is its own reward. Setbacks and lapses are new challenges, ultimately greater proof of one's survival skills. Popular culture provides a wide array of survivors to emulate (as well as examples of those who have been unable to get themselves together): from Katniss in *The Hunger Games*, to the winners of uncountable reality television competitions, to games like *Day Z* and *Fallout*, to victims of illness or crime. Emotions of anger, suspicion, and defensiveness are justified—one can rely only on oneself—and potentially useful as the psychic weapons that can help maintain an impossible individuality.

The survivor is a figure not for a culture of narcissism but for a psychotic culture. If narcissistic culture is characterized by the dislodging of symbolic authority, psychotic culture is characterized by its foreclosure.[26] In brief, Lacan defines psychosis in terms

---

24   Lane, *A Company of One*, 13.

25   Ibid., 51, quoting Andrew Ross, *No Collar*, Philadelphia: Temple University Press, 2003.

26   See my longer discussion in *Democracy and Other Neoliberal Fantasies*, Durham, NC: Duke University Press, 2009, ch 6.

of the foreclosure of the Name-of-the-Father or master signifier. That the master signifier is foreclosed means that it does not stabilize meaning; the signifying chain lacks an anchor that can hold it together. The generalized loss of symbolic power impacts the subject such that he feels this now-missing authority to be all the closer, more powerful, and intrusive. In a psychotic culture, then, mistrust is pervasive, all-consuming. Each confronts power directly and alone.

To compensate for the missing symbolic authority, the psychotic turns to the imaginary. He positions himself in relation to a "captivating image," perhaps of one whom he hates, admires, or fears.[27] This imaginary other would then be a rival to defeat or destroy. The psychotic may try to mimic those around him, particularly as he grapples with intense fear and aggression. And he may also become captivated by an image of himself. Here the psychotic imagines himself not *as* anyone or anything in particular: *I am my own worst enemy*. What matters is persistence, survival, for its own sake.

Whether rendered as caring for oneself or looking out for number one, the captivating image of the individual enjoins its own maintenance. For all their emphases on self-reliance, Silva's interviewees nonetheless want to be recognized. They want someone else to hear their stories, validate what they've accomplished. Communicative capitalism supplies the necessary infrastructure, the crowd of many who might view, like, or share.

Lasch's diagnosis of cultural narcissism has lost its currency: communicative capitalist society is less narcissistic than it is psychotic, oriented via an alliance of the imaginary and the Real in the wake of the loss of the symbolic. Rather than enduring a surfeit of expertise, we are awash in multiple, conflicting, irreconcilable opinions. Unable ever fully to determine which is right, we have to decide for ourselves. Algorithms and data render social science obsolete.

27 Jacques Lacan, *The Psychoses: 1955–1956, Seminar III*, ed. Jacques-Alain Miller, trans. Russel Grigg, New York: Norton, 1997, 204.

Power is backed by neither authority nor knowledge, appearing and manifesting instead as violence. Therapy offers neither justice nor cure. Militarized policing—arrests and shootings without accountability or cause—takes the place of the former; a wide array of pharmaceuticals takes the place of the latter, and when these fail there is depression, incapacity, addiction, and suicide. Finally, precarity, competition, and social networks supplant the antagonistic cooperation Lasch associates with the internal life of the corporation. Aggressive impulses need not be repressed under a veneer of cheerfulness. In the extreme inequality of communicative capitalism, multiple channels encourage their expression: hate and outrage circulate easily in affective networks.[28]

Nevertheless, Lasch's attention to the forces that simultaneously command and undermine individuality remains compelling for the way it opens up the growing weight placed on the individual form. As subsequent sociological research attests, the interiorization of this weight continues to unburden corporations and the state from social responsibilities, intensifying concentration on already stressed individuals. An effect has been the diminishing of expectations such that survival itself becomes the achievement worth celebrating.

Left Individualism

In the very moment when capital as a class was mounting what would come to be recognized as a deadly onslaught against unions, the welfare state, and suppositions of collective responsibility more broadly, commanded individuality appears in a surprising place: the communist party. More specifically, enamored of the apparent freedom and creativity offered under the guise of a network society, leftists in and around the Communist Party of

---

28 For a more detailed discussion see my *Blog Theory*, Cambridge, UK: Polity Press, 2010.

Great Britain appealed to individual responsibilities and capacities in terms much like Sennett's. The individual, rather than the class, would be the locus of freedom.

At the end of the 1980s, *Marxism Today*, a CPGB magazine, made itself into a platform for debates on the British Left over Marxism, Thatcherism, the legacy of communism, and the future of socialism. At the heart of the debate was the question of "new times." How could and should socialism adapt given the changes associated with post-Fordism and the political challenge of Thatcherism? For many writing in *Marxism Today*, the dissolution of the welfare state and the rise of information technology, and, later, the collapse of the Soviet bloc demanded the Left's reconstruction. The question, then, was what this reconstructed Left would look like. For what became the dominant voice, it looked liberal, offering little more than capitalism with a human face.

Charles Leadbeater's proposal for a "progressive individualism" emphasized putting individual interests at the center of socialist strategy: "If the Left stands for one thing, it should be this: people taking more responsibility for all aspects of their lives."[29] As a counter to Thatcher's culture of "individual consumerism," his Left would offer "individual citizenship." The point of collective action would be fulfilling individual needs. Leadbeater formulates the idea in market terms, saying that the Left "has to renegotiate the contract between those who finance collective services, those who provide them, and those who consume them, to ensure they provide value for money, efficiency, flexibility and choice."[30] This is a vision of social welfare as consumer good, a vision possible through the evacuation of collectivity and the suppression of class struggle. Leadbeater couples his call for the Left to reorient itself around individual rights and responsibilities with one for collective provision. Nonetheless his analysis repeats key elements of

---

29 Charles Leadbeater, "Power to the Person," *Marxism Today*, October 1988, 14.

30 Ibid., 15.

Thatcherism, from the attack on the welfare state for its ineffi-
ciency and paternalism to the assertion of the role of the market in
meeting individual needs.

Leadbeater's language and values are neoliberal. Thatcherism
establishes the place from which he sees the world. He says that
Thatcherism encourages "aspirations for autonomy, choice,
decentralization, greater responsibility." The Left needs to accept
these values and broaden them: "While Thatcherism confines
individual choice within the market, the Left should stress the
importance of wider social individuality, diversity and plurality in lifestyles which cannot be delivered by the market."[31] The
state should be both player and platform, guaranteeing rights
and providing alternatives in a larger field of choices. So not only
does the market have a role—competition efficiently coordinates
"lots of decentralized economic decisions"—but the public sector
needs to become consumer oriented, the benefits office having the
same "standards of the high street." The devolution of common
good into individual benefit goes unmarked, the assumption that
public services be treated like private consumer choices unex-
plored. Leadbetter, with Thatcher, just assumes the market as
the model for social relations.[32] Not only do individuals need
rights to consultation and participation in the workplace, but
they have a responsibility to accept "reasonable offers of employment" as well as "reasonable measures of labor flexibility."[33]
To adapt to the new times, the Left has to look like, see as, the
Right. Rather than championing working-class values of equality, solidarity, and collectivity, in Leadbeater's version the Left
stands for capitalist ones of efficiency, flexibility, and decentralization, held together by a celebration of the individual as a rational,

31   Ibid., 18.
32   For a critique of this assumption in the "new times" debate more generally, see Michael Rustin, "The Politics of Post-Fordism: or, The Trouble
with 'New Times,'" *New Left Review* 175, May–June 1985, 54–77.
33   Leadbeater, "Power to the Person," 19.

disciplined, and autonomous agent with the power to remake his world.[34]

Rosalind Brunt similarly pushed a left individualism.[35] For her, the "new times" demand a politics of identity. The examination of one's personal history, a beginning from oneself, is what made sexual politics exciting and what the Communist Party needs to embrace. Brunt argues that identity politics should be at the heart of a transformative politics because it gives a sense of difference, of the many identities offered in and by contemporary culture. It helps people think about how they relate to others, how they live and directly experience ideology. Instead of the Party providing a critical perspective from which to look at the world, breaking from the hegemonic capitalist culture and installing a gap within it, lived experience would be the perspective brought to bear on politics. In Brunt's version, which prefigures what would become a key feature of left thought for several decades, politics itself turns inward, the task of changing the world preceded by that of understanding oneself. Having listed the identities and relations important to belonging—race, class, gender, nation and colleagues, friends, children, lovers—Brunt writes, "And then there is the bedrock sense of the 'real me', the feeling that, however precarious these other identities, there is a secret hidden core, a completely unsocialised and essential self somewhere private and inside."[36] The implication is that this secret core should be the bedrock of a new politics of "unity-in-difference," a Bolshevik principle reimagined through an identity politics that refuses talk of priorities and socialism as a greater good. The effect is a resonance both with capitalist society's marketplace demographics and therapy culture's emphasis on an authentic self. The result is a change in the focus of communist politics such that it contracts rather than enlarges.

---

34 Idid., 17.

35 Rosalind Brunt, "Bones in the Corset," *Marxism Today*, October 1988.

36 Ibid., 21.

Although they voice themes that will come to dominate the post-Marxist and post-structuralist Left, Leadbeater's and Brunt's are of course not the only positions taken in *Marxism Today*'s debate over the "new times." Ellen Meiksins Wood, to use but one example, offered a powerful critique of the "new times" hypothesis, particularly as set out in the programmatic *Manifesto For New Times*. Wood rejects the premise of postmodern fragmentation underpinning emphases on personal identity, flexibility, and diversity. Such emphases give the impression that capitalism "has become infinitely more permeable, opening up huge spaces for people to carve out their own autonomous social realities."[37] The reality, she argues, is that capitalism has become more of "a total global system" than ever before. Subjection to the "expansionary logic of capitalism" and its coercive market forces is growing. Under Thatcher, class politics is more blatant, more extreme. Drawing from Michael Ruskin in *New Left Review*, Wood asks whose worldview is given expression in the *Manifesto*. The answer: those who attempt to manage capitalism in a project of modernization. The new times aren't new: the Left in retreat always presents itself as capitalist managers. And the *Manifesto*'s perspective isn't innovative: it's capitalism's own. Retroactively, no one can deny that Wood was right.

In step with the unleashing of the welfare state's restraints on capital accumulation, views such as Leadbeater's and Brunt's came to characterize the "left realism" broadly shared across the Anglo-European Left, theoretically developed by Ernesto Laclau and Chantal Mouffe and buttressed by cultural studies and post-structuralism (Habermasian critical theory provided the framework for a similar accommodation). As I detail below, left realists accept the market as necessary. They reject revolution, prioritizing democracy and citizenship. In effect, they fear politics, outdoing the Right in their excoriation of twentieth-century communism for

_____

37   Ellen Meiksins Wood, comment on the *Manifesto for New Times*, *Marxism Today*, August 1989, 31.

its crimes and their disavowal of its successes. Abandoned is anything like communism as a vision of justice. Confining themselves within a limited political field and accepting the state and market as given, left realists embrace the politics of identity: the individual is to be invested with the energy and attention formerly directed toward building the revolutionary people.

At the moment when capital was acting as a class to break unions, dismantle the welfare state, privatize public services, impose information technologies, transfer industrial production to cheaper labor markets, and facilitate expansions in financial services and capital flow, *Marxism Today* was trying to figure out how to make socialism attractive rather than how to fight back. Proceeding as if socialism were nothing but another product in a political marketplace, *Marxism Today*'s perspective on the political and economic challenges facing the Left was determined by a capitalist rather than a communist horizon. It embraced the capitalist appeal to individualism at the very moment when it should have emphasized solidarity and collective strength. Tragically, this embrace helped to shore up the individual form that, as we learn from Lasch, was already self-destructing. It no doubt seemed necessary to many at the time, but this is part of the tragedy. Now we know.

The Pressure Is Killing Me

The intensification of capitalism amplifies pressures on and for the individual. These pressures are political: the individual is called on to express her opinion, speak for herself, get involved. She is told that she, all by herself, *can make a difference*. Her responses to ubiquitous demands for feedback take the place of collective action, rendered as either impossible or too repressive to constitute a real alternative. The pressures on the individual are also economic: even in the absence of significant social mobility, the individual is offered up as the most significant determinant of success or failure.

In competitive labor markets, attracting buyers for one's labor power is a challenge. One has to distinguish oneself to get hired or, for some of us, to maintain the fantasy of something like a fair competition (it would be horrible to think that all that debt was for nothing). No wonder that communicative capitalism enjoins us to uniqueness: we are the product we make of ourselves. At the same time, specialization supports marketeers' interests in ever more granular access to customers, police efforts to locate and track, and capital's concern with preventing people from coalescing in common struggle. Identification is inseparable from surveillance, personalization absorbed in commerce. Capitalism's injunction to individuate is the most powerful weapon in its arsenal.

The pressures are also psychological, as we have already seen. Franco Berardi highlights the "conquest of internal space, the interior world, the life of the mind" endemic to communicative capitalism.[38] Informational intensification and temporal acceleration saturate our attention to "pathological levels." Berardi associates panic, aggressiveness, depression, and fear with this saturation. He finds symptoms of it in waves of suicide, escalating Viagara use among those with no time for affection, tenderness, and sexual preliminaries, "millions of boxes of Prozac sold every month, the epidemic of attention deficit disorders among youngsters, the diffusion of drugs like Ritalin to school children, and the spreading epidemic of panic."[39] People respond to overload with drugs and technology, trying to do more, be more, keep up and on top, but the pressure is relentless. The more they do, the more they are expected to do. Swamped under the overproduction of signs, the human receiver is overloaded to the point of breakdown.

I agree with much of Berardi's description, but I want to suggest an alternative approach to the psychopathologies he observes. Drugs, depression, ADHD, and panic are not merely pathologies.

---

38   Berardi uses the term "semio-capitalism." See Franco Berardi, *Precarious Rhapsody*, London: Minor Compositions, 2009, 69.

39   Ibid., 82.

They are also defenses. The real pathology is the individual form itself. Drugs attempt to maintain it, keep it going. The individual is pathological in the sense that it is incompatible with its setting, incapable of responding to the pressures it encounters without pain, sacrifice, or violence (psychoanalysis stems from this insight, hence the primacy of castration). The problem of contemporary subjectivity arises not from the extremes of a capitalism that has merged with the most fundamental components of communicativity. It's not that the saturated, intensified, and unbearably competitive circuits of communicative capitalism are making us depressed, anxious, autistic, and distracted and that we need to find ways to preserve and protect our fragile individualities. Depression, anxiety, autism, and hyperactivity signal the breakdown of a form that has always itself been a problem, a mobilization of processes of individuation and interiorization in a reflexive inward turn that breaks connections and weakens collective strength. The individual form is not under threat. It is the threat. And now it's weakening.

In *Alone Together: Why We Expect More from Technology and Less from Each Other*, Sherry Turkle documents some of the ways social media provide relief from individualist expectations. To be sure, she does not describe her findings in terms of such relief. Rather than construing the individual form as a problem, she presents it as a vulnerability in need of protection. So she echoes dominant injunctions to individuality. Nonetheless, her explorations of "networked life and its effects on intimacy and solitude, on identity and privacy" open up paths she doesn't follow, paths to collectivity.[40]

Reporting on her interviews with teenagers, Turkle describes young people waiting for connection, fearful of abandonment, and dependent on immediate responses from others even to have feelings. For example, seventeen-year-old Claudia has happy feelings

---

40   Sherry Turkle, *Alone Together*, New York: Basic Books, 2011, 169.

as soon as she starts to text. Unlike a previous generation that might call someone *to talk about* feelings, when Claudia wants *to have* a feeling, she sends a text.[41] Turkle reports the anxieties people express about face-to-face interactions as well as about expectations associated with the telephone, that is to say, about speaking to another person in real time.[42] The multitasking inseparable from contemporary communication, the fact that people may be texting and talking simultaneously, looking at something else while ostensibly listening to their interlocutor, implants an uncertainty as to whether another is even paying attention. Combined with pressures for immediate response and the knowledge that the "internet never forgets" (most of us are unable to eliminate all traces of our digital identities after they've been uploaded, archived, and shared), our new intimacy with technology, Turkle demonstrates, is affecting the kinds of selves we become. We experience solitude, privacy, connection, and others differently from how we did before.

For Turkle, these new experiences are pathological.[43] Drawing from Erik Erikson's work on personal identity, she argues that networked technologies inhibit the kind of separation necessary for maturation. Parents are always in reach, available, even if they are not actually present but themselves overworked, distracted, and overextended. Young people do not learn how to be alone, how to reflect on their emotions in private. Fragile and dependent, they fail to develop the sense of who they are that they need to have "before" they "forge successful life partnerships."[44] Rather than inner-directed and autonomous (Turkle refers to David Riesman), the culture of mobile phones and instant messaging has raised other-directedness "to a higher power."[45] The expectation

41   Ibid., 176.
42   Ibid., 205.
43   Ibid., 178.
44   Ibid., 175.
45   Ibid., 167.

of constant connectivity eliminates opportunities for solitude even as people are "increasingly insecure, isolated, and lonely."[46] Turkle concludes, "Loneliness is failed solitude. To experience solitude, you must be able to summon yourself by yourself; otherwise you will only know how to be lonely."[47]

There is nothing surprising in Turkle's account of contemporary "tethered selves." From her diagnoses of narcissism to her worries about the constant and even addictive character of networked communications, she repeats well-known criticisms of teens, media, and contemporary culture. But the language Turkle employs when she speaks of solitude signals something more than an updating of the critique of cultural narcissism for a networked age. She uses the second person—"you must be able to summon yourself by yourself"—and shifts from a descriptive to an imperative mode: "you must" if you are to know something besides how to be lonely. Turkle relies on this mode because she has described the reflective individual as threatened by networked technologies. She wants us to join her in defending the individual from this threat. Directly addressing the reader, she insists that the reflective individual be shored up (even as she rejects technologically mediated forms of this shoring up as themselves pathological). For Turkle, a self that is less bounded, more expansive, less separate, more connected, is immature, at risk of loneliness. It needs to form its identity, separate itself from others, and go through the stages of becoming an individual.

What Turkle links to technology, Dany-Robert Dufour (in *The Art of Shrinking Heads*) links to the acceleration of the process of individuation more broadly, particularly in connection with the decline in symbolic efficiency or change in the structure of the symbolic.[48] The contemporary subject, he says, is called upon to

---

46   Ibid., 157.

47   Ibid., 288.

48   Dany-Robert Dufour, *The Art of Shrinking Heads*, Cambridge, UK: Polity Press, 2008.

create itself.[49] Dufour repeats in a Lacanian register findings we already encountered in the research of sociologists Silva and Lane, namely, the overloading onto the individual of previously collective responsibilities and expectations. By the end of the twentieth century, in a setting Dufour characterizes as postmodern and neoliberal, the "I" is completely self-referential, grounded in nothing external to it, dependent on the acknowledgement of no other. But where Dufour grapples with the impossibility of self-individuation, locating the intensification of the injunction to be oneself in the alliance between the imaginary and the Real in the wake of the decline of symbolic efficiency, Turkle repeats the command: "you must be able to summon yourself by yourself."

Turkle's interviewees describe themselves in ways that rub up against Turkle's own concerns with separation and individuation. For example, a nurse, tired after eight hours at work and a second shift at home, says that she logs onto Facebook and feels less alone. A college junior explains, "I feel that I am part of a larger thing, the Net, the Web. The world. It becomes a thing to me, a thing I am part of. And the people, too. I stop seeing them as individuals, really. They are part of this larger thing."[50] The student's words here resonate with a line from Félix Guattari: "The collective engagement is at once the subject, the object and the expression. No longer is the individual always the reference point for the dominant significations."[51] The college junior feels himself and others to be part of a larger collectivity such that viewing himself and others as separate, as individuals, makes no sense; it loses the connection that arises through their mutual engagement.

For Turkle, though, connectivity is so pathological that she depicts it biochemically, as an addiction. Her argument relies on

49   Ibid., 16.
50   Turkle, *Alone Together*, 168.
51   Félix Guattari, *Molecular Revolution*, trans. Rosemary Sheed, New York: Penguin, 1984, 203.

Mihaly Csikszentmihalyi's work on "flow." Most references to flow are positive, descriptions of a desirable experience of focus, involvement, and immersion. Turkle's, however, is critical: "In the flow state, you are able to act without self-consciousness" (as I describe below and explore in greater detail in the next chapter, this absence of self-consciousness is an attribute crowd theorists associate with being in a group, mass, or crowd). For Turkle, acting without self-consciousness is a problem because "you can have it when texting or e-mailing or during an evening on Facebook" (again, the use of the second person pronoun points to Turkle's attempt to implicate us in practices that are threatening and must be combatted).[52] Melding game and life, that is, actual games like World of Warcraft, with email and Facebook, Turkle explains, "When online life becomes your game, there are new complications. If lonely, you can find continual connection. But this may leave you more isolated, without real people around you. So you may return to the Internet for another hit of what feels like connection."[53] She uses neurochemistry to justify the language of addiction:

> Our neurochemical response to every ping and ring tone seems to be the one elicited by the "seeking" drive, a deep motivation of the human psyche. Connectivity becomes a craving; when we receive a text or an e-mail, our nervous system responds by giving us a shot of dopamine. We are stimulated by connectivity itself. We learn to require it, even when it depletes us.[54]

Turkle's pathologizing treatment of connectivity blurs interaction with machines—phones, computers—with interactions with people. Our brains react to sounds by releasing—injecting—dopamine. But rather than this reaction being a valuable

---

52 Turkle, *Alone Together*, 226.
53 Ibid., 227.
54 Ibid.

reinforcement of our connections with others, it is a dangerous stimulant that we crave. Would happy neurochemical responses to seeing people face-to-face be similarly suspect? Is the thrill of contact with others at a party, in a rally, at a concert, or in a crowd also at risk of becoming a craving insofar as such intense and demanding contact might also deplete us?

If we do not give normative priority to the individual as the proper or exclusive form of subjectivity, we can read the evidence Turkle offers differently. We can read it as an indication that a political form of separation and enclosure is changing, mutating, becoming something else. Michael Hardt and Antonio Negri follow Gilles Deleuze in describing this change as the passage from disciplinary society to the society of control. They point out how disciplinary logics worked primarily within the institutions of civil society to produce individuated subjects.[55] By the end of the twentieth century, disciplining and mediating institutions— the nuclear family, the school, the union, and the church—were in crisis (Lasch's cultural narcissism is one diagnosis of this crisis). The spaces, logics, practices, and norms previously coalescing into social and economic institutions broke down and apart. In some instances, the release of an institutional logic from its spatial constraints gave it all the more force; in other instances, the opposite occurred. Thus, Hardt and Negri argue that pervasive institutional dissolution has been accompanied by an "indeterminacy of the *form* of the subjectivities produced."[56] Hardt and Negri conclude that the bourgeois individual—the citizen-subject of an autonomous political sphere, the disciplined subject of civil society, the liberal subject willing to vote in public and then return home to his private domesticity—can no longer serve as a presupposition of theory or action. They suggest that in its place, we find fluid, hybrid, and mobile subjectivities who are undisciplined, who have

55　　Michael Hardt and Antonio Negri, *Empire*, Cambridge, MA: Harvard University Press, 2000, 329.

56　　Ibid., 197.

not internalized specific norms and constraints, and who can now only be controlled.

Hardt and Negri are right to point to the changes in the settings that produced the bourgeois individual. Yet they underplay the emergent ferocity of commanded individuality. Their fluid, hybrid, and mobile subjectivities appear as loci of freedom, as if their singularity were a natural property rather than itself enjoined, inscribed, and technologically generated in the service of capitalism. As the decline of discipline weakened individuating structures, new technologically mediated techniques of individuation took their place. An easy example (one prominent in Turkle's discussion) is the adoption of mobile phones as personal communication devices for kids. Enabling parents to keep track from a distance, phones fill in for the direct supervision and contact that has diminished in the wake of increasing work demands on parents, particularly mothers. Additional such techniques and technologies of individuation include competition in intensified labor markets as they induce a marketing relation to oneself; targeted advertisements that urge consumers to differentiate and specify themselves; locative technologies associated with mobile phones and GPS; cookies and other data-gathering techniques associated with transactions on the internet; political injunctions to personal participation; and, in the US, a rights-based political culture focused on personal identity, harm, and exclusion as opposed to common, collective, and systemic injustice—within this culture, systemic problems such as exploitation in the workplace and amplified personal indebtedness are treated as the effects of individual choices, preferences, and luck. The fluidity that Hardt and Negri observe, then, is accompanied by the technologies and practices of commanded individuality. The result is that the expectation of unique individuality exerts demands that are as constant and unyielding as they are impossible to meet.

That the young people Turkle interviews express anxieties associated with autonomy and connection is not surprising. They are enjoined to individuality, told each individual is selfsame, self-creating, self-responsible: one is born alone and one dies alone; you can rely on no one but yourself. Yet the technologies that further individuation—smartphone, tablet, laptop—and the platforms that encourage it—Twitter, Facebook, Instagram, Tumblr—provide at the same time an escape from and alternative to individuation: connection to others, collectivity.

Crowds

As I explore more thoroughly in subsequent chapters, Elias Canetti's weird yet compelling anthropology of crowds (Adorno described it as a scandal) addresses an anxiety different from the one that concerns Turkle.[57] He considers not the fear of being alone but the fear of being touched: "There is nothing that man fears more than the touch of the unknown."[58] The one place where man is free of this fear is in a crowd. "The crowd he needs is the dense crowd, in which body is pressed to body," Canetti writes, "a crowd, too, whose psychical constitution is also dense, or compact, so that he no longer notices who it is that presses against him."[59]

Turkle thinks that people's aversion to talking on the phone (as opposed to texting) and conversing face-to-face reflects their need for filters, for ways to handle sensory and information overload. They reflect, she suggests, not only a longing for solitude but also the way that in a stimulation and simulation culture we have become cyborgs.[60] Canetti suggests an alternative interpretation: we may be coming to prefer the crowd, the presence of many

57   "Elias Canetti: Discussion with Theodor W. Adorno," *Thesis Eleven* 45, 1996, 1–15.
58   Elias Canetti, *Crowds and Power*, trans. Carol Stewart, New York: Farrar, Straus and Giroux, 1984, 15.
59   Ibid.
60   Turkle, *Alone Together*, 209.

that opens us to collectivity and relieves us of anxiety. One-on-one conversations may feel too constraining insofar as they enclose us back in an individual form. Rather than part of a group, of many, we are just ourselves.

If this is plausible, then we have an alternative way to think about preoccupations with numbers of friends, followers, blog hits, shares, and retweets. They do not indicate personal achievement or popularity. They mark our absorption in the crowd, how densely we are enmeshed in it. So, to be clear, we can think of these counts in the individualist terms given us by capital. We can also recognize them as something else, as markers of belonging to something larger than oneself. In this latter sense, they reassure us that we are not unique but common.

For Canetti, the relief we feel in a crowd is paradoxical. It arises from a fear of others, a feeling that others are threatening, which "reverses into its opposite" in the crowd.[61] In a discussion with Adorno, he explains that he believes that people like to become a crowd because of "the relief they feel at the reversal of the feeling of being touched."[62] From this vantage point, the craving for dopamine Turkle describes seems more like the relief we may feel when we shake off the fears associated with individuation—isolation, exposure, vulnerability.

One might object that Canetti's crowd is physical and the networked crowd is virtual. This objection is compelling—part of the power of the occupations of Tahrir Square, Syntagma Square, and the Occupy movement's multiple parks and sites came from the force of bodies out of doors in collectivities authorized by neither capital nor the state. But the objection implies a distinction between the physical and the virtual that crowd theory consistently destabilizes. Most crowd theorists attend to physical and virtual crowds. They draw out "crowd" as a verb, as dynamics, and as affects that traverse and constitute collectivity. Canetti himself describes

---

61   "Canetti: Discussion with Adorno."
62   Ibid.

invisible crowds of the dead and spermatozoa. As I detail in the next chapter, Gustave Le Bon's influential (albeit notoriously reactionary) work on crowds treats the crowd primarily as a psychological concept. Le Bon goes so far as to claim enigmatically that "crowds, doubtless, are always unconscious, but this very unconsciousness is perhaps one of the secrets of their strength."[63] Furthermore, technologies of presencing have developed so as to make our mediated interactions feel all the more present and intense. We are interacting with others, not just screens. When we register trending hashtags and multi-shared stories, we experience the force of many. In social media, the many flow across our screens, waves of images and expressions of feeling with effects that accumulate, resonate, and consolidate into patterns irreducible to any particular position or utterance. Canetti notes "how *gladly* one falls prey to the crowd."[64] The crowd, virtual and physical, moves and intoxicates. Canetti writes, "you were lost, you forgot yourself, you felt tremendously remote and yet fulfilled; whatever you felt, you didn't feel it for yourself; it was the most selfless thing you knew; and since selfishness was shown, talked, and *threatened* on all sides, you needed this experience of thunderous unselfishness like the blast of the trumpet at the Last Judgment."[65] The experience of flow that overwhelms the conscious experience of self that Turkle finds so threatening, then, might also be understood as a breaking out of the illusion that the individual is and can be a subject of action (rather than a form of enclosure and containment) and a giving-over to a crowd.

---

63 Gustave LeBon, *The Crowd* (1896), Kitchener, Ontario: Baroche Books, 2001, 6.

64 Elias Canetti, *The Torch in My Ear*, trans. Joachim Neugroschel, New York: Farrar, Straus and Giroux, 1982, 148.

65 Canetti, *Torch*, 94.

We've Got to Be We

The crumbling of capitalist realism—the shaking off of Margaret Thatcher's destructive mantra that "there is no alternative" to unfettered capitalist competition—has led to mainstream acknowledgement that capitalism is a system that takes from the many and gives to the few.[66] Today no one denies the fact that some always lose in the capitalist economy. The system produces losers—the unemployed, the homeless, the indebted, the conned, the wiped out, the abandoned, the sacrificed. It runs on debt, foreclosure, expropriation, eviction, dispossession, destruction—these are just other words for privatization. But then what? Ever since the Left started looking at itself and the world in terms of individual specificity and the efficiency of markets, it has seemed easier to imagine the end of capitalism than it is to imagine an organized Left.

Characterized by a perspective foreshadowed by *Marxism Today*'s debate over the new times, a left realism has congealed around a set of loosely held suspicions. This left realism may not be endorsed in its entirety by any particular political or theoretical tendency. No one that I know of has published an explicitly developed left realist position. Yet the fragmenting of left politics into an ever-expanding array of populist, liberal, progressive, trans, pluralist, green, multiculturalist, anti-racist, radical democratic, feminist, identitarian, anarchist, queer, autonomist, horizontalist, anti-imperialist, insurrectionist, libertarian, socialist, and communist persuasions is symptomatic of such a realism, the premises of which manifest as suspicions time and again—in arguments among activists and academics, retorts at meetings, and rejoinders in social media. These premises are that collectivity is undesirable and that collectivity is impossible.

Collectivity is undesirable because it is suspected of excluding possibilities, effacing difference, and enforcing discipline.[67] "What

---

66 Mark Fisher, *Capitalist Realism*, London: Zero Books, 2009.

67 As Jeremy Gilbert observes, "the tradition of derogatory descriptions

do you mean 'we'?" is one slogan of this suspicion, typically lobbed into contexts and discussions deemed insufficiently attentive to the specificities of each person's experience. "Diversity of tactics" sometimes comes up as another such slogan, particularly when invoked to secure space for small-group confrontations with the police at the expense of broader political coordination.

Some find collectivity to be undesirable because of its opposition to individual responsibility and freedom. Rejecting the communisms of Badiou as well as Hardt and Negri, Vanessa Lemm warns, "In both these trends, the process of subjectivation tends to dissolve the individual into a 'multitude' or a 'cause' that is supra-individual and that, far from assuming responsibility for one's freedom, demands that one surrender it."[68] Lemm offers a Nietzschean "counterforce to the radical egalitarianism" of the communists, emphasizing how Nietzsche's "aristocratic conception of culture" relies on "cultivating the responsibility of singular individuals." Others position collectivity as undesirable by insinuating that collectivity has to be imposed; any collective employs a state logic. Banu Bargu's bold deployment of Max Stirner's egoist view of liberation as an individual project of self-valorization best exemplifies this view: to realize their own uniqueness and potential, egoists "should direct their efforts not only against the state, but against any collectivity and collective project."[69]

In the place of an undesirable collectivity, left realism offers up diversity, plurality, and multiplicity. To this end, Eugene W.

---

of collectives—crowds, mobs, masses, etc.—always includes a reference to the group's supposed homogeneity in at least one dimension." See his *Common Ground*, London: Pluto Press, 2013, 70.

68   Vanessa Lemm, "Nietzsche, Aristocratism and Non-Domination," in *How Not To Be Governed*, eds. James Martel and Jimmy Casas Klausen, Lanham, MD: Lexington Books, 2011, 96.

69   Banu Bargu, "Max Stirner, Postanarchy *avant la letter*," in *How Not To Be Governed*, 114–15.

Holland wants to create a "multiplicity of multiplicities."[70] Jimmy Casas Klausen and James Martel likewise encourage expressions of human diversity and view thriving political and economic associations as those that are adaptable, contingent, and multiple.[71] And Andrew Koch claims that anarchism is the "only justifiable political stance" because of its defense of the infinite pluralism of individuated meaning.[72] Such views proceed as if such multiplicity were primarily ontological, rather than also stimulated by capitalism for its benefit and preservation.[73] They also underplay state interest in plurality, particularly the fragmentations that hinder collective opposition and the individuations that facilitate targeting, isolation, and control.

Left realism's second premise is that collectivity is impossible. We are so different, so singularized in our experiences and ambitions, so invested in the primacy of one set of tactics over another that we can't cohere in common struggle. At best we can find momentary affinities and provisional coalitions. Politics should thus involve cultivating our own unique point of view—or the point of view of our sect, tribe, or locale—rather than trying to organize these views into something like a strategy. Left realism implies that coming together itself should be exposed as a fantasy covering over a hidden Hobbesian impulse to transcendence, a myth some use to manipulate others into fighting for their interests.

---

70   Eugene W. Holland, *Nomad Citizenship*, Minneapolis, MN: University of Minnesota Press, 2011, xxiv.

71   James Martel and Jimmy Casas Klausen, "Introduction," *How Not To Be Governed*, xv.

72   Andrew M. Koch, "Poststructuralism and the Epistemological Basis of Anarchism," *Post-Anarchism: A Reader*, eds. Duane Rousselle and Süreyyya Evren, New York: Pluto Press, 2011, 38.

73   As I discuss in the following chapter, Silvia Federici and Michel Foucault provide powerful accounts of the processes of differentiation and individualization accompanying the emergence of the capitalist mode of production.

A further variation on the premise of impossibility is that fundamental changes in the world economy preclude collectivity.[74] Rather than concentrating workers in centralized locations, contemporary capitalism disperses them across the globe. It relies on long supply chains and global capital, using complexity to dissolve sites of accountability.[75] Workers in ever more sectors of the capitalist economy are thus isolated, immiserated, and politically disorganized. To be sure, immiseration and political disorganization also characterize the early decades of revolutionary socialism. Karl Marx, Friedrich Engels, and Rosa Luxemburg all emphasize how competition means that workers tend to remain isolated, lack solidarity, and take a long time to unite. This is why unions and parties have to be created and why creating them is a struggle. Left realism's one-sided emphasis on the objective dimension of our present capitalist setting fails to acknowledge the subjective dimension of perspective, organization, and will: our perspective is part of the setting it sees. This subjective dimension has always been crucial to the Marxist tradition. The communist response to isolation is not to let the reality that produces individualism determine our political horizon. Instead, it is to build solidarity.

The assumptions that collectivity is both undesirable and impossible derive from an even more insidious assumption of left realism: that politics involves the individual. Manuel Castells, for example, treats as a key cultural transformation "the emergence of a new set of values defined as individuation and autonomy, rising from the social movements of the 1970s, and permeating throughout society in the following decades with increasing intensity."[76] Exactly how politics involves the individual varies—*no one speaks*

---

74   See Joshua Clover and Aaron Benanav, "Can Dialectics Break BRICS?" *South Atlantic Quarterly* 113: 4, Fall 2014, 743–59.

75   See Jasper Bernes, "Logistics, Counterlogistics, and the Communist Prospect," *Endnotes* 3, September 2013.

76   Manuel Castells, *Networks of Outrage and Hope: Social Movements in the Internet Age*, Cambridge, UK: Polity Press, 2012, 230.

for me but me; the personal is political; if I can't dance, I don't want to be part of your revolution. But the premise remains the same: a left politics has to encourage and express the multiplicity of individual projects. Individuals have to choose and decide—even as the left fails to provide something anyone could actually choose. Leaders, vanguards, and parties are modes of politics for a time not our own, we are told. They are remnants of a political-economic assemblage that has already crumbled.[77]

Left realism feels realistic to some because it resonates with the prevailing ethos of late neoliberalism that tells us to do it ourselves, stay local and small, and trust no one because they will only betray us. It affirms capitalism's insistence on immediacy and flexibility and the state's replacement of long-term planning and social services by crisis management and triage. Left realism is good on spontaneous outrage. But it fails to organize itself in a way that can do something with this outrage. Disorganized, it remains unable to use crises to build and take power much less construct more equitable and less crisis-prone social and economic arrangements.

The realism in which the Left has been immersed in the neoliberal decades has meant that even when we are fully conscious of the deep inequity of the system in which we find ourselves, we confirm and conform to the dominant ideology: turn inward, enclave, emphasize the singular and momentary. Sometimes we don't feel like we can do anything about it (maybe we have too much work to do already). Or we find ourselves participating in individuated, localized, or communicatively mediated activities without momentum, duration, or a capacity for political memory. Or we presume that we have to focus on ourselves, start with ourselves and thereby redirect political struggle back into ourselves. In a brutal, competitive, and atomized society, psychic well-being is so difficult that success on this front can feel like a significant accomplishment. Trying to do it themselves, people are

---

77   Gilbert, *Common Ground*, 207.

immiserated and proletarianized and confront this immiseration and proletarianization alone.

This chapter has sought to dismantle the assumption of the political primacy of the individual that binds left politics to the dominant capitalist imaginary and that prevents us from seeing the concentration of politics onto the individual as symptomatic of left defeat. Rather than a locus for creativity, difference, agency, and responsibility, the individual is the overburdened remainder of dismantled institutions and solidarities. Commanded individuality obscures individual incapacity even as it amplifies the contradictions barely congealed in the individual form. At the same time, these commands and incapacities attest to another force, the power of collectivity that manifests in crowds.

2

Enclosing the Subject

"Subject" is a concept that continues to trouble political theory. Does "subject" direct us toward initiative and autonomy or subjugation and constraint? Efforts to decenter the subject—whether targeting Cartesianism, Hegelianism, Marxism, or humanism—grapple with the challenge of accounting for order *and* initiative, submission *and* resistance, freedom *and* determination. Theorists and activities inspired by other traditions get roped into these debates when they construe politics in terms of the thoughts, actions, or feelings of individuals. Not only is agency privileged over structure but the presumption that agents are individuals formats the alternative of autonomy or subjugation as an opposition between individual and collective. Collectivity comes to be associated with constraint, with preventing rather than enabling creativity and initiative. Liberal political theorists explicitly construe political agency as an individual capacity. Others take the individuality of the subject of politics for granted. I argue that the problem of the subject is a problem of this persistent individual form, a form that encloses collective political subjectivity into the singular figure of the individual.

The first part of the chapter sets up the idea of enclosure via an inversion of Louis Althusser's famous claim that ideology interpellates individuals as subjects.[1] The point of this inversion is less to critique Althusser than it is to provide a heuristic that can loosen the hold of the individual form on conceptions of political subjectivity. I demonstrate this point by putting the inverted formula, "the subject is interpellated as an individual," in conversation with work in post-structuralist and psychoanalytic theory. The second part of the chapter tracks the enclosing of the subject in the individual form as it appears in the encounter between psychoanalysis and crowd theory, more specifically, in Sigmund Freud's appropriation of the notorious Gustave Le Bon. Continuing the argument from chapter one, my goal is to break free from the individualizing assumptions that hinder understanding the political subject as a collective subject. The individual form encloses collective bodies, ideas, affects, and sensations into a singular, bounded body. The link between individuality and political subjectivity, however, is neither necessary nor natural. It is an effect contingent to the array of processes that converge in bourgeois modernity.

Just as the commodity is a form for value, so is the individual a form for subjectivity. It is a form that impedes collective political subjectivity by separating it into and containing it within individuated bodies and psyches. C. B. MacPherson's presentation of seventeenth-century liberalism is one of the clearest expositions of this vision of the individual. MacPherson argues that at the heart of liberal theory is a "possessive individual" conceived as "the proprietor of his own person or capacities, owing nothing to society for them."[2] He uses Thomas Hobbes and John Locke as his examples. In MacPherson's reading, for Hobbes and Locke the essence of being human is "freedom from dependence on the

---

1   See Louis Althusser, *On the Reproduction of Capitalism*, trans. G. M. Goshgarian, London: Verso, 2014, chapter 12, "On Ideology," and the appendix, "Ideology and Ideological State Apparatuses," 232–72.

2   C. B. MacPherson, *The Political Theory of Possessive Individualism: Hobbes to Locke*, New York: Oxford University Press, 1964, 3.

wills of others, and freedom is a function of possession."[3] They understand the individual neither primarily as a part or member, nor as fundamentally and irrevocably dependent on relations with others, human and nonhuman. Rather, the individual is in essence one who owns himself and his capacities.

What's at stake here is less MacPherson's reading of Hobbes and Locke (which is contestable), than his highlighting of liberalism's mutual constitution of individual and owner. Ownership relies on and is produced through a series of separations and enclosures. Capacities are separate from others as well as separate from a self, which encloses these capacities within its person. Instead of entailing collective reproduction for common good, training—whether moral or technical—is work on and for the self. Cut off from the settings that produce and enable them and enclosed within the individual, capacities are objects of individual concern, so many objects available for exchange and, as capitalism expands, for investment, stylization, and branding.

Although liberal theory treats the individual as an owner and therefore a locus of freedom, the codependence of the commodity form and the individual form works in another direction as well, one that enables elision between commodity and individual. In his gripping account of the antebellum slave trade in the United States, Walter Johnson describes the importance of individuation in the dismantling of slave families and the categorizing and fashioning of slaves for the market. Johnson writes, "On the one hand, they were to be transformed into exemplars of the category to which they had been assigned; but once the categories of comparison had been established and embodied, the slaves were supposed to once again become visible as individuals."[4] To be priced, slaves had to

---

3   Ibid., 3.

4   Walter Johnson, *Soul by Soul: Life Inside the Antebellum Slave Market*, Cambridge, MA: Harvard University Press, 1999, 119. I am indebted to Rob Maclean for alerting me to Johnson's work and elucidating the importance of the individual form for the slave trade.

be comparable. To be sold, they had to be distinctive enough, individuated enough, to stand out from the crowd. The individuality of the marketed slave was produced for purchase.

The elision between commodity and individual evidenced in the slave trade demonstrates that there is nothing necessarily or essentially liberating about the individual form. As I consider below, it emerges historically as an ideological mechanism for the de-subjectification of collectives. The individual—and, as we shall see, not only in its liberal, possessive variety—is a form of capture.

The Subject Is Interpellated as an Individual

Louis Althusser's reworking of the Marxian notion of ideology presents the category of the subject as constitutive of ideology. It is constitutive of ideology because the function of ideology is "'constituting' concrete individuals as subjects."[5] This function, Althusser argues, is a characteristic of ideology in general; ideology "transforms" individuals into subjects. He names the operation at work in this transformation "interpellation." Presenting interpellation as a "hail" or call, Althusser illustrates it with a policeman shouting "hey, you there!" and a person turning around in response. With this turn-in-response, the individual becomes a subject: "he has recognized that the hail was 'really' addressed to him, and that 'it was *really him* who was hailed' (and not someone else)."[6] Interpellation, then, is a process of subjection. Becoming subject, the individual both takes on and comes under ideology's structure of beliefs and expectations.

Althusser's account of interpellation does not imply that there are individuals "out there" prior to interpellation. Invoking Freud and the rituals and expectations accompanying the birth of a child,

---

5   Althusser, *On the Reproduction of Capitalism*, 262.
6   Ibid., 264.

"that happy event," he insists that an "an individual is always-already a subject, even before she is born."[7] A child is born into a structure that has already subjected it, a structure that gives it a name, a sex, and a place and expects it to fill this place, be this sex, and carry this name to become the subject it already is.

The example of the hail notwithstanding, ideological interpellation is not a singular event. It is constant and ongoing, embedded in material practices of recognition and misrecognition "which guarantee for us that we are indeed concrete, individual, unmistakable and, naturally, irreplaceable subjects."[8] As Elizabeth Wingrove writes, Althusser's theory of ideology thus explains how actors' "subjectivity—which is to say, their awareness of themselves as unique, (relatively independent), and capable of making choices—is achieved and sustained by virtue of their subjection to the rules, practices, and relations of the multiple apparatuses within a given social formation."[9] Subjectivity—or individuality, which in Althusser's discussion is the same thing—is an effect of the larger ideological material structure.

One of the most influential of Althusser's contributions, the idea of ideological interpellation has come under significant criticism.[10] Paul Hirst points out that "Althusser's concept of subject supposes that subjects and individuals correspond; that the subject is the unitary 'identity' of the individual, that the subject effect corresponds to the classic philosophical conception of consciousness."[11]

---

7   Ibid., 192.

8   Ibid., 189.

9   Elizabeth Wingrove, "Interpellating Sex," *Signs* 24: 4, Summer 1999, 869–93, 879.

10   For a detailed discussion of changes and developments in Althusser's theory of ideology see Warren Montag, *Althusser and His Contemporaries*, Durham, NC: Duke University Press, 2013.

11   Paul Q. Hirst, "Althusser and the theory of ideology," *Economy and Society* 5: 4, 1976, 385–412, 400. Additional commentators that associate the subjectivity acquired by the individual with identity include Judith Butler, *Excitable Speech*, New York: Routlege, 1997, 25; and Richard D. Wolff,

Judith Butler highlights the "unelaborated doctrine of conscience" underpinning Althusser's description of the individual's turn in response to the hail, finding there "a guilty embrace of the law."[12] And Jacques Rancière criticizes the Althusserian theory of ideology for its exclusion of class struggle, its positing of a function for ideology independent of the existence of classes.[13] He charges Althusser with missing what was already clear to Marx: ideological forms *are the forms in which a struggle is fought out.*"[14]

Approaching Althusser from the perspective of psychoanalysis, Mladen Dolar challenges yet another line of critique, one which faults Althusser for positing a "clean cut," a sudden passage from the individual—"a pre-ideological entity, a sort of *material prima*"—to the subject.[15] This critique misses its mark, Dolar argues, because the real problem with Althusser's version of subjectivization is that the subject's illusory belief in its own autonomy is never as total as Althusser implies. Interpellation itself produces a remainder for which Althusser cannot account. Psychoanalysis proceeds from this remainder, the flaw at the heart of the individual subject. Dolar writes, "For Althusser, the subject is what makes ideology work; for psychoanalysis, the subject emerges where ideology fails. The illusion of autonomy may well be necessary, but so is its failure; the cover-up never holds fast."[16] As Slavoj Žižek emphasizes, the difference between the Althusserian

"Ideological State Apparatuses, Consumerism, and U.S. Capitalism: Lessons for the Left," *Rethinking Marxism* 17: 2, April 2005, 223–35, 226.

12   Judith Butler, *The Psychic Life of Power*, Stanford, CA: Stanford University Press, 1997, 106–15.

13   Jacques Rancière, "On the Theory of Ideology: Althusser's Politics," appendix to *Althusser's Lesson*, trans. Emiliano Battista, London: Continuum, 2011, 149. See also the contributions to "The Althusser-Rancière Controversy," *Radical Philosophy* 170, November/December 2011, 8–35.

14   Rancière, "On the Theory of Idelogy," 151, italics in original.

15   Mladen Dolar, "Beyond Interpellation," *Qui Parle* 6: 2, Spring–Summer 1993, 73–96, 76.

16   Ibid., 78.

and psychoanalytic views of the subject is that psychoanalysis emphasizes the ineliminable gap between ideology and individual. It does so not to naturalize an individual specificity perpetually out of ideology's reach but to treat the subject itself as nothing but this gap.[17]

My wager is that Althusser got it backwards. Ideological interpellation makes more sense as a theory of individuation than as a theory of subjection (which would account for the identity of subject and individual that remained a thorny problem in Althusser's different theorizations of ideology).[18] Warren Montag provides support for this inversion. He highlights Althusser's claim that ideology "recruits" its bearers: "individuals are picked from an undifferentiated mass, singled out, removed from it and endowed with a unique identity, as if such a singling out or separation of individuals were necessary to the functioning of the economy."[19] Confronting a crowd or mass, the ideological hail fragments it into singular elements. Montag notes the specific resonance of Althusser's use of the term "interpellate" in the context of the protests and demonstrations of the 1960s. One would be stopped by the police "and therefore singled out from the crowd or singularized in relation to a background."[20] What was a crowd becomes so many separable individuals.

Rather than following Althusser's emphasis on ideology in general, inverting his claim to attend to the interpellation of the subject as an individual narrows the focus to bourgeois ideology (and thereby returns class conflict to the theory of ideology). I use "bourgeois ideology" to refer to the loose set of ideas and apparatuses associated with European modernity, an instrumental

---

17 Slavoj Žižek, "Class Struggle or Postmodernism? Yes, please!" in *Contingency, Hegemony, Universality*, Judith Butler, Ernesto Laclau, and Slavoj Žižek, London: Verso, 2000, esp. 114–20.

18 Montag, *Althusser*, 104.

19 Ibid., 137.

20 Ibid.

concept of reason, and the emergence of the capitalist mode of production. The Protestant Reformation exemplifies bourgeois ideology's interpellation of the subject as an individual. Breaking with the communality of Catholicism, Protestant theologies hail believers as singular souls responsible for their own salvation. Effects of the interpellation of the subject as an individual include the reduction of agency to individual capacity, freedom to individual condition, and property to individual possession. They include as well the supposition that aggregates—groups, tribes, collectivities, and crowds—are unavoidably primitive, barbaric, irrational, and atavistic.

The advantage of reversing the Althusserian account is that the subject is not pre-constrained to the individual form, a form that psychoanalysis teaches is always already as failing and impossible as it is assumed and demanded. With this reversal, the individual form itself becomes a problem, the coercive and unstable product of the enclosure of the common in never-ceasing efforts to repress, deny, and foreclose collective political subjectivity. The individual is a form of capture. Rather than natural or given, the individual form encloses into a singular bounded body collective bodies, ideas, affects, desires, and drives.[21]

Althusser's claim that "ideology represents the imaginary relationship of individuals to their real conditions of existence" should be reread with the emphasis on *individuals*. What is imaginary is that the conditions ideology organizes relate primarily to an individual. The individual is itself an imaginary figure, as we learn

---

21   See also Jobst Welge's discussion of the challenges of representation and individuation in early twentieth-century European literature, especially with regard to the relation between the writer and the masses. Even as some modernist writers focus on the search for the self amidst the turmoil of the city, "the crowd exists, as it vibrates with its complex multitude of personalities, yet it exists primarily inside the subject." Welge, "Far from the Crowd: Individuation, Solitude, and 'Society' in the Western Imagination," *Crowds*, eds. Jeffrey T. Schnapp and Matthew Tiews, Stanford, CA: Stanford University Press, 2006, 335–58.

from Lacan.[22] Bourgeois ideology treats conditions that are collective and social—embedded in histories of violence and systems of exploitation—as if they were relationships specific to an individual, as if states arose through individual consent, as if politics were a matter of individual choice, and as if desires and capacities, affects and will naturally originate from and reside in an individual form. But just as collective experience of antagonism—the "social substance"—underlies what Marx calls the "phantom-like objectivity" of the commodity, so too does it underlie the phantom-like subjectivity of the individual.

Enclosing the Common

Inverting Althusser helps us conceive the individual as a form of enclosure. As Marx describes in *Capital*, enclosure is an operation through which what is common is seized and put into service for capitalism. Judith Butler's account of the constitution of the subject in language, an account that itself draws from Althusser, provides a way to access this operation insofar as the linguistic category of the subject designates a condition of common belonging.[23]

Butler writes,

> The genealogy of the subject as a critical category ... suggests that the subject, rather than be identified strictly with the individual, ought to be designated as a linguistic category, a placeholder, a structure in formation. Individuals come to occupy the site of the

22   Lacan makes this point most famously in "The Mirror Stage as Formative of the Function of the *I* Function, as Revealed in Psychoanalytic Experience," *Ecrits: A Selection*, trans. Bruce Fink, New York: W. W. Norton, 2002, delivered originally in 1949. See also Jacques Lacan, *My Teaching*, trans. David Macey, London: Verso, 2008, 79.

23   Pierre Macherey also explores interpellation in terms of the constitution of the subject in language. See his "Figures of Interpellation in Althusser and Fanon," *Radical Philosophy*, May 2012, 9–20.

subject ... The subject is the linguistic occasion for the individual to achieve and reproduce intelligibility, the linguistic condition of its existence and agency.[24]

That individuals come to occupy the place of the subject implies that more than one necessarily occupies this place at the same time. Because "subject" is the linguistic condition for intelligibility and its function is to hold open a place, the utterly singular and unique would have no place. The utterly singular would be illegible within the available terms of existence and agency. "Individual" thus designates a specific occupation of the subject understood as a common place. As a subject, the individual can only be one occupant among many. The singularity of its subject-status is purely imaginary. "Subject" is a condition for agency because the individuality of agency is a fantasy occluding the material and collective conditions for action, contracting them into an imaginary ego.

Butler associates the individual's occupation of the position of the subject, its subjection, with foreclosure.[25] As the individual is subjectified, it loses something of itself (even if this is something it never had). To be a subject is to be, in a way, bereft. Butler suggests that the subject is a condition of freedom at the cost of freedom, where this lost or sacrificed freedom is a kind of authenticity or potential for love and desire that would be available to the subject were it not for the law to which the subject is beholden: "One cannot criticize too far the terms by which one's existence is secured."[26] Understanding the subject as interpellated as an individual, however, opens up another possibility. The bereavement accompanying interpellation arises from the loss of others. The individual is the one cut off from, cut out of, the collective. Caught in the isolation of the imaginary ego, the individual tries to do and be alone what she can only do and be with others.

---

24 Butler, *The Psychic Life of Power*, 10.
25 Ibid., 23.
26 Ibid., 129.

Already in *Discipline and Punish*, Michel Foucault treats the individual as an effect of power and knowledge as he details the making of the individual through the extension of disciplinary formulae of domination in eighteenth-century Europe.[27] Discipline involves a range of mutually reinforcing techniques employed to solve the problem collective people create for authority. The state needs the army, but an armed assembly of the people can overthrow the state. Capital needs labor, but the concentrated power of the workers can render useless, destroy, and effectively abolish capitalist investment in raw material and means of production. Over the course of the eighteenth century, processes of enclosing, partitioning, functionalizing, and ranking spread throughout the social to turn the motley, amorphous, unruly mass into a docile, useful, combination of forces. Vagabonds and paupers are confined.[28] Workers are closed off into factories. A monastic model becomes the ideal for secondary schools. The "army, that vagabond mass," is regularized into a more regimented military, separated into barracks in order to prevent looting and violence.[29] The enclosed are then partitioned off from one another: "Each individual has his own place; and each place is individual. Avoid distribution in groups; break up

---

27   Michel Foucault, *Discipline and Punish: The Birth of the Prison*, trans. Alan Sheridan, New York: Vintage, 1979. For a schematic overview of nineteenth-century American and European individualisms, see Steven Lukes, *Individualism*, New York: Harper & Row, 1973. Montag argues that Althusser's thesis that ideology interpellates individuals as subjects "only takes on its full meaning in relation" to Foucault's description of the material conditions of interpellation in *Discipline and Punish*, 163–70. Noting how Foucault "opens an entire dimension that Althusser's essay unwittingly presupposes: a history of the body, the history of the individual itself," Montag provides further support for the utility of inverting Althusser, 167.

28   Already in *Madness and Civilization* (trans. Richard Howard, New York: Vintage, 1973), Foucault describes the great confinement of the seventeenth century.

29   Foucault, *Discipline and Punish*, 142.

collective dispositions; analyze confused, massive or transient pluralities."[30]

As Foucault makes clear, enclosure and segmentation accompany not only technological developments, the punctuation and measuring of time, and the correlation of bodies and gestures, but also important changes in the work of power on bodies. These changes in the mode of power's operation on bodies increase opportunities to observe and gain knowledge of them and to put this knowledge to use in securing their combined utility and docility. "Discipline 'makes' individuals," Foucault writes.[31] "The crowd, a compact mass, a locus of multiple exchanges, individualities merging together, a collective effect, is abolished and replaced by a collection of separated individualities."[32] Observed and compared, bodies, aptitudes, and capacities are individuated as they are "classified in relation to one another." Evaluated and rewarded, they shed their quality as mass and take shape as trained, specified, and knowable individuals.[33] As an effect of the enclosure of the crowd, individuation is fundamentally—and deliberately—depoliticizing, the fantasies of liberals notwithstanding.[34] Put back in

30   Ibid., 143.

31   Ibid., 170. Foucault notes that disciplinary power reverses the "axes of individuation." Procedures of "ascending" individuation mark the individuated as possessing more power than others, as great and privileged. Hence, portraits are painted and tales are told of kings and nobles. Ascending individuation is not exactly an individuation. It is a glorification, a process for the generation of prestige and immortality so that the glorified is an exemplar of a group, whether that group be family, tribe, or nation.

32   Ibid., 201.

33   Ibid., 162.

34   In a nuanced discussion of the ways gender, race, and class become imbricated in a new notion of individual identity in eighteenth-century Europe, historian Dror Wahrman writes, "In the *ancien régime* of identity … the preference for generic categorization had meant that collective categories that identified groups had primacy over categories that identified individuals … But in the new configuration of the late eighteenth century such categories contributed to the generation of unique identity before they generated

terms of a question Althusser poses in his discussion of ideological state apparatuses: "What do children learn at school?" They learn that they are individuals.

Silvia Federici deepens and extends Foucault's account of the material production of the individual in modern Europe. Tracing the peasant uprisings, popular heresies, and witch hunts inseparable from the bloody processes of capital accumulation, Federici connects the disciplinary enclosure of the workforce with the "accumulation of differences, inequalities, hierarchies, divisions, which have alienated workers from each other and even from themselves."[35] She attends to demographic and economic crises in the first decades of the seventeenth century (crises involving dramatic population declines in Europe and the New World and leading to the establishment of the transatlantic slave trade), situating there the emergence of reproduction and population growth as matters of intellectual and state concern.[36] A particular focus of the mercantilists, state preoccupation with population growth results in attempts to expropriate from women their reproductive labor, rendering them literally and physically a source of labor power as it differentiates between men's and women's work, devalues the work of women, and demonizes their knowledge of reproduction and the body. Moreover, as the ruling classes endeavor to impose ever stricter discipline on an unruly workforce, inefficient social activities like gaming and drinking come under heavy scrutiny and regulation; unproductive sexuality is forbidden.

Federici affiliates these developments with the rationalism of Descartes and Hobbes. She attributes the popularity of Cartesianism among middle- and upper-class Europeans to its

---

the identicality of a collective group, and were thus closer to the new understandings of self." See his *The Making of the Modern Self*, New Haven: Yale University Press, 2004, 278.

35   Silvia Federici, *Caliban and the Witch: Women, the Body and Primitive Accumulation*, Brooklyn, NY: Autonomedia, 2004, 115.

36   Ibid., 86.

provision of a model of self-management crucial for capitalism's need for a reliable, predictable, and calculable workforce.
Cartesianism provides "a new model of the person," where the
self works on its self, training, controlling, and stylizing its body,
now configured as something other, something possessed. "The
product of this alienation from the body," Federici writes, "was the
development of individual *identity*, conceived precisely as 'otherness' from the body, and in perennial antagonism with it." As she
concludes, this emergence of an *alter ego* represents "the birth of
the individual in capitalist society."[37] Rather than belonging to the
world, the world exists in order to belong to it.

Foucault's and Federici's explorations into the disciplinary production of the individual supply ample reason to replace the idea
of the individual's interpellation as a subject with that of the subject's interpellation as an individual. The individual is a product of
European modernity, the form through which collective economic
force is politically secured so as to facilitate the processes of its
own exploitation. Bourgeois ideology, manifest in the disciplinary
techniques that make individuals, hails the collective subject, the
mass of workers, vagabonds, soldiers, and students, as individuals
(even as the capacity of the common people for individuated self-
discipline in the service of capital accumulation and liberal order
will persist as a problem). It singles out and separates, producing
the very individuals it extracts.

Nonetheless, Foucault cannot explain how disciplinary techniques and processes subjectify or de-subjectify the individuated.[38]

---

37 Ibid., 151–52.

38 Molly Anne Rothenberg writes, "As purely external (and discursive)
productions, subject positions have no interiority from which they might
mount resistance to their own conditions of determination. Where Althusser
conceives of subjects as mis-recognizing (and therefore in principle capable
of recognizing) the truth about their relations to real conditions of their production, Foucault conceives of subjects as nothing more than the conditions
of their production and so incapable of misrecognition or recognition." See

Where is the gap of subjectivity in the web of its determinations? We gain an understanding of bourgeois ideology's regime of individuation at the cost of the foreclosed collective. Federici takes a step toward such an explanation when she gestures to an emergent *alter ego*—an incomplete individuation or individual that remains somehow plural. Psychoanalysis, built around the failures of the individual form, helps carry the explanation further. "For psychoanalysis there is no such thing as an individual," Dolar writes. "The individual only makes sense as a knot of social ties, a network of relations to others, to the always already social Other, the Other being ultimately but a shorthand for the social instance as such."[39] Below, I turn to Freud's discussion of *Group Psychology and the Analysis of the Ego* as a resource for a psychoanalytically attuned inquiry into political subjectivization, excavating from his account the collectivity enclosed in the individual.

The Subject Is the Gap in the Structure

Before I turn to Freud, however, I want to mention an additional advantage to rethinking ideology as the interpellation of the subject as an individual, namely, making political sense out of the idea from Dolar and Žižek that the subject is nothing but the gap in the structure. Because Althusser takes as his problem the compliance of individuals with a system that oppresses them, he has trouble conceiving the system as itself a social product (or product of conflict). Institutions are external to the subjects they produce. Dolar and Žižek, in presenting the limits of interpellation *as* the subject, could be seen as making the problem worse in that they have to

her *The Excessive Subject*, Cambridge, UK: Polity Press, 2010, 26. My goal is to demonstrate the sense in which this interiority is transindividual, a crowd at the heart of the person.

39   Mladen Dolar, "Freud and the Political," *Theory & Event* 12: 3, 2009, 15–29.

posit the continuity of interpellating institutions that always fail. After all, they suggest that the subject as such is hysterical, resisting the interpellative hail, perpetually refusing the identity offered to her. How, though, would an institution continue if its hail were persistently resisted?

One possible answer would be that the subject is rare, the *unique* individual (or individual in the moment of uniqueness), the heroine capable of going to the limit, doing the impossible. Institutions would then be understood as persisting because most of the time they work, but this working is not through the successful production of subjects; it's through the production of objects. Another answer would shift registers altogether, reconceptualizing the problem in terms of the concept of subjectivity: if for Althusser subjectivity consists in the identity that emerges in response to the hail, for Dolar and Žižek subjectivity consists in the gap produced and occluded by answering the hail. These two options of unique or void, unconditioned or ineliminable, are politically unsatisfying.[40] Politics diminishes into waiting for the impossible arrival of one who cannot make much of a difference anyway.[41] Fortunately, these are not the only options.

Reversing Althusser's formulation so as to understand ideology as interpellating the subject as an individual provides another option: the subject emerges where ideology fails because the subject is collective. When bourgeois ideology fails, individuation fails and the fact of collectivity impresses itself. A problem faced by one becomes a condition shared by many. Correspondingly, the subject is a gap in the structure because the people are the subject of politics. "Subject" is therefore not primarily a linguistic site of individual freedom, decision, or choice. Nor does it index the unconscious fantasies that fill in and direct the never complete

---

40   See Bruno Bosteels's critique of Žižek on this point in *The Actuality of Communism*, London: Verso, 2011.

41   James Martel, *Textual Conspiracies*, Ann Arbor, MI: University of Michigan Press, 2011.

structure. Rather, subject is a gap in three other intertwined senses: structure's inability to ground or posit itself, its dependence on something external to it, and the torsion of the Real in the excess of its self-relation.[42]

In their self-relating, the people always come up against themselves. They encounter the practical, material limits of their association, the psychic and affective pressures of their commonality, and the effects of histories of conflict and conquest. The excess of their reflective relation to themselves as *the people* is the torsion of politics. Politics takes place in the non-identity, gap, or torsion between people and their self-governance.[43] Political subjectivization involves forcing this non-identity, making it felt as an effect of a subject. As Bruno Bosteels puts it in a discussion of Alain Badiou, "subject consists in the coherence of a forced lack."[44] But not just any gap is that of the subject. Subject appears through the active occupation of the constitutive lack in the people.

There is politics because the political subject is collective and it is split. This split is practical and material, the condition of our physical being. The people can never be politically (or, differently put, the "people" is not an ontological category). They are only present as parts, as subsets. This is the case with crowds occupying public squares, elected assemblies, armies in battle, and opinion polls. All are necessarily parts. Their partiality—the gap between parts and (imaginary) whole—is the exciting cause of political subjectivization. Moreover, even as parts, the people are only present temporarily. They may try to inscribe their presence, their having been, in documents, practices, and organizations which will take their place and operate in their stead, a taking and

---

42   See Slavoj Žižek's discussion of the Mobius strip in *Organs without Bodies*, New York: Routledge, 2003; see also Rothenberg's explication of the logic of the empty set as the addition of a negation, 30–45.

43   Jodi Dean, "Politics without Politics," *Parallax* 15: 3, 2009, 20–36.

44   Bruno Bosteels, "Alain Badiou's Theory of the Subject: The Recommencement of Dialectical Materialism," Part 2, *Pli* 13, 2002, 172–208, 185.

operating which is also and unavoidably partial. Some degree of alienation is unavoidable: making something ourselves, building collectives, creating new institutions cannot eliminate the minimal difference between the collectivity and the people. The condition of politics, then, is this practical material split between the people and the collective that actually comes together. Expressed in Rousseauian terms: the general will does not follow from the will of all.

The split in the people is also an effect of the group on its members in the sense that the people are never fully identical with their sovereignty. Groupness exerts a force that is more than the sum of individual expectation. The expectations of groups work back upon their members. People have them of each other as well as of themselves, and they have them of each other and themselves in ways of which they are never fully conscious. This excess manifests itself in the point of reference from which a collectivity views itself as a collective, a point sometimes occupied by a leader or held in place by a proper or common name. A name forces a gap in the collectivity it names, inscribing the non-all character of the collectivity and providing a new terrain of struggle: we argue over the name. The common name can never fully designate—capture and enclose—the collectivity even as the collectivity cannot relate to itself absent a structuring form.[45]

The split in the people *goes all the way down*. It can't be limited to the idea that some are excluded from the people (and hence that including them would solve the problem of the gap). Nor can it be rendered as the problem of representation (and hence addressed via ontology). Rather, the people do not know what they want. They are not fully present to themselves. Conflicting and contradictory desires and drives render the people a split subject perpetually pushing to express, encounter, and address its

---

45   I provide a more extensive elaboration on this concept of the sovereignty of the people in *The Communist Horizon*, London: Verso, 2012. I am indebted to Jason Jones for discussion on this point.

own non-knowledge. Returning to the idea given by Žižek and Dolar, as the collective subject of politics the people is nothing but this gap.

I have proposed an inversion of the Althusserian account of ideology and suggested some of the conceptual benefits that accompany it. An understanding of the subject as interpellated as an individual resonates with linguistic ideas of the subject, better fits with Althusser's own description of ideological recruitment, and attends to the historicity of the individual in bourgeois modernity.[46] Even more, it lets us begin to explore the gaps constitutive of collective subjectivity and thereby further loosen the grip of the individual form. Insofar as he fails to uncouple subject and individual and consider the crowd out of which the hailed individual is recruited, Althusser naturalizes enclosure. To be sure, he is working on the terrain of a psychoanalysis that has already enclosed the collective subject in the individual form. If we turn to Freud's *Group Psychology and the Analysis of the Ego*, we can see how this enclosing is accomplished. There Freud presents the individual form as a product of the enclosure of the crowd.[47] A return to Freud, and to his primary interlocutor in *Group Psychology*, the notorious Gustave Le Bon, reanimates the crowd as it highlights the displacement of many by one. Attending to this crowd contributes to the dismantling of the phantom-like subjectivity of the individual by locating in the crowd the dynamics of a collective subject.

---

46   Etienne Balibar introduces the concept of the *"differential forms of historical individuality"* already in part 3 of Louis Althusser and Etienne Balibar, *Reading Capital*, trans. Ben Brewster, London: Verso, 2009, 282–84. Parts 1 and 2 are authored by Althusser.

47   Gilles Deleuze and Félix Guattari raise a similar point regarding the crowded Freudian unconscious in their reading of the Wolf Man in *A Thousand Plateaus*, trans. Brian Massumi, Minneapolis, MN: University of Minnesota Press, 1987.

The Unconscious Is a Crowd

In *Group Psychology and the Analysis of the Ego* (1921), Freud concerns himself with man as a member, man in his belonging to: how is it that that to which man belongs, belongs to him? These concerns lead Freud to discuss problems of identification, attachment, and the intensification of affect.

Freud's turn to group psychology brings psychoanalysis into dialogue with crowd theory, a field of work emerging in late nineteenth-century social science out of discussions in biology, criminology, psychology, and sociology and out of fears incited by the revolutionary crowds of the Paris Commune of 1871.[48] Crowd theorists wanted to understand what they saw as the dangerous irrationality of the crowd, why people in large groups seemed to become more emotional, instinctual, and even primitive. In predisciplinary or even interdisciplinary style, crowd theorists used evolution to rank human civilizations, hypnosis to explain imitation in groups, and medicine to diagnose crowd pathology.[49] At the time of Freud's intervention, crowd theory was well established and widely accepted. Freud enters the conversation as a way to expand the influence of the newer field of psychoanalysis

---

48   The German title refers to *Massenpsychologie*. The English "group" could have been translated as "mass" or as "crowd." Readings of the text in its relation to crowd theory vary. Serge Moscovici argues that Freud provided analytic rigor to crowd theory (*The Age of the Crowd: A Historical Treatise of Mass Psychology*, trans. J. C. Whitehouse, Cambridge, UK: Cambridge University Press, 1985); Daniel Pick argues for its relevance to interrogating nationalism and national identity ("Freud's *Group Psychology* and the History of the Crowd," *History Workshop Journal* 40, Autumn 1995, 39–61); Ernesto Laclau reads Freud as unifying a dualism in crowd theory (*On Populist Reason*, London: Verso, 2007). Laclau emphasizes the notion of identification in Freud but fails to associate it with Freud's enclosing of the crowd in the individual.

49   Susanna Barrows, *Distorting Mirrors: Visions of the Crowd in Late Nineteenth-Century France*, New Haven, CT: Yale University Press, 1981, 43–44.

by demonstrating how psychoanalysis better accounts for group behavior.[50]

While he engages several different crowd theorists, Freud relies most heavily on the work of Gustave Le Bon. Le Bon was a pessimistic conservative who presented his racist, elitist, and misogynist ideas as scientific discoveries.[51] His immensely popular 1895 book, *The Crowd: A Study of the Popular Mind*, consolidated literary and historical accounts of the crowd from Émile Zola and Hyppolite Taine with work on criminal crowds from Scipio Sighele and Gabriel Tarde.[52] *The Crowd* announced to its readers that they were entering an Era of Crowds (capitalization in the original). It instructed them to fear it. It was certainly possible, Le Bon warned, "that the advent to power of the masses marks one of the last stages of Western civilization, a complete return to those periods of confused anarchy which seem always destined to precede the birth of every new society."[53] The masses were now in charge and the most likely result was the collapse of civilization.

The Crowd appeared at a time of increasing worker militancy.[54] In France, the number of workers in syndicates tripled between 1890 and 1900. The number of strikes quadrupled over two decades. In 1886, in the dramatic miners' strike in Decazeville, workers threw a deputy director of the company out of a window; he was then

---

50 J. S. McClelland, *The Crowd and the Mob: From Plato to Canetti*, London: Unwin Hyman, 1989, 242.

51 Robert A. Nye, *The Origins of Crowd Psychology: Gustave Le Bon and the Crisis of Mass Democracy in the Third Republic*, London: Sage Publications, 1975; Barrows, 162–66.

52 Gustave Le Bon, *The Crowd: A Study of the Popular Mind*, Kitchener, Ontario: Batoche Books, 2001. Widely translated and reprinted, *The Crowd* has been credited as an originating text for social psychology. See Robert A. Nye, "Two Paths to a Psychology of Social Action: Gustave Le Bon and Georges Sorel," *Journal of Modern History* 45: 3, September 1973, 411–38.

53 Le Bon, *The Crowd*, 10.

54 This point and the following are indebted to Barrows, *Distorting Mirrors*.

mauled to death by the crowd. In 1890, plans for massive May Day demonstrations prompted the government to garrison 38,000 troops in Paris to avert what some feared would be a resurgence of the Commune. Le Bon offered his theory of the crowd as guidance for understanding this new era even though he thought little could be done to shape it. His subsequent fascist admirers try to disprove this second point by drawing from his work in their efforts to stir and channel mass feeling.

Le Bon's account of crowds arises out of his antipathy toward the transformation of the popular classes into governing classes. Lamenting that the "divine right of the masses is about to replace the divine right of kings," Le Bon decries the way *association*, far more than universal suffrage, is making the masses conscious of their strength. They are founding syndicates and labor unions, before which authorities capitulate. They aim to limit the hours of labor, nationalize mines, railways, factories, and soil, equalize the distribution of products, and eliminate the upper classes. The claims of the masses, Le Bon warns, "amount to nothing less than a determination to utterly destroy society as it now exists, with a view to making it hark back to that primitive communism which was the normal condition of all human groups before the dawn of civilization."[55] Le Bon's findings confirmed and amplified already intense anxieties among the elite.

A primary concern of the nineteenth-century crowd theorists was how it was that law-abiding individuals could act like criminals when they were combined together in a crowd. Le Bon's answer is that a crowd is a new collective being. Assembly into a crowd results in new psychological characteristics as all the thoughts and feelings of the collectivity are turned in an identical direction.[56] Under conditions that Le Bon attributes to "exciting causes," something emerges that is not present in individuals alone, "just as in chemistry, certain elements, when brought into

---

55   Le Bon, *The Crowd*, 8–9.
56   Ibid., 15.

contact—bases and acids, for example—combine to form a new body possessing properties quite different from those of the bodies that have served to form it."[57] Despite his claims to originality, Le Bon steals this idea from Sighele, who had been involved in a public dispute with Tarde over who deserved credit for originating crowd theory.[58] Plagiarizing both, Le Bon schematizes the tropes that had by that time become inseparable from the crowd concept—contagion, suggestion, affective intensification, and de-individualization.[59]

The vehicle for Le Bon's schematization is the unconscious. He writes, "The substitution of the unconscious actions of crowds for the conscious activity of individuals is one of the principal characteristics of the present age."[60] It is this emphasis on the unconscious that provides the opening for psychoanalysis. In *Group Psychology*, Freud joins the crowd theory discussion via a twist: not only is the crowd unconscious but the unconscious is itself a crowd. Freud thus accepts Le Bon and inverts Le Bon. The inversion is possible because Le Bon's own concept of the crowd is psychological.

Le Bon does not view crowds as a mass of bodies in the street. "Crowd" involves a concentration and directionality that encompasses people in a specific place and that extends to a wide array of structured institutions (parliament and jury) and imaginary communities (race and nation). More than a set of social relations, "crowd" for Le Bon is a process ("like those microbes which hasten the dissolution of enfeebled or dead bodies") or force in which individuals get caught ("Ideas, sentiments, emotions and

---

57   Ibid., 16.

58   Jaap Van Ginneken, "The 1985 Debate on the Origins of Crowd Psychology," *Journal of the History of the Behavioral Sciences* 21:4, Oct. 1985, 375–382; McClelland, 163-173; Barrows, 137–88.

59   See also Christian Borch and Britta Timm Knudsen, "Postmodern crowds: re-inventing crowd thinking," introduction to a special issue of *Distinktion: Scandanavian Journal of Social Theory* 14: 2, August 2013, 109–13.

60   Le Bon, *The Crowd*, 4.

beliefs possess in crowds a contagious power as intense as that of microbes").[61] Early twenty-first century commentators will describe the same phenomena with terms like "cascade effects," "band-wagoning," "confirmation bias," and "bubbles." Informed by nineteenth-century science, Le Bon affiliates crowd processes with hallucination, barbarism, and the direction of the spinal cord instead of the brain.[62] He correlates the strength of these processes with the dangers of crowd power: the "last surviving sovereign force of modern times" and "the only force that nothing menaces."[63]

Le Bon conceives the unconscious racially as a hereditary substratum of similarity upon which individual differences are built. The unconscious encompasses a wide array of instincts and passions, affections and aversions, passed down through the generations. Vastly more influential than the mind's conscious life, the unconscious always threatens to subsume the individual's independent intellectual aptitudes, themselves the fragile achievements of reason, education, and elite culture. In a crowd, common characteristics overpower the rare achievements of intelligence. Ordinary qualities triumph over distinction and specialization. As Le Bon puts it, these qualities "in crowds become common property."[64] No matter their differences in occupation, intelligence, character, or mode of life, individuals in a crowd possess a collective mind, what Le Bon attributes to the "psychological law of the mental unity of crowds."[65] I should add that anxiety about subjection to the crowd, or, differently put, the fragility of the individual as a form of subjectivity, comes to characterize over a century of inquiry into the crowd, from Durkheim, through Mill,

---

61   Ibid., 10, 73.
62   McClelland, 168. This is another point Le Bon steals from Sighele.
63   Le Bon, *The Crowd*, 8.
64   Ibid., 17.
65   Ibid., 13. Tarde theorizes the same phenomena under the heading of "imitation."

through twentieth-century American sociology's emphases on the mass and conformity.[66]

In *Group Psychology and the Analysis of the Ego*, Freud treats the unconscious as a crowd in two senses. The first is an analytic or structural sense of the repressed product of history, whether of family or species, as it impresses itself within the individual. Freud commends Le Bon's discussion of the unconscious because it resonates so well with his own (adding that "as a matter of fact none of the author's statements bring forward anything new").[67] The second is a more analogical sense where the unconscious is described in terms of the affective dynamics of the crowd. The forces in the unconscious are *like* the directed intensities of crowd processes. Freud shifts back and forth between these two senses in his attempt to explain the nature of group ties and the emergence of individual from group psychology. These explanations never quite cohere.

Mikkel Borch-Jacobsen challenges the Freudian postulate of the unity of the subject of the unconscious, suggesting instead that it is multiple, unascribable, and unidentifiable.[68] In a deconstructive

66 In an analysis of the rise of "mass" as a sociological category in France, Stefan Jonsson identifies four (loose and overlapping) moments: mass as innumerable individuals, mass as the violent and criminal mob of the poor, mass as organized movement of workers, and, finally, mass as political sickness, the madness of all collectivity. See "The Invention of the Masses: The Crowd in French Culture from the Revolution to the Commune," *Crowds*, 47–75. Eugene E. Leach recounts crowd psychology in the US, tracing the reception of the work of Le Bon and Tarde as well as the work of Boris Sidis, "America's only original crowd psychologist," a student of William James who linked the "mob-self" to the highly suggestible, immoral, will-less, and de-individuated "sub-waking self." See "'Mental Epidemics': Crowd Psychology and American Culture, 1890–1940," *American Studies* 33: 1, Spring 1992, 5–29.

67 Sigmund Freud, *Group Psychology and the Analysis of the Ego*, Standard Edition, New York: W. W. Norton, 1990, 19.

68 Mikkel Borch-Jacobsen, *The Freudian Subject*, trans. Catherine Porter, Stanford, CA: Stanford University Press, 1988. He writes, "the

reading of psychoanalysis's binaries of subject and other, desire and object, Borch-Jacobsen draws from René Girard to treat desire as primarily mimetic, positing a "primordial tendency" to identification.[69] The details of this discussion exceed my purposes here. What's compelling, though, is Borch-Jacobsen's attunement to the ineluctable problem of individuation in psychoanalysis, the problem of being apart when one is always a part. As parts, we remain inextricably interconnected: every attempt to be apart, to separate, involves connection at another point or on another plane.[70] Following a nuanced treatment of Freud's writing on narcissism as symptomatically deploying sexuality in the context of Freud's own professional rivalries, Borch-Jacobsen turns to *Group Psychology*. He asks whether *Group Psychology* is premised on a possibility Freud can't let himself think and that he has

---

cleavage or division of the subject that psychoanalysis keeps talking about takes place against the background of unity, a unitary subject," 6. Borch-Jacobsen presents his account as an alternative to Lacan's association of desire with interdiction. He overstates the difference between them insofar as he and Lacan both conceive desire as the desire of the Other, enjoyment as indirectly accessible, and the object of desire as separate from the object-cause of desire. Žižek's version of Lacan, moreover, suggests an even greater compatibility with Borch-Jacobsen in that he, too, emphasizes that desire has no object prior to an intervention that establishes desireability, as in, for example, Žižek's discussions of ideology as a matrix of desire, of enjoyment as originally stolen, and of the ego ideal. Although a thorough exploration of the possible convergences is beyond the scope of my analysis, a potential benefit in Borch-Jacobsen's emphasis on desire as imaginary is that it opens up a thinking of desire in the wake of the decline of symbolic efficiency, allowing for an understanding of the rivalry, hatred, and violence that Žižek associates with the alliance of the imaginary with the Real.

69   Ibid., 47.

70   Borch-Jacobsen writes, "The so-called subject of desire has no identity of its own prior to the identification that brings it, blindly, to occupy the point of otherness, the place of the other (who is thus not an other): an original alienation (which is thus not an alienation); and an original lure (which is thus not a lure, either)." Ibid., 48.

perpetually to displace, namely, that of "a mass-ego, a primordial crowd."[71]

There is much to admire in Borch-Jacobsen's reading. I want to note where mine diverges from his. Rather than attending to the two different senses of the unconscious as a crowd in Freud, Borch-Jacobsen absorbs the dynamic in the structural. He treats the crowd unconscious (for Le Bon and Freud) as a womb, "a soft, malleable, plastic, infinitely receptive material without will or desire or any specific instinct of its own."[72] Crowd as "matrical mass" fits with Borch-Jacobsen's emphasis on the imaginary. It also fits with his critique of Freud insofar as Freud attempts to enclose the crowd within the form of the individual. The problem, however, is that neither Le Bon nor Freud presents the crowd as infinitely receptive and incapable of desire. Le Bon notes that influencing the crowd takes skill; the crowd senses its own strength and is thus intolerant of contradiction in those who speak before it.[73] Since neither truth nor argument make a difference to crowds (they are not infinitely receptive), Le Bon emphasizes affirmation, repetition, and contagion as more promising methods of influence. Likewise Freud says that the crowd "may desire things passionately" and that it can tolerate no delay "between its desire and the fulfillment of what it desires."[74] His primary argument is that crowds are tied together libidinally; they are products of desire. In short, the unconscious processes associated with the crowd are more subjectal than Borch-Jacobsen acknowledges. The collectivity desires and wills, destroys and creates. These attributes precede Freud's attempts to contain them in the unconscious of an individual whose own becoming-subject is contingent upon this containment.

Dolar advances beyond Borch-Jacobsen when he suggests that the unconscious as Freud describes it in *Group Psychology* takes

71 Ibid., 133.
72 Ibid., 139.
73 Le Bon, *The Crowd*, 30–31.
74 Freud, *Group Psychology*, 13.

place *between* the individual and the collective, "in the very establishment of the ties between an individual (becoming a subject)
and a group to which s/he would belong."[75] Dolar declines to read
Freud in terms of a collective unconscious because that "would
demand a defined collectivity, a community to which it would
pertain, but no such pre-given community exists." Because Le
Bon's crowds are heterogeneous as well as homogeneous, criminal
as well as moral, forming a collective mind "doubtless transitory,
but presenting very clearly defined characteristics," however, I see
no reason to presume a "defined collectivity."[76] "Defined collectivity" implies a collectivity that is known and inscribed rather than
crowd characteristics, dynamics, and attributes that are themselves
definable. It suggests bounded groups rather than momentary collectivities formed through a concentration of forces the exciting
causes of which can only be retroactively determined. In *Group
Psychology*, the unconscious is nothing but collective, an insight
Freud attempts repeatedly to repress by enclosing its processes in
an individual form never adequate to its task. Psychoanalysis as a
field is possible and can contribute to the debates in crowd theory
because the dynamics it investigates are already collective even as
they are enclosed in the generic form of the individual.

"A provisional being formed of heterogeneous elements"

Freud quotes extensively from *The Crowd*. Two ideas significant
for Le Bon's crowd concept appear in the first passage Freud lifts:
the crowd as a source of new feelings, thoughts, and ideas; and the
crowd as the novel consistency of a provisional being. First, individuals in a group are

---

75   Dolar, "Freud and the Political."
76   Le Bon, *The Crowd*, 13.

in the possession of a sort of collective mind that makes them feel, think, and act in a manner quite different from that in which each individual one of them would feel, think, and act were he in a state of isolation. There are certain ideas and feelings which do not come into being, or do not transform themselves into acts except in the case of individuals forming a group.

Second, the psychological group is a

provisional being formed of heterogeneous elements, which for a moment are combined, exactly as the cells which constitute a living body form by their reunion a new being which displays characteristics very different from those possessed by each of the cells singly.[77]

Freud doesn't question the emergence of previously inexistent ideas and feelings. Nor does he challenge the notion of a new, provisional being. He fully assumes the idea that in a group, individuals combine into a temporary unity, a collectivity that did not exist prior to this combining. Freud wants to know what unites people in a crowd, what the character of the ties that bind them together is.

Le Bon had not concerned himself with what unites people in a crowd because he begins from the fact of collectivity—the provisional being of the crowd—seeking to understand its effects. He thus tries to explain why actions and affects not previously possessed by individuals emerge in a crowd.[78] Freud recounts Le Bon's three explanations. The first is that a crowd feels itself to

---

77   Freud, *Group Psychology*, 7.

78   "How is it that these new characteristics are created?" Le Bon, 17; Freud, *Group Psychology*, 9. Borch-Jacobsen misreads Le Bon and Freud here. He treats as descriptive characteristics of the crowd what Freud and Le Bon present as explanations why new characteristics appear, 139. McClelland makes the same mistake, misreading the causes of new characteristics as the new characteristics themselves, 203.

have enormous power. This feeling of invincibility makes a person less likely to hold himself in check which means that he yields to instincts he would otherwise restrain. Freud writes this off as unimportant: of course our deepest selves lack responsibility; the crowd enables the individual to "throw off repressions."[79] Le Bon is mistaken in taking the sentiment of invincible power as a cause for the appearance of something new—nothing new is appearing. Rather, the impulses repressed in the unconscious have simply become free to manifest themselves. As Freud notes, his disagreement with Le Bon here stems from their differing accounts of the unconscious. Le Bon's "racial mind" lacks the dimension of the "unconscious repressed" conceptualized by psychoanalysis, so for him the crowd does give rise to something new, something that cannot be reduced to the substratum of hereditary influences. Freud's objection thus treats the dynamic Le Bon describes as a structure, shifting between the two senses of "unconscious" such that behavior in a crowd manifests what is contained in the human mind.

More interesting to Freud is the second explanation Le Bon provides for the change effected by crowds: contagion. Contagion is kin to hypnosis in that it induces people to act in unexpected ways. Freud quotes Le Bon: "In a group every sentiment and act is contagious, and contagious to such a degree that an individual readily sacrifices his personal interest to the collective interest."[80] The third is suggestion. Freud fills the next page with Le Bon's description of the "magnetic influence given out by the group," the vanishing of conscious personality and loss of will, "the turning by means of suggestion and contagion of feelings and ideas in an identical direction, the tendency to immediately transform the suggested ideas into acts."[81] Freud notes an asymmetry in Le Bon's account. Contagion refers to members' effects on each other. Suggestion,

---

79   Freud, *Group Psychology*, 9.
80   Ibid., 10.
81   Ibid., 11.

particularly when understood in terms of hypnosis, implies something else entirely, the operation of a hierarchical relation of influence. Who is the hypnotist? I should add here that even today nearly everyone who writes about crowds describes crowds in terms of contagion and suggestion. We see the language of contagion, for instance, in discussions of networked media as well as in depictions of the movements, protests, occupations, and riots erupting in the second decade of the twenty-first century.

Momentarily setting aside the matter of the hypnotist (just as he did the question of group ties), Freud includes another long quote from Le Bon:

> by the mere fact that he forms part of an organized group, a man descends several rungs in the ladder of civilization. Isolated, he may be a cultivated individual; in a crowd, he is a barbarian, that is, a creature acting by instinct. He possesses the spontaneity, the violence, the ferocity, and also the enthusiasm and heroism of primitive beings.[82]

Freud approves, commending not just Le Bon's "identification of the group mind with the mind of primitive people" but also noting the convergence between crowd theory and psychoanalysis. What crowd theory has found in crowds, psychoanalysis has observed "in the unconscious mental life of individuals, of children and of neurotics."[83] The processes that Le Bon describes as changing the man in the crowd are for Freud indications of the crowd already in the man. He then repeats multiple elements of LeBon's description, saying that the group is changeable, irritable, impulsive, credulous, incapable of persevering, desirous, intolerant of delays in the satisfaction of its desire, open to influence and that it thinks in images. "It has a sense of omnipotence;" "no personal interest, not even that of self-preservation, can make itself

---

82 Ibid., 12.
83 Ibid., 15.

felt."[84] The group is inclined to extremes, lacks a critical faculty and respects force. It has a thirst for obedience: "It wants to be ruled and oppressed and to fear its masters."[85] Groups demand illusions. Distinctions between truth and falsity matter little. Words function more magically than rationally. A group "knows neither doubt nor certainty," a phenomenon of unconscious life that Freud reminds his readers he has already discussed in *The Interpretation of Dreams*.

To reiterate, insofar as Le Bon conceives the crowd in terms of a dynamic wherein energies are concentrated in a single direction, he sees the force of crowds expressed in races, castes, classes, nations, juries, parties, and parliamentary assemblies. All these can override individual judgment and opinion, eliciting effects that exceed what an individual would rationally decide to do on his own. These are psychological crowds where "crowd" names the novel consistency temporarily formed from interlinked processes. The last third of *The Crowd* examines the particular characteristics that arise when different collectivities are "transformed into a crowd under the influences of the proper exciting causes."[86] Most commentators on Le Bon miss this transformative dimension of Le Bon's crowd concept. They criticize him for blurring the boundaries of the crowd such that there is no difference between juries and mobs when they should commend him for drawing out the dynamics shaping collectivities. Freud doesn't miss this point because he doesn't share the sociologists' concern with classifying groups. His interest is in establishing the reputation of psychoanalysis by demonstrating its explanatory power. For Freud, whether an individual is physically in a group—in the crowd or in an institution—is no different from whether the group manifests itself in the individual—as with the nation or race. From the perspective of psychoanalysis, the individual in a crowd and subject

84   Ibid., 13.

85   Ibid., 15.

86   Le Bon. *The Crowd*, 90.

to its emergent dynamics is just another instance of the individual as such, a fragile ego grappling with unevenly repressed desires and drives.

From Group Psychology to Individual Psychology ... and Back

Although Freud praises the brilliance of Le Bon's depiction of the group mind, he's not satisfied with Le Bon's discussion of what ties the group together. This is where Freud thinks that psychoanalysis can contribute to crowd psychology. It can *explain* the desires and instincts that underlie group cohesion instead of *taking for granted* the primacy of an instinct to sociality. The liability to affect and intellectual inhibition that alters the individual in a crowd, Freud argues, should not be attributed to number, to a quantity of people. Instead, it can be explained with basic psychoanalytic concepts. Moving from many to one, Freud's explanation encloses the directed intensities of Le Bon's crowd into an individual unconscious. Collective desire is reduced to an amplification of frustrated individual desire. Forces associated with the crowd become unconscious processes within an individual. Freud works to prevent these processes from rupturing the individual, but his efforts at containment never quite succeed, held in place, ultimately, through the reassertion of the "scientific myth" of the primal horde.

In his initial step toward enclosure, Freud criticizes the authorities on group psychology for appealing to "suggestion" in their attempts to understand crowd processes such as imitation and contagion, in other words, "influence without logical foundation."[87] Freud finds these accounts of suggestion circular: they rely on the idea that suggestibility is a fundamental mental fact (*ein weiter nicht reduzierbares Urphänomen*). As Borch-Jacobsen writes, "when

---

87   Freud, *Group Psychology*, 29.

Freud rises up against the tyranny of suggestion, he is of course militating in favor of the autonomy of the individual subject."[88] Already in his shift from the active process of "suggestion" (*die Suggestion*) to the more passive, receiving "suggestibility" (*die Suggerierbarkeit*), Freud takes a group process and makes it into an attribute of an individual.[89]

Looking "behind the shelter, the screen, of suggestion," Freud finds love. Group ties are libidinal ties. The individual gives up his distinctiveness to the group because he wants to be in harmony with its members. Given the violent, disruptive, and volatile crowds Le Bon describes, this is a very strange move. Freud justifies it by faulting Le Bon for paying insufficient attention to the leader and by attending himself to groups that crowd theory typically ignores: the church and the army. This enables Freud to oedipal-ize the crowd, to enclose it into the oedipal relationships crucial to his theory of individual psychology. Church and army are each headed by a leader (Christ, commander) "who loves all the individuals in the group with an equal love." The illusion of equal love is absolutely essential, Freud tells us. Everything depends on it. Christ stands in relation to the individuals in the church as an elder brother or "father surrogate." Because of the equality of members—each shares equally in Christ's love—the church is like a family. Members call each other brother: "the tie which unites each individual to Christ is also the cause of the tie which unites them with one another."[90] The army is basically the same, with the fundamental difference being that this familial structure is repeated in a hierarchical fashion (sections, units, squadrons, etc.). What matters here to Freud is the double nature of the libidinal tie of the group: individual to leader, individual to individual. Group ties have to be libidinal if they are to be strong enough to limit the narcissism that Freud attributes to the individual.

---

88   Borch-Jacobsen, *The Freudian Subject*, 157.
89   Freud, *Group Psychology*, 27; paragraph 40 in the original German.
90   Ibid., 33.

Yet the forces Freud describes exceed the structure in which he wants to place them. He has been attempting to remedy the problem of the circularity of suggestion by appealing to libido. To cement his case, he considers the complicating example of panic (as discussed by another crowd theorist, William McDougall). On the one hand, panic "means the disintegration of the group." On the other, it is an intensification of affect through contagion. This produces the paradox that what binds unbinds. Freud thinks that understanding group ties libidinally solves the problem insofar as panic is analogous to anxiety and is thus manifest because of an increase in danger or a cessation of emotional ties. Borch-Jacobsen points out the resulting contortions this results in for Freud:

the disappearance of the libidinal-political bond that ensured the cohesion of the group does not liberate narcissistic egos in a pure and simple unbonding. In a way, it liberates nothing at all, and especially not autonomous subjects (individuals), since panic consists precisely in an unmasterable overflowing of ego by way of (affects of) others; or, put somewhat differently, panic consists in a mimetic-contagious epidemic narcissism. The example of panic is thus not the counter-example of the group, and Freud's argument can easily be turned around: by making panic the exemplary example of individual psychology, a paradoxical result is achieved—namely, that narcissism does away with itself in one of its most striking manifestations, since panic is tantamount to a gaping, more or less bewildered opening toward others.[91]

Another way to describe this same contortion is to note that it results from Freud's structuring of process. Panic is an affective force, a flow that disrupts as it moves. It is not the counterexample to the group or crowd because it is itself unleashed as a dispersion of crowd intensity. The problem Freud encounters is the result of

---

91 Borch-Jacobsen, *The Freudian Subject*, 166–7.

his attempt to enclose this intensity in the form of the individual. Freud focuses on the scattered elements rather than the common dynamic that scatters them.

There are further challenges Freud encounters as he deploys psychoanalysis against crowd theory and explains group ties as a reinforcing combination of aim-inhibited object love and mutual identification. At key points he illustrates his argument by appealing to girls and women: the hysterical sympathetic identification of boarding school girls longing for secret love affairs and the "troop of women and girls" crowded around a singer or pianist with whom they are all in love. Le Bon's fierce and powerful crowds ready "to pillage a palace, or to die in defense of a stronghold or a barricade" are diminished and truncated, enclosed in the bourgeois sites of boarding school and concert hall, the ferocity of collective power turned inward as identification through love for a shared object. Collective desire becomes nothing but common frustration.

Borch-Jacobsen explores Freud's discussion of the imbrication of identification and object love, drawing out the strange loops in Freud's efforts to shore up an individual ego the emergence of which perpetually eludes him. Freud presents a graphic representation of these loops at the close of chapter eight. I limit myself here to noting Freud's acknowledgement that "We cannot for long enjoy the illusion that we have solved the riddle of the group with this formula."[92] He recognizes that his discussion of church and army unfairly emphasizes the leader and keeps "the other factor of mutual suggestion too much in the background."[93] And he wonders whether it would have been simpler, more modest, just to accept the idea of a herd instinct (he invokes Wilfred Trotter, *Instincts of the Herd in War and Peace*, 1916). But he concludes no. There's no such thing as a primary herd instinct. What's at work is the more complex structure he already outlined, the one where multiple individuals identify with one another in their love for the

92   Freud, *Group Psychology*, 62.
93   Ibid., 63.

same object. The reason the herd instinct doesn't explain groups is that it leaves no room for the leader, which Freud has already asserted to be crucial. The leader is necessary because he is that point in relation to which all the others are equal to one another. The members assert their equality to one another in light of the leader's superiority to them all. Freud presents the demand for equality as a reaction-formation arising out of envy; if one can't have the special relation to the leader, no other shall either. The equality of the crowd is thus a kind of negative solidarity of rivals. Freud substitutes for the herd instinct a horde. Man is a horde animal, "an individual creature in a horde led by a chief."[94]

For Freud the primal horde is the originary form that the crowd revives. He notes that the dynamics associated with crowds—"the dwindling of the conscious individual personality, the focusing of thoughts and feelings into a common direction, the predominance of the affective side of the mind and of unconscious psychical life"—are contained in his idea of the primal horde.[95] Freud thereby morphs crowd processes into a closed, mythic, ur-form of sociality. Group behavior corresponds to a regression to a primitive mental state.

According to Freud's myth of the primal horde, because of the strong emotional ties connecting the group, "there was only a common will, there were no single ones."[96] Freud thus posits that the oldest psychology is group psychology. Individual psychology comes out of it "by a gradual process which may still, perhaps, be described as incomplete."[97] But he quickly corrects himself, making individual and group psychology co-primary. Why? Because of the leader, the free, strong, and willful father of the horde. This reintroduces the problem of individual psychology at another level: not just where this primal father comes from but how a member

94 Ibid., 68.
95 Ibid., 70.
96 Ibid., 70.
97 Ibid., 71.

can become a leader. "There must therefore be a possibility of transforming group psychology into individual psychology"— which is precisely Freud's own task in *Group Psychology*.[98] But his answer is nearly nonsensical. It turns back in on itself by suggesting that the sons were initially individuals forced by the primal father's sexual jealousy into group psychology, which would mean that individual psychology comes first. And, it posits a successor who will be allowed access to women, breaking his libidinal ties to the group. Succession is force in reverse, as if the sons in the horde retained their initial individual desires rather than merging them in group psychology. Freud uses the myth to hold in place and conceal the disruption of the individual form of psychic structure by crowd processes. The myth narrates the processes together in a story where division is forced no less than connection and where the affective dynamics that disrupt are the same as those that bind.

In a postscript to *Group Psychology*, as if compelled to make his myth itself more dynamic, Freud supplements his abbreviated discussion of the horde. He brings in the patricidal story from *Totem and Taboo*, which lets him add dissatisfaction, new developments, breakdown, and compensation to the myth. Freud does so in order to provide another origin for, a mythic myth of, the emergence of the individual from the group.

In the elaborated myth, the first to break free of the group is the poet. The poet disguises the truth of the slaying of the father, putting a hero in the place of the crowd (present in fairy tales as the small animals and insects who help the hero accomplish his tasks). By creating the hero myth, the poet gives the group an idealized individual with whom each can identify. Each can imagine himself as the hero, acting alone and abolishing the one who oppresses them all. The poet, an imaginary figure of imagining, writes the individual into being, much as Freud himself does when he asserts the primacy of the father of the horde.

---

98   Ibid., 72.

The figures of leader and poet take the place of the crowd, becoming themselves models of subjectivity in its individuated form. As I mentioned, Freud finds Le Bon's discussion of the leader insufficient. In *The Crowd*, Le Bon doesn't talk about leaders until midway through the text. When he does, he treats the leader as the nucleus of will around which a crowd forms, what we could also express in Lacanese as an object-cause of crowd desire. The crowd doesn't desire the leader; the leader incites and directs the desire of the crowd. The leader is an instigator, an agitator whose intensity inspires the crowd and concentrates its attention. And even as Le Bon allows for the rare, great leaders of history, those whose will is so powerful and enduring that "nothing resists it; neither nature, gods nor man," he focuses primarily on the fact that the leader begins as one of the led and that he is led himself, hypnotized by the idea as Robespierre was by Rousseau.[99] The idea possesses the leader such that nothing else exists for him, which explains why leaders of the crowd "are recruited from the ranks of the morbidly nervous, excitable, half-deranged persons who are bordering on madness." For Le Bon, the leader concentrates and transmits an idea, turning it into a cause of action. Indeed, he considers the possibility that mass periodicals may even be replacing the leader in that they, too, can simplify, consolidate, and transmit ideas.

Rather than conceiving the leader as hypnotized, Freud treats the leader as hypnotist: "the hypnotist asserts that he is in possession of a mysterious power that robs the subject of his own will; or, which is the same thing, the subject believes it of him."[100] He argues further that the very uncanniness of hypnosis suggests something familiar but repressed, whether that of the child's relation to his parents or of the primal horde to the primal father. Freud thereby transfers a certain passivity in Le Bon's leader—fascination with the idea—to the crowd. The leader becomes active in their place. As primal father, the leader acquires a freedom, independence, and

---

99   Le Bon, *The Crowd*, 71, 68.
100   Freud, *Group Psychology*, 73.

intellectual capacity altogether missing in Le Bon even as he bears traces of the excesses of the crowd in his own furious enjoyment. Freud emphasizes that the father of the horde needs no reinforcement from others. Le Bon makes the leader himself a follower, a conduit for the natural instincts of a crowd no longer obedient to governmental authority.

Just as Freud transposes the activity of the crowd onto the leader, so too does he transfer the crowd's creativity to the poet. Early in *Group Psychology* he acknowledges the genius of groups "as is shown above all by language itself, as well as by folk-song, folklore and the like."[101] Le Bon had credited crowds with the creation of language. By the end of *Group Psychology*, creativity is the province of the individual, the singular poet who invents the heroic myth of the slaying of the father.

Freud presents psychoanalysis as capable of explaining aspects of behavior in groups central to crowd theory. Where crowd theorists see numbers, contagion, and suggestion as innovating, as producing actions that are unexpected and uncontrollable, Freud finds the explicable patterns of individual psychology: nothing new here, except Freud's own findings. The collective subjectivity of Le Bon's powerful, sovereign, often criminal and sometimes heroic crowd is incorporated in an individual figured as leader or poet, and the individual form becomes itself the site of struggling desires, drives, ideals, and anxieties, organic processes localized at best in a provisional being formed of heterogeneous elements. So rather than explaining the crowd, Freud encloses it, fragilely and awkwardly. Where there were many, there appears one. Psychoanalysis's attempt to account for collective desire condenses and displaces it into the individual form. Perhaps surprisingly, we learn more about collective subjectivity from the notorious Le Bon than we do from Freud.

---

101   Ibid., 20.

Conclusion

If the subject is interpellated as an individual, the strengths of many become the imaginary attributes of one. The individual appears as the locus of a capacity for innovation and interruption that is only ever an effect of collectivities. If bourgeois ideology is the imaginary relationship of individuals to their real conditions of existence, as we learn from Althusser, these conditions will be represented repeatedly as individual matters of individual preference and choice, belief, and circumstance. The contradictions constitutive of capitalist relations will exist side by side, appearing as so many dreams or neuroses. Collectivity, in turn, will be figured derivatively, in the shadow of the individual such that the subjectivity it evinces fails to appear as an effect of a subject. Rather than as the dynamic force of the crowd, desire appears as personal longing. Rather than an inescapable circuit of activity, drive appears as addiction. While the subject of psychoanalysis is not the reasonable, self-aware subject of liberalism, when the unconscious is rendered as that of an individual, psychoanalysis is drafted into its service as covert support for an individuated subjectivity conceived in terms of a rational and knowable will. Recognizing the collective as a subject becomes all the more challenging because the terms of what counts as the act of a subject are truncated and distorted. Rather than heterogeneous, conflictual, temporary, unbounded, and in need of support from objects and figures that exceed it, the subject as individual is impossibly, fantastically independent and enduring. The crowd becomes unconscious again in the continued operation of enclosure effected by the individual form.

Althusser asks why the relation given to individuals of their collective material life is an imaginary relation. My answer is that it is imaginary because it is given to them as individuals. Althusser, though, tries a different explanation, one that emphasizes practices of belief—kneeling, praying, shaking hands. He wants to get at the material dimension of ideology in practices, but he misses the ways these practices are collective, generic. In themselves, they are not individuating but rather the practices of a body of believers, a collectivity. Deploying Freud as backup, Althusser nevertheless asserts that individuals are always-already subjects, particularly to the extent that they are born into a family, a place: "it is certain in advance that it will bear its Father's Name, and will therefore have an identity and be irreplaceable."[102] His assertion points not to the inevitability of subjection but to the specificity of interpellation as an individual in the bourgeois family. In this regard, Althusser intermixes generic and naming practices, failing to distinguish between those that involve groups and those that single out an individual by name.

Le Bon is an odious reactionary. *The Crowd* sounds the alarm, alerting elites to the threat of mass power and giving the rest of us a window into the will formed, expressed, and unleashed as that of a collective subject. Collectivity brings with it a sense of invincibility, an immense courage and capacity to put self-interest aside. It is accompanied by an unshakeable equality, a demand for justice that Freud acknowledges even as he derives it from an original envy. The "exciting causes" of the crowd's directed intensity are unpredictable and temporary, which adds to the anxiety of elites endeavoring to hold onto the privilege they associate with their individuality before they are themselves swept up, compelled into thoughts and actions they abhor. Destructive, creative, unpredictable, temporary, and intense: the crowd expresses the paradoxical power of the people as subject.

---

102   Althusser, *On the Reproduction of Capitalism*, 119.

3

The People as Subject:
Between Crowd and Party

Attention to the disruptive crowd event breaks through the impasse the individual presents to left politics. Signaling the paradoxical power of the people as political subject, the crowd presses forward unexpectedly, then dissipates. We feel the force of many, even as we know they are not all. There are always more. Insistent and opaque, the crowd illuminates attributes of political subjectivity distinctive to the contingent, heterogeneous unity of collectives, attributes missed in mistaken characterizations of the political field as consisting of individuals. Rather than a matter of deliberation, choice, and decision, politics manifests as breaks and gaps, in the unpredictability of an exciting cause, and through collective courage, directed intensity, and capacities to cohere.

This does not mean, however, that the crowd *is* a political subject. I argue in this chapter that the crowd rupture is the Real that incites political subjectivization. The crowd is a necessary but incomplete component of political subjectivity, the opening cut by the concentrated push of many, the disruptive power of number. Whether this push will have been an emancipatory egalitarian expression of the people as a collective political subject depends on the party. The crowd is not the people. The crowd is not a political subject. Rather, the people appear as the subject of politics when the rupture of the crowd event can be attributed to them retroactively as an effect of and in fidelity to the egalitarian crowd discharge.

What Do Crowds Want?

From the preceding chapter's reading of the notorious Le Bon we gained an opening into political dynamics, affective flows of contagion, suggestion, and imitation that exceed the conscious will of individuals as they form a provisional being out of heterogeneous elements. Crowd phenomena are irreducible to specific "contents," that is to say, to the ostensible topics or complaints occasioning their emergence. They have dynamics of their own, collective drives and desires. Le Bon presents the political unconscious as the crowd of diverse and indeterminate others to whom we belong and the force this belonging exerts. Sometimes the crowd is physically present. Sometimes it is not.

Freud encloses the crowd's tumultuous belonging into the fragile yet enduring structure of the psyche. He makes one out of many, losing in the process a capacity to analyze the force of collectivity. Insofar as he treats the crowd as the product of individual desires, Freud nonetheless acquires an ability to say something about collective desire. Group ties form out of an individual's identification with another through love for a common object.

Le Bon doesn't theorize crowd desire. He takes it as a given, enfolding it in the masses' determination to destroy society and restore primitive communism. Crowd desire is inseparable from the will to collectivity formed out of its provisional being. The crowd phenomena that interest Le Bon define a new political era of mass political involvement. The very fact that crowds amass, that the people can be seen as having left their proper place, disrupts one social order and creates the possibility of another. What the people desire is less significant than the fact that they desire.

Crowd desire registers in the concentration that negates, in the positivity of a negation of the boundaries and separations ordering social being.

Crowd observers and commentators generally react to large political crowds with combinations of anxiety and enthusiasm. Social order disrupted, anything can happen. Exemplary here is Hyppolite Taine's account of crowds in the French Revolution. Written in the aftermath of the Paris Commune of 1871, Taine's portrayal influenced Le Bon. It continues to serve as a prototype for crowd description. We hear its echo in contemporary reports of riots. Taine describes a tumultuous buzzing swarm. "The starving, the ruffians, and the patriots all form one body, and henceforth misery, crime, and public spirit unite to provide an ever-ready insurrection for the agitators who desire to raise one."[1] Taine's crowd doesn't *have* a politics. It's an *opportunity for* politics. Need, violence and a sense of justice reinforce each other. The crowd manifests the desire of the people, but without telling us what it's for, telling us instead that it can never be one thing, never one and never a thing, that until it is dispersed it will remain beyond satisfaction. Taine ventriloquizes in advance twenty-first-century internet commentary:

> In this pell-mell of improvised politicians, no one knows who is speaking; nobody is responsible for what he says. Each is there as in the theatre, unknown among the unknown, requiring sensational impressions and transports, a prey to the contagion of passions around him, borne along in the whirl of sounding phrases, of ready-made news, growing rumours, and other exaggerations by which fanatics keep outdoing each other.[2]

---

1   H. A. Taine, *The Revolution*, "Les origines de la France contemporaine" vol. 1, trans. John Durand, London: Daldy, Isbister & Co, 1878, 30–1.
2   Ibid.

Here in the upheaval of the political crowd there is no clear or singular demand, no person of known responsibility. The setting is one of rumor without knowledge and rhetoric without basis. People in the crowd are speaking, and their collective desire exceeds what is individually spoken.

In the contemporary United States, it could seem that what the people desire most are cheap consumer goods. Our most prevalent image of crowds is that of Black Friday shoppers surging through the doors of Walmart. Ubiquitous screens feature chaotic hordes cohering through the concentration of personal wants for things before the closed doors of big box stores, but nothing that looks much like collective desire. In these crowd images, capitalism formats our setting so that only consumers and commodities appear, the consumers welded into a single mass through the erasure of social space, the commodities now so desirable as to have been magically able to effect this erasure. A fantasy of demands that goods can satisfy occupies the place of the object of collective desire. Black Friday shoppers know the role they play. Decades of media coverage have made that clear enough with interviews of bargain hunters braving bitter cold and long lines, excited in the press of bodies against glass and desperate enough to punch, kick, and grab in this scene of shopping staged as looting. That someone might be trampled to death adds to the thrill of the stampede of capitalist enthusiasm. The form of crowd action that capital expects in these spectacles of consumption— wait, press, rush—has been well established, scripted to generate a crowd energy that capital can direct and exploit.

Late twentieth-century Britain offered a similar crowd experience for those standing in stadium terraces watching football. As Bill Buford describes it:

> the physicalness was constant; it was inescapable—unless you literally escaped by leaving. You could feel, and you had no choice but to feel, every important moment of play—through the crowd. A shot

on goal was a felt experience. With each effort, the crowd audibly drew in its breath, and then, after another athletic save, exhaled with equal exaggeration. And each time the people around me expanded, their rib cages noticeably inflating, and we were pressed more closely together. They had tensed up—their arm muscles flexed slightly and their bodies stiffened, or they might stretch their necks forward, trying to determine in the strange, shadowless electronic night-light if this shot was the shot that would result in a goal. You could feel the anticipation of the crowd on all sides of your body as a series of sensations.[3]

Buford attempts to understand the violence of English football fans, a violence not only of fighting (beating, kicking, knifing) and property damage (smashing, burning, throwing), but also of crush, stampede, collapse, and suffocation. Crowd violence is more a product of design, architecture, patterns of ticketing and transportation than it is a spontaneous expression of anger.

A crowd forms in a place. It depends on the boundedness of a setting to concentrate its intensity. On the one hand, the boundaries demarcate the permissible: "the crowd can be here, but not there."[4] They establish the divisions that en-form the crowd. On the other, these very limits invite transgression, directing the crowd's attention. They provide the thresholds that, once crossed, enable the crowd to feel its strength and renew its assertion of power. Buford attends to this crowd feeling, the exhilarating moment when a sense of individuality is obliterated as all the mediators of social interchange that maintain our separateness give way to the "jubilant authority of suddenly being in a crowd."[5] Charge, atmosphere, pressure, expectation, excitement: the affective sensibility of the collective becomes desirable in itself, the shared sense

---

3   Bill Buford, *Among the Thugs* (New York: Vintage, 1993), 166. Thanks to Joe Mink for bringing this book to my attention.

4   Ibid., 190.

5   Ibid., 194.

of the power of numbers. This sense lets us construe the crowd as the positivity of negation, a positive expression of the negation of individuality, separateness, boundaries, and limit.

The Egalitarian Discharge

Buford's depiction of the violent crowds associated with English football supporters repeats key elements of Elias Canetti's classic work, *Crowds and Power*. I mentioned in chapter one that Canetti associates the crowd with a primal fear, the fear of being touched, particularly by the strange or unknown. Only in a crowd—the denser the better—is this fear shed. "As soon as a man has surrendered himself to the crowd, he ceases to fear its touch," Canetti writes. "Suddenly, it is as though everything were happening in one and the same body. This is perhaps one of the reasons why a crowd seeks to close in on itself: it wants to rid each individual as completely as possible of the fear of being touched." The crowd provisionally coalesces into its heterogeneous being. Norms of appropriate proximity dissolve. Conventional hierarchies collapse. In place of the distinctions mobilized to produce the individual form, there is a temporary being of multiple mouths, anuses, stomachs, hands, and feet, a being comprised of fold upon fold of touching skin.

Canetti describes the moment of the crowd's emergence as the "discharge." This is the point when "all who belong to the crowd get rid of their differences and feel equal."[6] Up until that point, there may be a lot of people, but they are not yet that concentration of bodies and affects that is a crowd. Density, though, as it increases, has libidinal effects:

---

6 Elias Canetti, *Crowds and Power*, trans. Carol Stewart, New York: Farrar, Straus and Giroux, 1984; original German publication in 1960, 17.

In that density, where there is scarcely any space between, and body presses against body, each man is as near the other as he is to himself, and an immense feeling of relief ensues. It is for the sake of this blessed moment, when no-one is greater or better than another, that people become a crowd.[7]

Canetti gives us the crowd as a strange attractor of *jouissance*, a figure of collective enjoyment.[8] The libidinal energy of the crowd binds it together for a "blessed moment," a moment Canetti renders as a "feeling of equality" in the shared intensity of belonging. The feeling won't last. Inequality will return with the dissipation of the crowd. Very few give up the possessions and associations that separate them (those who do form what Canetti terms "crowd crystals"). But in the orgasmic discharge, "a state of absolute equality" supplants individuating distinctions.[9]

Canetti's crowd equality has nothing to do with Freud's imaginary equality of rivals. Nor does it resemble *bourgeois equality* of the sort Marx excoriates in "The Critique of the Gotha Program." This is not the formal equality of a common standard applied to different people, objects, or expenditures of labor. Rather, the equality Canetti invokes is one where "a head is a head, an arm is an arm, and the differences between individual heads and arms is irrelevant."[10] De-individuation accompanies intense belonging. Just as Marx parenthetically notes that unequal individuals "would not be different individuals if they were not unequal," so does Canetti associate inequality with differentiation, with the siphoning off of the fluid, mobile substance of collectivity into the form of distinct individuals. The force of equality in the crowd breaks down the always fragile and imaginary enclosure of the individual

---

7   Ibid., 18.

8   See my *Democracy and Other Neoliberal Fantasies* (Durham, NC: Duke University Press, 2009) for a discussion of strange attractors, 67–70.

9   Canetti, *Crowds and Power*, 29.

10   Ibid.

form, enabling the collective to experience its collectivity. Canetti argues that the crowd's equality infuses all demands for justice. Equality as belonging—not separation, weighing, and measure— is what gives "energy" (Canetti's term) to the longing for justice. As I argue below, a communist party organizes fidelity to this equality, this justice, this blessed moment of joyous belonging.

Too many castigate the crowd for its destructiveness without looking into why the crowd destroys. Canetti associates destructiveness with the discharge, almost as if the crowd were crying out in ecstasy: "the noise of destruction adds to its satisfaction." Sounds of shattering glass augment the jubilation of the crowd, testifying to its strength prolonging enjoyment by promising continued growth and movement: "the din is the applause of objects."[11] Particularly satisfying is the destruction of boundaries. Nothing is off limits because there are no limits. The windows and doors that make houses into separate spaces, spaces for individuals apart from the crowd, are smashed.

> In the crowd the individual feels that he is transcending the limits of his own person. He has a sense of relief, for the distances are removed which used to throw him back on himself and shut him in. With the lifting of these burdens of distance he feels free; his freedom is the crossing of these boundaries.[12]

Canetti's crowd desires. It wants to grow, to increase and spread. It will persist as long as it is moving toward a goal. In addition to equality and density, then, Canetti attributes to crowds traits suggestive of what psychoanalysis treats as desire: growth and direction. The urge to increase is a push to be more, to eliminate barriers, to universalize and extend the crowd feeling such that nothing is outside it. Direction intensifies equality by providing a common goal. If the crowd is to continue to exist, the goal must

11   Ibid., 19.
12   Ibid., 20.

remain unattained. Expressed in Lacanian terms: desire is a desire to desire.

In the contemporary United States, political crowds, crowds authorized by neither capital nor the state, rarely manifest out of doors. Increase seems a desire limited to capital. 2011 was a year of hope and disruption because protesters from Madison, Wisconsin and then the multiple Occupy encampments shot a hole in the wall of expectations that enabled us to glimpse radical collective possibilities. For the most part, though, political crowds occur elsewhere—Tunisia, Egypt, Greece, even Canada. The December 2, 2013 headlines for the news program *Democracy Now!* expressed this status quo as they highlighted the thousands demonstrating in the occupied territories against potential Israeli expulsion of Bedouin Arabs, the thousands rallying in Honduras for an election recall, the tens of thousands protesting in Mexico against their president, the hundreds of thousands in Ukraine protesting the government's refusal to boost ties to the EU, and the "Republican Tweet Mocked for Racist Claim." The Republican National Committee had tweeted a photo of Rosa Parks with the message: "Today we honor Rosa Park's bold stand and her role in ending racism." Thousands retweeted it with the hashtag #RacismEndedWhen.

In the *Democracy Now!* headlines, domestic social media snark, contained in and channeled through networked communications, appears at the same level as mass protests in other countries as if to stand in for the missing crowd, the many invoked in terms like "crowd-sourcing." Yet again political energy is captured in communicative capitalism's circuits of drive. But this contained and limited media moment still indicates the necessity of the crowd for politics. The millions of repetitions under a common name— marked by the hashtag—push back against the Republican Party's rebranding efforts, demonstrating its failure to comprehend ongoing racism in the US. For a little while, the Twitter crowd turns lack into a common object. They disorder the Republican social media plan, their intrusion via a common name denegating the minimal difference of communicative capitalism's personalized media. Their force comes from their provisional being-many-as-one—until it is swept back into the engulfing media flow. Even here, even in communicative capitalism's virtual crowds, we can glimpse an expression of crowd desire, a desire irreducible to either a specific object or specific individuals counted up as the force of their aggregation counts for nothing. Social media is thus a second site of permissible, laudable increase: everyone wants more friends, forwards, and followers.

Crowds exert force or, better, they are a force of desire exerted by collectivity. When they amass in spaces authorized by neither capital nor the state, they breach the given, installing a gap of possibility. The presence of a crowd is a positive expression of negation. People act together in ways impossible for individuals, a phenomenon that preoccupied the early twentieth-century crowd theorists. Pushing against dominant arrangements, the crowd prefigures a collective, egalitarian possibility—but "prefigures" in a completely literal way: "prior to figuration." The crowd by itself, unnamed, doesn't represent an alternative; it cuts out an opening by breaking through the limits bounding permitted experience. It mis-assembles what is present and threatens what is not yet there (I say "mis-assemble" because "assemble" would imply order and "dis-assemble" would imply destruction without subjectivization). People are there, but, through the active desire of the crowd, differently from how they were before, combined into a state of such absolute equality that "differences between individual heads and arms are irrelevant."[13] Together, previously separate people impress the possibility of the people as the collective subject of a politics.

The energy of the crowd opens to political subjectivity, but it is not the same as political subjectivity. It's necessary but insufficient,

---

13   Ibid., 29.

an incomplete part of a politics not yet the politics of a part, half a split subject. For the crowd to become the people, representation is necessary, representation faithful to equality, to the "blessed moment" of the discharge. Some on the Left—autonomists, insurrectionists, anarchists, and libertarian communists—so embrace the energy unleashed by the crowd that they mistake an opening, an opportunity, for an end. They imagine the goal of politics as the proliferation of multiplicities, potentialities, differences. The unleashing of the playful, carnivalesque, and spontaneous is taken to indicate political success, as if duration were but a multiplication of moments rather than itself a qualitative change. For the fantasists of politics as beautiful moment, any interpretation of a crowd event is to-be-contested because of its unavoidable incompleteness, its partiality. They forget, or disavow, the fact that the non-all character of the people is the irreducible condition of struggle. And so they treat organization, administration, and legislation as a failure of revolution, a return of impermissible domination and hierarchy rather than as effects and arrangements of power, rather than as attributes of the success of a political intervention.

The politics of the beautiful moment is no politics at all. Politics combines the opening with direction, with the insertion of the crowd disruption into a sequence or process that pushes one way rather than another. There is no politics until a meaning is announced and the struggle over this meaning begins. Most of us have experiences in everyday life that confirm this point: we come across a bunch of people in an unexpected place and want to know what's going on. What are they doing, what is everybody looking at, why are police there? Have we come across a protest, a crime, an accident, a film set? Explanations of what is happening may diverge. Their divergence, the conflict between accounts, marks the political division. Insistence on remaining within the infantile fantasy of the beautiful moment of indeterminacy attempts to forestall politics and its necessary division. Even more, it denies or even betrays the crowd's expression of equality, the collective desire for collectivity that incites the crowd.

A crowd provides an opportunity for the emergence of a political subject. It doesn't determine this emergence. It can't control the politics to which it gives rise. But this politics can itself proceed with more or less fidelity to the crowd event, attempting to carry on and out its equality or trying to repress, deny, and dissipate it.[14] The crowd's chaotic moment is indeterminate, but to fetishize this indeterminacy dematerializes the crowd, extracting the affective intensities rupturing a given setting from the rupture itself, as if a crowd event were nothing more than semantic confusion. The cacophony of impressions and transports of the unknown among the unknown releases a sense of the many channeled in the everyday along set paths, igniting possibilities that will appear in retrospect to have been there all along. The political challenge is maintaining fidelity to this sense of the many—the crowd discharge—without fetishizing the cacophonous rupture. The party is a form for meeting this challenge, maintaining fidelity even as its position is itself an effect of the crowd. In Marxist theory, treatments of the Paris Commune—a key touchstone for grappling with the political form of rule by the working people—illustrate this point.

The Paris Commune

A feature of every discussion of the Paris Commune is the crowd, the people, the working class, the shocking presence of those who have been excluded from politics now in its place and the confounding of politics that results. In the Commune event, crowd

---

14 "To be faithful to an event is to move within the situation that this event has supplemented, by thinking (although all thought is a practice, a putting to the test) the situation 'according to' the event," Alain Badiou, *Ethics*, trans. Peter Hallward, London: Verso, 2001, 41.

and Commune overlap in an expression of the desire of the people. Interpretations of the Commune read this desire, making claims about who the people are and what it is that they want.

It's not quite right to say that what the people wanted was the Commune: prior to March 18, 1871 clubs and associations throughout Paris had repeatedly called for elections to a new Commune. People had rioted. But the protests and dissent hadn't yet broken the connection with the National Government. That doesn't happen until the National Government attempts to disarm the Paris National Guard and the crowd emerges to stop it. In the wake of this rupture, advocates for a new municipal government, a Commune, present the Commune as answer and object, answer to the question of the political form for Paris (and perhaps all of France) and object of the desire of the people. The desiring people are an effect of the positing of the object of their desire. They don't precede it. What precedes it is the crowd.

An eyewitness describes the crowd on March 18 as it defended the cannons from the troops sent in to take them:

The women and children were swarming up the hill-side in a compact mass; the artillerymen tried in vain to fight their way through the crowd, but the waves of people engulfed everything, surging over the cannon-mounts, over the ammunition wagons, under the wheels, under the horses' feet, paralyzing the action of the riders who spurred on their mounts in vain. The horses reared and lunged forward, their sudden movement clearing the crowd, but the space was filled at once by a backwash created by the surging multitude.[15]

The collective people manifest as a force of nature. Like the sea, they engulf all that's around them in waves.

Canetti describes the sea as a crowd symbol. He writes:

15 Stewart Edwards, ed., *The Communards of Paris, 1871* (Documents of Revolution), Ithaca, NY: Cornell University Press, 1973, 62–3.

The dense coherence of the waves is something which men in a crowd know well. It entails a yielding to others as though they were oneself, as though there were no strict division between oneself and them. There is no escape from this compliance and thus the consequent impetus and feeling of strength is something engendered by all the units together.[16]

The impetus and feeling of strength, the will, arises out of the collective. Attempting to reduce it to the thoughts or decisions of individuals is as senseless as treating the sea in terms of aggregated drops of water. The press of bodies forward and back supersedes individual thought and decision. Sounds, smells, and combined reaction reinforce the sense of a new powerful collective.

The National Army yields to the crowd. The troops are absorbed in it, becoming non-troops as they shed the distinctions of place and rank: they fraternize and intermingle.[17] The crowd offers wine and meat rolls, which are eagerly accepted by men who'd had no breakfast and had been standing in the cold for hours.[18] *The Times* of London reported:

> There was something intensely exciting in the scene. The uncertainty for a moment whether the men were meeting as friends or enemies, the wild enthusiasm of the shouts of fraternization, the waving of the upturned muskets, the bold reckless women laughing and exciting the men against their officers, all combined to produce a sensation of perplexity not unmingled with alarm at the strange and unexpected turn things were taking.[19]

---

16   Canetti, *Crowds and Power*, 80.

17   Prosper Olivier Lissagaray, *History of the Paris Commune of 1871*, trans. Eleanor Marx, London: New Park Publications, 1976, 65.

18   Frank, *The Paris Commune of 1871*, New York: Grosset and Dunlap, 1965, 112.

19   Edwards, *The Communards of Paris*, 59.

As the crowd increases and engulfs the troops, it intensifies. Through the addition of more, through the abolition of its outside, the crowd becomes stronger, more confident. When the general, Lecomte, arrives, he orders his troops to fire on the crowd. The troops refuse. He orders twice more. "Then the troops turned up the butts of their rifles, and amid the wild joy of relief, handed over them to the crowd in exchange for a mug of wine, a kind word, a fraternal embrace. 'Long live the Republic!' they shouted; and the crowd replied, 'Long live the Line!'"[20] The eyewitness account I mention above similarly evokes the egalitarian power of the crowd as it concludes: "The General gave in. He realized the full meaning of the situation. His faith in military power, his contempt for the people, his hopes and ambitious dreams, all had vanished in the face of stark reality: he had been taken prisoner."[21]

After March 18, there would be argument over who the Commune is—a working-class government?—and what it wants, but no one will dispute the fact that the situation had turned on the actuality of an insistence and a desire. The crowd forces an opening, an interruption that changes the political setting. It ruptures suppositions of order, inciting thereby attempts to expand, enclose, and target the unleashed intensities in one direction rather than another.

That the March 18 crowd event was followed by the Commune does not mean that the crowd creates the Commune or that the Commune expresses the constituent power of the people. The Commune form precedes the crowd event. It was an already existent political possibility, attempted yet thwarted in revolts in October and January. Throughout the fall and winter of 1870–71, militants organized as vigilance committees in the districts of Paris debated proposals and planned demonstrations. Yet when in their attempts to establish the Commune they pushed for revolt, the people weren't with them. In the elections following the October

20   Jellinek, *The Paris Commune of 1871*, 113–14.
21   Edwards, *The Communards of Paris*, 65.

31 march on the Hotel de Ville, over 322,000 Parisians voted in support of the National Government. 54,000 voted against.[22] In January, only a few hundred people responded to the "red poster" calling for insurrection that was distributed by the delegation of the Twenty Districts, which "saw itself as the Commune to be constituted."[23] Later that month, even as thousands were dying from the Prussian siege, only a few insurgents showed up for a new insurrection planned for January 22. The insurrection was brutally suppressed, and the National Government cracked down on clubs, public meetings, and newspapers. The national elections held in February, however, made it clear that while the majority of the French countryside supported monarchy, the cities favored a republic. Resulting anxiety over the restoration of a monarchy, the convening of the National Assembly in Bordeaux, the Assembly's failure to pay the National Guard in Paris, and the exodus of the bourgeoisie, not to mention the ongoing destitution of the people because of the siege, produced conditions more auspicious for an uprising. The previous efforts on behalf of the Commune establish in advance the idea of what an uprising would produce even as they can't themselves produce it. Commune could name a division, "the direct antithesis to the empire," in Marx's words.[24] Yet until the crowd creates the opening for it, it was just this "vague aspiration" denoting a fundamental opposition. As antithesis and aspiration, the Commune form precedes its arrival.

The struggle for the Commune is also a struggle over its meaning. It has been offered as a figure for republicanism, patriotic nationalism, federalism, centralism, communism, socialism, anarchism, even secessionism. Marx views the multiplicity of its interpretations, "and the multiplicity of interests which construed

---

22   Martin Breaugh, *The Plebian Experience*, trans. Lazer Lederhendler, New York: Columbia University Press, 2013, 177.

23   Ibid., 178.

24   Karl Marx, "Civil War in France," *Selected Writings*, ed. Lawrence H. Simons, Indianapolis: Hackett Publishing, 1995, 304.

it in their favor," as indicative of the thorough expansiveness of the Commune form.[25] This same excess can also be read as a lack, as the gap of the political. For example, although Charles Beslay's opening speech depicts the Commune as a municipal government concentrating on local matters, its decrees quickly encompassed national affairs. As Prosper Olivier Lissagaray observes in his definitive account, it was "Commune in the morning, Constituent Assembly in the evening."[26] Contention over the political form of the Commune is inseparable from, indicative of, the Commune event.[27] Multiplicity isn't attributable to institutional innovations specific to the Commune. It's an index of political division and the struggle over the Commune name: would the Commune be animated by fidelity to the crowd discharge or would another politics appropriate crowd energy in a direction antithetical to equality and collectivity?

Consider reception of the Commune in the United States. Rather than animated by fidelity to the egalitarian crowd event, it was configured through the politics of Reconstruction.[28] Political commitments antithetical to equality and collectivity attempted to appropriate the energy of the Parisian crowd. Some in the US North saw Paris as wrongfully seceding from France, just as the Southern

---

25   Ibid., 307.

26   Lissagaray, *History of the Paris Commune of 1871*, 130.

27   Frederick Busi writes, "From its inception the Commune was plagued with indecisiveness and a confusing diversity of aims and ideas. An American observer in Paris remarked, 'It's a madhouse inhabited by monkeys.' From its beginning, lack of discipline and direction hampered its development, and understandably so, for it could never quite decide if it were the vanguard in the struggle against social injustice or for the restoration of national honor through war." "The Failure of Revolution," in *Revolution and Reaction: The Paris Commune 1871*, ed. John Hicks and Robert Tucker, Amherst: The University of Massachusetts Press, 1973, 14–25; 19. The book is a reprint of *The Massachusetts Review* XII, 3, Summer 1971.

28   Philip M. Katz, *From Appomattox to Montmarte: Americans and the Paris Commune*, Cambridge, MA: Harvard University Press, 1998.

states wrongly left the Union. Commune and Confederacy both rejected legitimate centralized government. Others in the North, increasingly mistrustful of popular sovereignty, used the Commune as an emblem of the failure of Reconstruction. An editor of *The Nation* railed against the "Socialism in South Carolina" that came from "allowing incompetent black men to govern and vote."[29] As he saw it, neither Paris nor the South had the political capacity to govern itself. Some Southerners embraced the parallel between Paris and the Confederacy, particularly the revolt against a repressive governmental authority. Weirdly, in 1880 a former vice president of the Confederacy identified himself as a communist—Alexander Stephens, who became a member of Congress after the war. For Stephens, to be a communist means to favor home rule, the sovereignty of the local government.[30] He explicitly rejects the abolition of private property, capturing communist desire in a racist *ressentiment* that substitutes for and attempts to displace class struggle. In any case, the point is clear: *contra* Marx, the multiplicity of Commune interpretations has nothing to do with the expansiveness of the commune form. Rather, this multiplicity points to the struggle over the name incited by the rupture of the crowd event.

Marx suggests that the Paris Commune provides a glimpse of a solution to the problem of the political form of the people. While all previous forms of government had been repressive, the Commune is a "thoroughly expansive political form."[31] Marx's rhetoric is stirring, polemically suited to struggle over the meaning of the Commune. "Commune" names aspiration and antagonism; it designates the alternative to the empire. Within the ongoing struggle over the positive realization of that alternative, Marx prioritizes one among the multiple interests that tried to see itself in the Commune form, presenting the Commune "essentially" as the

---

29　Ibid., 97.
30　Ibid., 108–10.
31　Marx, "The Civil War in France," 307.

political form "under which to work out the economical emancipation of labor."

Analytically, Marx's account is less satisfying insofar as it equates
proletarian self-government with a federal system comprised of
local communes, district assemblies (comprised of delegates elected
from the communes), and a National Delegation of deputies sent
from these assemblies to Paris. That this arrangement presented
itself does not make it uniquely suited for the emancipation of
labor. Distributed and federal political arrangements have served
bourgeois and imperial power quite well. Marx even acknowledges that in the Commune's governing schema rural producers
were brought under the lead of the towns, so the Commune did
not eliminate repression. To the extent that "Commune" names
a governing body, apparatus, or schema, one comprised of an
arrangement of offices, the rules for their maintenance and distribution, as well as a set of dictates connecting this arrangement
to the people it would govern, "Commune" institutionalizes some
possibilities and excludes others. It puts repression to work. Marx,
faithful to crowd rupture, presents the Commune as a continuation of the egalitarian moment. My point is that the institutional
specificity of the political form of the Commune matters less than
the fidelity of its presentation. We should attend to Marx's rhetoric
rather than his (weak) analysis. Marx's rhetoric signals his fidelity to the egalitarian rupture of the crowd event. The Commune
incites a partisan subjectivization, an event in the political expression of the working class.

In the different accounts of the Paris Commune, the referent of
"Commune" is unstable. It shifts from all of Paris, to the people of
Paris who voted representatives to the Commune, to the working
class, to those elected to the Commune, to those who served in it,
even to particular sets of voices in the Council. While a politics can
and should be traced in these shifts—for this movement is nothing
but the expression and enclosure of a political subject—we might
also note that the fact of shifting indexes an irreducible feature

of the people as non-all, non-totalizable, and never fully present to itself. The people is only present as few, some, or many. The substitutionism about which Trotsky warned is not a danger particular to communist or working-class parties. It's an unavoidable condition of any popular politics with emancipatory egalitarian ends. Neither people nor class (nor movement nor mass) exists as a unity. Every attempt to invoke, create, or speak in behalf of such a unity comes up against an ineliminable, constitutive division.

Instead of solving a political problem, the Commune poses one: the sovereignty of the people. Is it possible and what forms can it take? The non-all character of the people has been a consistent sticking point in democratic theory. If the people are not a unity, how can they rule themselves? How can they speak or legislate? And how do we know? The theoretical discussions occur under various headings—foundings, constituent power, and the possibility of bringing something new into being. Taking the place of the mythic social contract, the power of the people to make their own history comes up against its grounding in what cannot be other than a crime against the prior order.

In contrast, Marxist theory makes the prior order itself the crime, repeating the series of need, crime, and justice Taine associates with the crowd. The revolutionary class gives its ideas "the form of universality" and represents these ideas "as the only rational, universally valid ones." Marx explains, "The class making revolution emerges at the outset simply because it is opposed to a *class* not as a class but as a representative of the whole of society."[32] This is the sense in which class struggle is a political struggle. Rather than determined within the economic conditions in which class confronts class as two distinct forces with particular interests, the class making revolution represents its interests as general over and against the particular will of the oppressing class. More

---

32   Karl Marx and Friedrich Engels, "The German Ideology," *Selected Writings*, 130.

precisely, class partisans and allies struggle to present the Real of the crowd's destructive interruption as expressions of the desire of the people.

Marx premises the revolutionary break within existing conditions of production, nevertheless Marxist theory doesn't escape the problem of the people. Whether as the limits of working-class struggle in trade union consciousness, the failure of the masses to revolt, or the betrayals by elitist vanguard parties, Marxist theory and communist movement run up against the disorganized, disagreeable, divided people. The people resist and evade the very forms on which their political subjectivity depends. When it appears, which isn't often, the movement for the majority isn't necessarily in the immediate interest of the majority. Since they can never be fully present, no revolution or revolutionary movement can actually *be* that of the people. It always entails the imposition of the ideas of some upon many.

In sum, the Commune gives form to the break with the National Government effected by the crowd even as the people's elusive desire propels a new subjective process, a process of inserting the people into history as an active subject and rereading history in terms of the actions of this subject.[33] Interpretations of the Commune thus grapple with how to understand the power of the people. Marx suggests as much in the letter to Kugelmann that Lenin cites in *State and Revolution*: heroic party comrades in Paris are attempting "real people's revolution."[34] As I argue above, the multiple, opposing treatments of the Commune are not indications of an expansive political form, and they are not reflections of specific features of institutional design. Rather, they underscore the irreducibility of the *gap between the people and their political forms, the gap constitutive of the people's subjectivity*. Badiou writes, "The

33   Alain Badiou, *Theory of the Subject*, trans. Bruno Bosteels, London: Continuum, 2009.

34   V. I. Lenin, "The State and Revolution," in *The Lenin Anthology*, ed. Robert C. Tucker, New York: Norton, 1975, 336.

subject glides between the successive partial representations of that whose radical lack institutes it as articulated desire."[35] Badiou is glossing Lacan. What I find suggestive is seeing in the partial representations of the Commune traces of the people as a political subject. The point is not to fetishize rupture or celebrate the pluri-potentiality of infinite modes of becoming. It is to see in the overlap of the Commune form and the crowd event the specificity of an emancipatory egalitarian politics. Because it is a form for the expression of the people's desire, the Commune is necessarily lacking.

The Destruction of Social Space

In her classic treatment of the Paris Commune as the transformation of social space, Kristin Ross enables us to feel the Commune as the expression of a new politics.[36] This felt politics, though, is not quite the politics of a subject. It's more a foreshadowing of the politics that hijacked and dismantled the sense that collectivity is a necessary attribute of the political subject. Ross's Commune looks like Paris in 1968, more specifically, like the Paris Commune presented by the Situationists in their "Theses on the Commune." The Situationists highlight the "biggest festival of the nineteenth century." The Commune was an explosion of inventiveness, an experiment in revolutionary urbanism that, for those who lived it, was a fully consummated political experience (not a failed attempt at establishing a new form of working-class rule). This version of the Commune, developed and extended by Ross as a celebration of individuality, continues today as a key image of radical politics. It's how we imagine revolution. And it's what we have

---

35 Badiou, *Theory of the Subject*, 138.

36 Kristin Ross, *The Emergence of Social Space: Rimbaud and the Paris Commune*, London: Verso, 2008; originally University of Minnesota Press, 1988.

to get beyond, a possibility latent in Ross's own attention to the crowd.

For Ross, the Commune's most profound elements are horizontality, emancipation from social division, and the politicization of everyday life. She finds the horizontality of the Commune in its "largely leaderless revolutionary government." This horizontality manifested itself symbolically in the destruction of the Vendome column. Social divisions broke down as workers asserted themselves as artists and authors, as all governmental agents received workers' wages, and as barricades blocked previous patterns of urban circulation and created new ones. Both horizontality and the elimination of social division figure into the politicization of everyday life as centralized state power is replaced by the Commune, a political form that did not concentrate power into an excrescence parasitic on society but operated as society's own politicization.

Critical of what she calls "the 'mature' Marx, author of scientific socialism," Ross distances the politics of the Commune from the politics of a working class inexorably marching toward communism. Exceeding the limits of class and property, the revolutionary praxis of the Commune came from its "challenge to the boundaries *between* work and leisure, producer and consumer, worker and bourgeois, worker and intellectual."[37] This challenge disrupts the linear, centralizing movement of capitalism's development into communism, a disruption Marx recognizes in *The Civil War in France*. Ross brackets *Capital* in order to link Marx's account of the civil war in France to his early critique of Hegel. The significance of Marx's writing on the Commune, for Ross, is its acknowledgement of a displacement of politics from "a specialized set of activities, institutions, and occasions" into "concrete problems of work, leisure, housing, sexuality, and family and neighborhood relations."[38] She thus uses Marx against Marx in order to present the Commune in terms of variegated, multiform revolution

---

37 Ibid., 20.
38 Ibid., 23, 33.

traversing the social field. Ross writes, "Revolutionary struggle is diffuse as well as specifically directed, expressed throughout the various cultural spheres and institutional contexts, in specific conflicts and in the manifold transformations of individuals rather than in some rigid and polar opposition of capital and labor."[39] Revolution isn't the expression of class struggle. It's a matter of multiple differentiated "transformations." In Ross's version of revolution, what happens to an individual takes the place of what a class makes happen.

If the unique contribution of the Commune was the challenge to boundaries between work and leisure, producer and consumer, worker and bourgeois, worker and intellectual, then it pre-enacts communicative capitalism. To see in Ross's depiction of the Commune a precursor to our mediated present isn't even a stretch. She emphasizes the "astounding abundance of newspapers, pamphlets, tracts, propaganda brochures, professions of faith, declarations of intentions, manifestos."[40] During the two months of the Commune, over seventy new periodicals were introduced. The policy of the Commune was "instant information." Posters covered the walls of Paris. Proclamations were often read aloud to people in the streets. Cartoons, caricatures, satires, and insults—often highly sexual—circulated widely.

In a setting where networked personalized media devices tether us to work without end, where our consumer activities are traced, bundled, and resold as so much searchable data, and where the achievements of middle-class, bourgeois life have collapsed in a proletarianization of the waged and indebted who confront new and extreme forms of inequality, an erasure of boundaries looks more like capitalist real subsumption than it does the revolutionary praxis of the oppressed. Ross's own categories further the diminution of questions of capital and labor: she wants to diminish this opposition so that other sites of politics can appear. Retroactively,

39   Ibid., 33.
40   Ibid., 136.

this diminution is the gesture of capitalist restoration enacted under the heading of neoliberalism. The redirection of politics throughout cultural spheres and specific conflicts was the form of its dispersion into loci capital could more easily swallow. The enclosure of politics in individuals was the index of working-class defeat. Ross gives us revolution in and as a form already captured by capitalism, easily dispersed throughout fantasies of the power of creativity to transform individuals.

Ross's account of the Commune is also an account of the crowd.[41] Her nuanced reading of the crowd in the poetry of Arthur Rimbaud opens up the possibility of repeating the move she makes with Marx and using Ross against Ross. Ross brings out the ways Rimbaud's poems render the crowd as a swarm. Some ways are acoustic: the distant drone, an indistinct buzzing that reverberates in the background, "the frantic, busy immobility of latency," the rustling of trees, of material against itself, and of stars, the murmur of agitation sweeping through a crowd. Others are tactile: "the sensation of being covered with enormous swarms of tiny insects," the "awakening of the colonies of the skin," "the dispersion of the body's surface into a thousand microsensations." Still others are lexical, fantastic juxtapositions of words (such as "rustling stars") in a "swarm of relations" suggesting "the premonition of a change in the relations of elements to each other."[42] For Ross, treatments of Rimbaud as a poet of sensation generalize a more specific feature of his poetry: the erotic as "predicated on the effectuation of the power of the crowd, a power both destructive and generative."[43] The crowd decomposes the body, making the body itself become a crowd, "as if it were peopled by multiplicities."

Ross links Rimbaud's crowd to changes at the level of the individual. The crowd effects a de-individuation "that signals a devaluation of individual subjectivity in favor of the construction

41   Ibid., 100–21.
42   Ibid., 103.
43   Ibid., 113.

of a (virtual) group subject."[44] She continues: "something is happening that cannot be seized without letting go of the power to say 'I.'" I don't know why Ross includes "virtual" parenthetically. I suspect that it has something to do with her critique of the "mature" Marx and her rejection of class politics. Ross is looking for a subjectivity emancipated from the confines of bourgeois life, the structured expectations of capitalism, and the "ordered disorganization" of consumer culture. She associates this subjectivity with "the anarchist notion of individual liberty, of individual*ity*" against capitalist individual*ism* (italics in original).[45] Ross wants to affirm this anarchist individuality, to retain it as a locus of emancipation over and against a Marxist emphasis on work. The problem of capitalism in this view isn't the exploitation of some for the enjoyment of others; it's the violence done to individuality. Capitalism commodifies and anonymizes. It dulls perception, enclosing desire into a narrowness fit only for work and consumption. Rimbaud's poetry multiplies the senses in order to break the hold of capitalism on the individualized body. It offers the "more-than-human" of the "transformed utopian body of infinite sensation and libidinal possibility as figure for the perfected community, for associative or collective life."[46] The group subject is virtual because it is a marker for a potential collectivity of unlimited individuality.

A quarter century since Ross's initial publication of her reading of Rimbaud, emphases on individuality and potentiality resonate less with freedom than they do with the dominion of capital. Individuality is communicative capitalism's primary value. We are told that each of us is unique, and enjoined to amplify, advertise, and accelerate this uniqueness. Our media is personalized, and we are encouraged to personalize it even more, for example, with apps and mobile phone cases that meet our singular needs and express our singular brands. Those looking for work are advised to make

---

44 Ibid., 113.
45 Ibid., 101.
46 Ibid., 120–21.

themselves stand out from the crowd, to distinguish themselves from others by offering that special something that will catch an employer's eye. Capital accumulation depends on cultivating and monetizing the new and different. In an informational milieu in which images and events are quickly absorbed in an infinite media flow, attracting and retaining attention is extraordinarily difficult. Social media experts and data analytics attempt to harvest and harness future possibilities, reminding us that coming up with a unique personal brand, getting noticed, getting heard is no simple matter. "Potential" is entrepreneurial buzzword and securitizable wager. Corporations capture it and hedge funds bet on its algorithmic variations. Individuality and potentiality point less to new experiences of freedom than to new means of entrapment within capitalist circuits.

When the group marks only the potential of unlimited individuality, it loses its political efficacy. It fails to make division appear, covering it over with the unifying screen of multiplicity.[47] In Ross's version embodied sensation replaces the collective body of the working class. Crowd affect displaces militant political association.

At the same time, Ross's insights into Rimbaud's figuring of the crowd suggest another reading of the crowd, one that treats the devaluation of individual subjectivity as a component of a process of collective subjectivization. Something is happening such that the capacity to say "I" is being replaced by the will to say "we." This something is the crowd effect rupturing the individual form. In another parenthetical, Ross writes:

the anonymous, blurry face in the crowd, the "man in the street," as we say, is always one step away from becoming "people in the streets": the crowd, the demonstration, the insurrection. The man

---

47   See Gavin Walker, "The Reinvention of Communism: Politics, History, Globality," *South Atlantic Quarterly* 113: 4, Fall 2014, 671–86.

in the street, the indistinct element in a swarm of people, stripped of individual subjectivity, faceless, is always on the point of becoming "political man," always just at the limit of action.[48]

Anonymity marks the de-individuation necessary for collective subjectivity, the power number exerts in excess of individual conscious decision. The blurring of distinctions that concentrated urban life provides perches cities on the brink of riot. On the one hand, insofar as a single figure stands in for a rebelling swarm, "political man" is a misnomer. On the other, that the swarm is not yet a political subject, not yet a collectivity, not yet present to itself as a provisional being highlights the indeterminacy of the crowd. Ross finds potential in the unformed. She values latency. Her rich descriptions of Rimbaud's crowds bring out the destructuring capacities of swarms in ways that need not be rearticulated with a freeing of individuality but can instead be associated with the emergence of collective subjectivity.

Ross positions the "half-real, half-fantastic" crowd as an alternative to a politics rooted in the well-defined interests of the class. It's not an alternative. The beautiful in-between of infinite potentiality can't last forever. People get tired. Some want a little predictability, reliable food sources, shelter, and medical care. Others realize they're doing all the work. Without a politics that targets capitalists as a class, the rest of us continue to be exploited (even when this exploitation is self-exploitation). Common work, knowledge, achievements, and resources are expropriated from us and channeled into the coffers of the very, very few. Ross herself fully recognizes the brevity of the Commune moment. Two months after the March 18 uprising, twenty-five thousand Communards were slaughtered in a massacre far exceeding any of the events of the Terror.[49] The crowd isn't an alternative political arrangement; it's the opening to a process of re-arrangement.

---

48   Ross, *The Emergence of Social Space*, 108.
49   Ibid., 4.

What Ross celebrates is the exciting cause of popular rupture with a dominant order, the crowd event that ignites a subjective process. What she avoids, sometimes disavowing, is the subject support of this process in a collective, partisan body. For example, even as Ross highlights the erasure of divisions and the proliferation of political engagements across diverse social classes, she nonetheless emphasizes the working-class nature of the Commune, as if in covert fidelity to that party that would insist on the egalitarian link between crowd discharge and Commune form. She lauds the reappropriation of drunkenness, laziness, and licentiousness on behalf of the workers against those who disparage them. A partisan position infuses Ross's text (the foreword is by Terry Eagleton), yet she pushes it aside in a fetishistic embrace of destabilization for its own sake. She concludes: "the force of an idea lies primarily in its ability to be displaced." At first reading this is unconvincing, requiring us to agree that the force in the Commune idea, for example, lies in its ability to be displaced and not in its expression of popular power. Any idea, image, or symbol can be displaced, resignified, reappropriated, ironically redeployed, turned into a meme. At second glance, Ross's claim is simply wrong: the force of a brand like Coke persists in its ability to resist displacement, its capacity to retain its symbolic efficiency across multiple registers and continue to designate a knot of beverage, culture, and thirst-quenching, corporatized contemporaneity even when other words and proper names occupy the place of its brand name, as we saw at the beginning of chapter one. Better, then, is appropriating Ross's sentence against itself: the force of an idea appears in the struggle over it, in its capacity to serve as a site worth contesting. The force expresses the subjectivity of a collective.

Our Party

In *Theory of the Subject*, a book that grew out of a seminar given from 1975 to 1979, Alain Badiou says that the Marxist tradition has given us two assessments of the Paris Commune. The first, from Marx, objectively considers the Commune in terms of the political goals of the working class with respect to the state. The proletariat has to smash the old state machinery and build new organs of political power. It has to take a place and exert force. How exactly force is concentrated, Marx neglects to explain.

The second assessment of the Commune, from Lenin, takes up this concentration. Lenin brings out the subjective aspect of force. Reading *What Is to Be Done?* for its "silent assessment" of the Commune, Badiou tells us that Lenin draws four consequences from the Commune's defeat: 1.) "it is necessary to practice Marxist politics, and not some local romantic revolt;" 2.) "it is necessary to have some overall view of things ... and not be fragmented into the federalism of struggles;" 3.) "it is necessary to forge an alliance with the rural masses;" and, 4.) "it is necessary to break the counter-revolution through an uninterrupted, militarily offensive, centralized process."[50] Lenin conceives the party by inferring a certain kind of subjective force from the Commune. That is to say, he reads the Commune as an effect or consequence of a political subject and builds his idea of the party from this reading. The party is an "operator of concentration" of the four consequences, "the system of practical possibility for the assessment of the Commune." The party provides the vehicle enabling assessment of the Commune even as it is an effect of this very assessment. Or, the place from which the Commune is assessed itself results from the Commune.

Badiou uses Lacan's notion of the Real to express the function of the Commune for Marxists. More than an historical event or

---

50   Badiou, *Theory of the Subject*, 46.

political institution, the Commune serves as a concept that enables us "to think the relation of the political subject to the real." Badiou writes, "The Marxist status of the revolutions is their having-taken-place, which is the real on the basis of which a political subject pronounces itself in the present." Expressed in the crowd terms I've been developing here, the crowd rupture can be the exciting cause of a political subject, but its pronouncement or appearance as such a cause is a separate, analytically distinct move. The crowd rupture has to be politicized, tied to a subject. The crowd provides a material opportunity for the expression of a political subject, a moment that has happened and the happening of which can be attributed to the workings of this political subject. We saw this in Marx's attribution of the Commune event to the working class.

The political subject exceeds the combination of event and interpretation. Badiou demonstrates that the Marxist approach remains incomplete. *How* event and interpretation are combined matters if an event is to be the cause of a subject. The Real of the Commune event consists in the crowd's rupture with the state, both the official state and the Marxist conception of the state. Confronted with the Commune event, Marx is surprised. He has to change his thinking. Badiou writes,

> It is by putting into effect a point of the impossible in this theory that it reveals its status as real, so that Marx, who logically disapproves of the triggering of the insurrection, can only *encounter* in it the vanishing Parisian masses. Whence the obligation, to which he remains faithful, of being wholly on the side of that of which he disapproves in theory, so as to find the new and retroactive concept of his practical approval.[51]

The people as a collective subject appear through the disruption of the crowd insofar as there is something about the insurrection that

---

51   Ibid., 220.

was unimaginable prior to its enactment. The impossible happens, compelling Marx to take a stand: whose side is he on? The subject forces a previously unimaginable interpretation of an event; the crowd doesn't look like what it had been before. Now it looks like the people. With the appearance of the people as a political subject, the entire situation changes.

Here is the unpredictability of an exciting cause, the people forcing a change of theory and practice. Riotous crowd, available political form, force of the impossible: the political subject impresses itself at the effervescent site of their convergence. Marx responds to this appearance of the people with fidelity. As he says in his letter to Kugelmann, no matter the Commune's multiple tactical and policy errors, "the present rising in Paris—even if it be crushed by the wolves, swine and vile curs of the old society—is the most glorious deed of our Party since the June insurrection in Paris."[52]

Marx nonetheless criticizes the Commune in this same letter. After praising the elasticity, historical initiative, and sacrifice of the Parisians, he chides them, first, for missing the moment when they fail to march on Versailles. He faults them, second, for eliminating the Central Committee of the National Guard and holding elections to institute the Commune.

The order Marx lists his criticisms is odd, seemingly backwards in that the first is a consequence of the second; the second happened first. Badiou, drawing from Lacan's discussion of anticipation and certainty in "Logical Time and the Assertion of Anticipated Certainty," explains why it is not. Marx is using Versailles's reaction (or what he imagines Versailles's reaction would have been) to register the Commune event. Versaille's reaction validates the hasty or anticipatory move that created the Commune. A subject had acted and Versailles had no choice but to respond. Badiou writes:

---

52   "Marx to Dr Kugelmann Concerning the Paris Commune," April 12, 1871, marxists.org.

Marx judges the Commune to be precipitated—subjectivizing in its political haste—and blames it for not marching onto Versailles. But this is in order to indicate retroactively the nature of the certainty (of victory) of which this haste itself could be the bearer, insofar as it could be deciphered in the other: in the initial disorder and surprise of the inhabitants of Versailles, and in the possibility of changing the lack into reason by a second haste, that of the military offensive against Versailles. The latter would then be finally caught up in the subjective process, that is to say, in a consequent political direction, which is the only validation of the vanishing algebra of the Parisian masses into a consistent subject.[53]

In other words, to understand an event as the effect of a political subject, Badiou conjoins two operations: subjectivization and the subjective process. *We will win. We will be shown to have been right.* The certainty of the political subject—we will win—is always too soon, an anticipation of results it cannot guarantee but pursues nonetheless. Precipitous certainty is another name for political will. Rather than an amorphous combination of multiple possibilities, which is just a description of a manifold, the subject is a direction that cuts through this manifold. We find evidence of this direction in the other. The response of the other, its disorder and surprise, indicates the presence of a subject. The other's response reads the disorder as an effect of a subject. It attributes to this subject a consistency of action, purpose, and will. That the other can do nothing but respond, that it cannot proceed as it had, is the work of the subject. In Badiou's formulation: "In subjectivization, certainty is anticipated. In the subjective process, consistency is retroactive. *To put into consistency the haste of the cause*: therein lies the whole enigma of the subject."[54]

Each operation—subjectivization and subjective process—involves political struggle. Militants, organizers, agitators, and

---

53   Badiou, *Theory of the Subject*, 251.
54   Ibid., 251.

vanguards try to set things in motion. They produce actions. They try to bring people out, get them to feel their collective power, and incite them to use it. They are alert to possibilities, to protests that may become ruptures. And consequent to the gap of a disruption, militants, organizers, agitators, and vanguards work to render the disruption as an effect of a subject. They fight on the terrain of the other, endeavoring to insure that the gap remains and to give this gap meaning and direction, to make it consistent. Enemies fight back. Enemies—and even allies—may deny that a disruption occurred: nothing significant happened; the demonstration or event was within the field demarcated by capital and state, part of business as usual, an expected and permitted protest, child-friendly and within the demarcated free-speech zone. They may deny that the disruption was the effect of a subject: it was hooligans; it was a motley and contingent array of disparate voices (here empirical sociological data that identifies and fragments crowd elements comes in handy). They may attribute the disruption to the wrong subject, another state, class, or agency. For the militants, organizers, agitators, and vanguards, establishing the collectivity as the subject of a politics, inscribing it in a process and rendering it consistent, politicizes the rupture, forcing it in one direction rather than another.

Subjectivization and the subjective process are connected by an anticipation and a lag. To disrupt and surprise, subjectivization has to come too soon. It can't be predicted, expected, or natural, for that would mean that it remained within the order of things. Rather than the intrusion of a subject, the subject would not have appeared at all. Correlative to anticipation is a lag, the gap between a move that may or may not disrupt and the disruption as it registers in the other. The lag means that effects seem to precede their causes. Only after an effect registers is its cause brought into consistency with it.

Badiou associates four "categories of the subject-effect" with subjectivization and the subjective process. Anxiety and courage respond to the gap of anticipation. The former wants to fill in the void in the old order, to restore things to their proper place, to put the law back where it belongs. The latter wants to extend the hole, to force it forward in the direction of justice. Courage leaves behind (and no longer feels) the former sense of proper place. It looks ahead to the building of something new. Correlative to anxiety and courage, then, are super-ego and justice, which are themselves effects of the subjective process, reactions to the rupture of anticipation.

That perspective which gives body to the political subject is the party. Marx describes the Commune as a glorious achievement of "our Party." This is not a descriptive empirical claim regarding membership in a political organization. It is the point from which he responds to the subjectivization effected by the Commune event, positioning it within a process oriented to justice.

Politicizing the People

Thirty years subsequent to his analysis of Commune, subject, and party, Badiou revises his analysis. In an essay included in *The Communist Hypothesis* (a slightly revised version of material presented in *The Logic of Worlds*), Badiou presents the Marxist discussion of the Commune in terms of the state. Rather than reading the party as the subject support of a politics, he figures it as the realization of the ambiguity of the Marxist account of the Commune.[55] On the one hand, the Commune is a clear advance in proletarian struggle insofar as it smashes the machinery of the state. On the other, it ultimately fails *because* it smashed the machinery of the state—it's unorganized, incapable of decision, unable to defend itself. To resolve these problems, the party takes a statist form. It

---

55   Alain Badiou, *The Communist Hypothesis*, trans. David Macey and Steve Corcoran, London: Verso, 2010, 182.

is a vehicle of destruction and reconstitution, but reconstitution within the constraints given by the state.

Badiou's rejection of party and state is familiar. Bruno Bosteels and Slavoj Žižek compellingly demonstrate the political inadequacy of this rejection. Arguing for the actualization and organization of communism in real movement, Bosteels criticizes the leftist idealism of the later Badiou's emphasis on the pure Idea.[56] Žižek likewise rejects the alternative of seizing or abandoning the state as a false one: the real challenge is transforming the state itself.[57] I agree with Bosteels and Žižek. I want to add, moreover, that for leftists to make state-centeredness the problem now is to short-circuit the discussion that matters. The Left in the US, UK, and EU—not to mention communists—is struggling just to register as a political force. To worry about our seizing the state, then, is a joke, fantasy, and distraction from the task at hand. Rather than a concentration of political will, communist possibility remains diffuse, dispersed in the multitudinous politics of issues, identities, and moments of action that have yet to consolidate in the collective power of the divided people. What matters for us here and now is the galvanization of such a communist will.

In his effort to reduce the Marxist discussion of the Commune to the problem of the party-state, Badiou neglects the more fundamental question posed by the Commune, namely, that of the relation of the party to the people, the collective political subject. The Commune is less the form of a state than it is the form of a break with a previous state, both the state as in the National Government and the state of political incapacity associated with the workers, as Badiou himself emphasizes in the later work. As such a break, it opens up and disorders. The people are disassembled,

---

56 Bruno Bosteels, "The Leftist Hypothesis: Communism in the Age of Terror," in *The Idea of Communism*, ed. Costas Douzinas and Slavoj Žižek, London: Verso, 2010.

57 Slavoj Žižek, "How to Begin from the Beginning," in *The Idea of Communism*.

suggestible, strong, and mobile as crowds. It is a mistake, then, for
Badiou to reduce the Commune to a state form (as Ross powerfully demonstrates) and the Marxist tradition to commentary on
and reaction to this state form. Badiou seems to have fallen prey
to the fatalism his younger self criticizes—parties will be parties;
"we will always be fucked over."[58] Marx himself analyzes the
Commune in terms of the subjectivization of the people. In the
letter to Kugelmann, Marx treats the Parisians, the people of Paris,
as "our heroic Party comrades." Their advances are teaching new
lessons in political struggle, namely, that smashing the bureaucratic-military machine is essential "for every people's revolution
on the Continent."[59] In *The Civil War in France*, as he presents the
Commune as the "direct anti-thesis to the empire," Marx describes
it as the positive form of a republic in which class rule itself is
superseded. He draws out the politics of constituting the people
under the leadership of the working class, noting the replacing of
the standing army by the armed people, the establishing of universal suffrage, the opening of education to all, and, of course,
the replacing of the parasitic excrescence of the old state organization with the self-government of the producers. Marx writes,
"The great social measure of the Commune was its own working
existence. Its special measures could but betoken the tendency of a
government of the people by the people."

The people "storming heaven" don't preexist the revolutionary event of the Commune. The Commune produces them as its
cause. The middle class, which had helped put down the workers'
insurrection of June 1848, finds itself enrolling "under the colors
of the Commune and defending it against the willful misconstruc-
tions of Thiers." Marx explains this support as resulting from the
Commune's abolition of interest on debts and extension of time for
repayment. The peasantry had Louis Bonaparte, but this support
started to break down under the Second Empire. Were it not for

58   Badiou, *Theory of the Subject*, 328.
59   Marx Letter to Kugelmann.

the blockade around Paris, Marx argues, the French peasantry
would have had to recognize that the Commune was its only hope,
its only source of release from blood tax, gendarme, and priest.
Again, the temporality is important: the peasantry "would have
had," had the Commune process been able to continue, a process
that Marx presents as the subjectification of the people as party.

Lenin's discussion of the Commune in *State and Revolution*
takes up a similar problematic of people and party. Lenin observes
that the idea of "a people's revolution seems strange coming from
Marx."[60] But to Lenin this idea is crucial—and crucial to understanding the role of the party—insofar as it points to the active
and independent activity of the majority, "the very lowest social
groups, crushed by oppression and exploitation," imprinting the
revolution with their own demands. Because in 1871 the proletariat
was not a majority anywhere in Europe, a "people's revolution"
had also to embrace the peasants. Lenin writes, "These two classes
then constituted the 'people.' These two classes are united by
the fact that the 'bureaucratic-military state machine' oppresses,
crushes, exploits them."[61] For Lenin, where the Commune fails
and where its failure impresses itself on (en-forms) the party is
in the constituting of the people, that is, in actually producing the
alliance between peasants and proletariat necessary for revolution.
Lenin commends Marx for seeing that, insofar as the "smashing of
the state machine was required by the interests of both the peasants and the workers," it united them and placed before them a
common task. Smashing the state, or eliminating a "special force"
of oppression, requires that the majority (workers and peasants)
suppress the minority (the bourgeoisie), which means that the
majority have to be organized to carry this out. This is the role of
the party: concentrating and directing the energies of the people.
The party shapes and intensifies the people's practical struggles.

Given Lenin's interests in establishing the revolutionary action

60   Lenin, "The State and Revolution," 337.
61   Ibid., 338.

of the Russian working class within the historical trajectory of proletarian struggle, that he highlights the idea of a people's revolution isn't surprising. The parallel with the Commune helps him here, providing a form by which to understand the Russian 1905 revolution. In an earlier text, "Lessons of the Moscow Uprising," published in 1906, Lenin examines the revolutionary events in Moscow in December 1905.[62] And while he does not look specifically at the Commune, he does highlight the action of the crowd, seeing in the crowd the march of practice ahead of theory, or, the anticipation effect of the subject.

For Lenin, the December movement in Moscow demonstrates that the general strike, as a predominant mode of struggle, is outmoded: "the movement is breaking out of these narrow bounds with elemental and irresistible force and giving rise to the highest form of struggle—an uprising." He argues that even as the unions and revolutionary parties "intuitively felt" that the strike they called for December 7 should grow into an uprising, they weren't prepared for this; they spoke of it as something remote. At the same time, a general strike was already contained within the parameters of the expected. The government was ready for the strike, organizing its countermeasures accordingly. These counter-revolutionary measures on the part of the government pushed the masses of people to insurrection. As the government escalated its repression, "the unorganized street crowds, quite spontaneously and hesitatingly, set up the first barricade." Lenin traces the move from strike, to isolated barricades, to the "mass erection of barricades and street fighting against the troops." At each point, the revolutionary movement compels the reaction to further violence, further attack, further extension and exhaustion of its troops. The workers demand more resolute action: "what is to be done next?" The Social Democratic leaders are left behind, perhaps because

62   V. I. Lenin, "Lessons of the Moscow Uprising," *Proletary* 2, August 29, 1906. In *Lenin's Collected Works*, vol. 11, Moscow: Progress Publishers, 1965, 171–78. Available at marxists.org.

they are arguing over what is to be done even as the revolutionary masses have already destroyed the previous setting of action and are rapidly creating a new one.

Lenin's excoriating critique of Plekhanov puts "into consistency the haste of the cause," that is, it retroactively assigns consistency to the revolutionary workers in anticipation of the certainty of their ultimate victory. Lenin writes:

> Thus, nothing could be more short-sighted than Plekhanov's view, seized upon by all the opportunists, that the strike was untimely and should not have been started, and that "they should not have taken to arms". On the contrary, we should have taken to arms more resolutely, energetically and aggressively; we should have explained to the masses that it was impossible to confine things to a peaceful strike and that a fearless and relentless armed fight was necessary. And now we must at last openly and publicly admit that political strikes are inadequate; we must carry on the widest agitation among the masses in favour of an armed uprising and make no attempt to obscure this question by talk about "preliminary stages", or to befog it in any way.

Plekhanov failed to respond to the masses as subject; he failed to note how their haste brought into being another phase of political conflict. What if the party had not lagged behind the workers? As he makes the party the subject support of the revolutionary people, Lenin makes it responsive to the lessons they teach.

In a passage evocative of descriptions of the March 18, 1871 crowd event that made way for the Commune, Lenin praises the crowd:

> In the December days, the Moscow proletariat taught us magnificent lessons in ideologically "winning over" the troops, as, for example, on December 8 in Strastnaya Square, when the crowd surrounded the Cossacks, mingled and fraternised with them, and persuaded

them to turn back. Or on December 10, in Presnya District, when two working girls, carrying a red flag in a crowd of 10,000 people, rushed out to meet the Cossacks crying: "Kill us! We will not surrender the flag alive!" And the Cossacks were disconcerted and galloped away, amidst the shouts from the crowd: "Hurrah for the Cossacks!"

The party is the bearer of the lessons of the uprising. It is both the perspective from which the uprising is assessed and is itself, as an organization capable of learning and responding, an effect of the uprising. The party learns from the subject it supports—and that it is the support of this subject is clear insofar as the subject necessarily exceeds it. Whether posed as crowd or Commune, the political form of the party cannot be reduced to a problem of the state. It must also be thought in terms of the subjectivization of the people and their process as the subject of a politics.

In his classic account of the Commune, the French journalist and revolutionary socialist Lissagaray likewise links crowd and party such that movements in the street are legible as the actions of a subject. He describes the weeks and months prior to the Paris Commune—the defeats in the war with Prussia, negotiations toward surrender, substitution of plebiscite (an up or down vote of confidence in the provisional government) for elections, and increase of political clubs in working class areas of the city. As he does so, Lissagaray attends to the poor, the working men and the faithful children of 1789, and the young men from the bourgeoisie who "have gone over to the people." In 1863, he tells us, these people scandalously affirm themselves as a class. In 1867, their demonstrations in the streets are the "appearance of a revolutionary socialist party" (which will be asserted more directly in a resolution adopted by a meeting of the vigilance committees in February 1871).[63] In 1870, they alone in a paralyzed summer

---

63   Lissagaray, *History of the Paris Commune of 1871*, 11; Edwards, *The Communards of Paris*, 53.

exhibit political courage. Yet this class, this party (Lissagaray doesn't think it necessary to make distinctions here, implying, perhaps, the open, changing, and interconnected dimensions of each), remains unable to channel the energies of the crowd. They may be a "party of action," but they are in a "chaotic state," criss-crossed by different currents (and, again, "party" here suggests a collective that is part of a changing situation).[64] So even as the crowd riots against the armistice, the people nonetheless endorse the government in the plebiscite that follows: 558,000 *yes* and 62,000 *no*.[65] Lissagaray explains that this happened because those who were "clear-sighted, prompt, and energetic" were wanting in "*cadres*, in method, in organizers."[66] Jacobins like Blanqui "lived in an exclusive circle of friends." Still other potential leaders "care-fully kept aloof from working men." Even the Central Committee of the Twenty Districts, while "daring, eloquent," treated "every-thing by manifestos" and so remained "only a center of emotions, not of direction."[67]

Lissagaray establishes the setting of the Commune in the chal-lenge of responding to the opening the active crowd produces, in

---

64   Lissagaray, *History of the Paris Commune of 1871*, 13.

65   Jellinek, *The Paris Commune of 1871*, 80; Breaugh gives different numbers.

66   Lissagaray, *History of the Paris Commune of 1871*, 25.

67   Ibid., 25. The Central Committee of the Twenty Districts aimed toward centralizing democratic and socialist forces in Paris; the Committee met in the headquarters of the Federation of Trade Unions and the Federation of the International. Eugene Schulkind writes, "Potentially, this commit-tee and the constituent vigilance committtees in each arrondissement were revolutionary organizations in the modern sense of the word, capable of mobilizing extensive popular support around a concrete programme and a long-range strategy as well as developing an experienced cadre for an even-tual revolutionary government. In fact, a number of concrete efforts were initiated in this direction by some of the leaders, only to peter out soon in random activity and endless neighborhood discussions." *The Paris Commune of 1871: The View From the Left*, New York: Grove Press, 1974, 36.

the consequences of the gap effected by the crowd for organizing the people. At stake is not the specificity of a form of government, municipal or national. Nor is it a matter of the legitimacy of elections, representatives, or decisions. Instead it concerns the movement from people, to class, to party, the movement at stake in politicization. The stakes of this movement, moreover, are not those of substitution, vanguardism, or domination—they are arrangements of intensity, courage, and will. The relation of the people to the party is a question of organization in the context of those who might steer the people against themselves, making them a means of a revolution not their own. Lissagaray suggests that a class enters politics as a scandal, a scandalous insistence on equality. When this insistence makes itself felt on the streets, a revolutionary socialist party appears, a party characterized by action, even by a concentration of emotions. But action and emotion, subjective capacity, aren't enough. The capacity, to persist as the capacity of a subject, has to be organized, incorporated into a form. Thus, the problem of the party is organizing the people in one direction rather than another, but always retroactively.

Conclusion

The crowd event is the Real that incites the people as a collective, partisan subject. The party is the body that renders the subjectivizing crowd event into a moment in the subjective process of the politicized people. The people as subject is neither crowd nor party but between them, in the overlap of anticipation and retroactive determination with respect to a political process. Lissagaray, Lenin, Marx, and Badiou—from them we see in the Commune the movement of a subject. Their perspective is not reducible to a static place or position. It is instead a consequence of the appearing of the subject to which this perspective responds. More than a stationary moment pregnant with potential yet exhausted in the crowd's dissipation, the Commune erupts to surprise and mis-assemble the social with the certainty of justice. We see this mis-assembly in the reaction of the other forced to respond, to react, to do things differently from the ways they were done before. As Badiou writes, "There is no subjectivization without anticipation, which in turn can be measured by the subjective process."[68] It's the people as political subject that concerns the party. How can it hasten their advance, how can it not stand in their way, how can it inscribe and extend their victories?

More than a body focused on the state, the party is a form for the expression and direction of political will. It concentrates disruption in a process in order to produce political power: *these acts are connected; they demonstrate the strength of the collective*. It endeavors to arrange the intensity unleashed by the crowd, to keep it present as fervent desire. Ross's attention to the crowd in the Commune enables her to draw out the opening of collective desire, the lack that maintains it as a desire to desire. This attention rightly prevents us from reducing the Commune to an arrangement of offices or list of edicts, focusing us instead on the disruptive presence of the people where they should not be. At the same time, the Marxist tradition crucially sees the people as a subject and its struggle as enduring. The subject that expresses itself in the Commune event is not the diffusion of creative individuality; dominant power always allows for the carnivalesque. It is rather the people as a political subject manifest in the closure of directed intensity within the revolutionary opening. Because the party looks for them, the people are found. As Badiou writes,

> When Marx takes it upon himself to listen to the revolutionary activity of his time, to the popular historical disorder, it is a matter of pinpointing in the latter, pursuant to harsh theoretical and practical work, the dialectical form of the political subject as such. The

---

68   Badiou, *Theory of the Subject*, 251.

deduction of its general activity presupposes only the riots of the nineteenth century.[69]

Whether he names this subject people, proletariat, party, or Paris, Marx finds it where it will have been.

---

69   Ibid., 279.

4

More Than Many

Many on the Left think that the party is an outmoded political form. For them, what '68 inspired and '89 ostensibly confirmed is the conviction that radical left politics necessarily exceeds the constraints of the political party.

Often voiced as a criticism of specific parties, the conviction that the party is useless for the Left swallows up an array of historical particulars. The rejected communist party is not simply the ossified bureaucracy of the Communist Party of the Soviet Union and the other ruling party-states of the former East. It is neither China's Communist Party, unable to free itself from its inner bourgeoisie, nor France's and Italy's compromised and complicit parties. It's the party form as such. Specific parties are rejected for errors singular or aggregate. They pushed for revolution at the cost of unnecessary violence and loss of life. They pulled back from revolution, selling out the working class and setting back the communist cause. Errors become evidence of the hierarchy, exclusion, and discipline irrevocably staining the party form as such, preventing it from being responsive to our changing times. Criticism of specific parties for the betrayals accompanying their acquiring of or participation in state power merges with a more general critique of the party as an ultimately authoritarian political association. The party is reduced to the actuality of its mistakes, its role as concentrator of collective aspirations and affects diminished if not forgotten.[1]

Consider the shift in radical politics marked by "1968" and characterizing key tendencies over the next decades. Leftists turned away from the party politics targeting the state and toward the social movements targeting society.[2] This turn expressed itself in multiple ways, indeed, multiplicity can be said to be its primary characteristic. Whether highlighting oppression based in sex and gender, exclusion anchored in race and ethnicity, the disciplinary mechanisms of institutions (university, church, family, union, party, clinic), patterns of hierarchy in organizations ostensibly committed to its abolition, the stultifying effects of bureaucracy, the deadening normativity of consumerism, or the overarchingly machinic character of militarized industrial life, the critical project at the end of the sixties was marked by the rejection of the state and the constitution of a new terrain of struggle at the level of the social. How to live freely and authentically became a, if not the, primary political question, one that state politics could not answer. Remarkably, the rejection of party and state cut across state socialist and capitalist societies, across East/West and North/South divisions. Whether the critique was issued from a liberal, democratic, feminist, socialist, anti-racist, anarchist, Maoist, or militant perspective, the underlying supposition was the same: politics exceeds the narrowness of class and party; it thus requires turning

---

1 Gavin Walker, "The Body of Politics: On the Concept of the Party," *Theory and Event* 16: 4, 2013.

2 In addition to the debate over the "new times" in *Marxism Today* discussed in chapter one, differing instances of this same turn can be found in Ernesto Laclau and Chantal Mouffe, *Hegemony and Socialist* Strategy, London: Verso, 1985; Jean Cohen and Andrew Arato, *Civil Society and Political Theory*, Cambridge, MA: MIT Press, 1992; Félix Guattari and Antonio Negri, *New Lines of Alliance, New Spaces of Liberty*, New York: Autonomedia, 2010; originally published in French in 1985.

away from the state and toward everyday life in all its unique specificity.

Forty years later, the suppositions of this critique continue to frame left politics. Despite their otherwise acute differences, communist theorists such as Alain Badiou and Antonio Negri beat the same anti-state, anti-party drums. Radical democratic activists emphasize global summits and events, NGOs and CSOs, communities and the local. Militants refuse and subtract, as if nothing had changed, as if politics were a matter of the micro-pure, as if the setting of politics remained that of a centralized state and dominant party instead of a combined and uneven mix of centralizing and decentralizing forces in various distributed combinations of state use of market and market reliance on state. The Left repeats a forty-year-old critique, as if its rejection of mediating institutions like the party did not serve capitalism's interest in preventing the buildup of the solidarity necessary for the collective power of the proletarianized.[3]

The problem with the Left's entrapment in repetition is not the repetition. It's that the repetition prevents us from acknowledging how struggles at the level of the social come up against their limits in the state and market. David Ost's account of the Polish Solidarity movement provides the best political analysis of this encounter with the limit. Documenting the deep connections between the spirit of '68 and the Polish movement in the seventies and eighties, Ost describes its goal of a "permanently open democracy," a political field irreducible to the oppositions between state socialism and market liberalism.[4] Solidarity emerged as a post-modern anti-politics that deliberately abjured state power, seeking instead the strengthening of citizens in civil society. A left politics

---

3   See the contributions to the debate "Communist Currents," eds. Bruno Bosteels and Jodi Dean, *South Atlantic Quarterly* 113: 4, Fall 2014, 659–835.

4   David Ost, *Solidarity and the Politics of Anti-Politics: Opposition and Reform in Poland since 1968*, Philadelphia: Temple University Press, 1990, 14.

outside the party, Solidarity appeared as a fascinating experiment in a new political form, as Badiou puts it.[5] What Ost makes clear is that the movement "became irrelevant the moment it succeeded."[6] Legalization, official recognition of an organization by a monopolistic state, was unavoidably an encroachment on that state. There was no way that Solidarity could pursue its program of societal democratization without touching state power, as it realized shortly before the December 1981 crackdown.

Slavoj Žižek makes an analogous argument with respect to capitalist societies. Anti-sexist, anti-racist, anti-homophobic, and other such social politics founder against the hard rock of the market. Žižek writes,

> The domain of global capitalist market relations is the Other scene of the so-called repoliticization of civil society advocated by the partisans of "identity politics" and other postmodern forms of politicization: all the talk about new forms of politics bursting out all over … ultimately resembles the obsessional neurotic who talks all the time and is otherwise frantically active precisely in order to ensure that something—what *really matters*—will *not* be disturbed, that it will remain immobilized.[7]

Newness and experimentation, not to mention preoccupations with changes at the level of the individual and actions focused on media and culture, take the place of a politics targeting capitalism and the state, ensuring that they continue doing what they do. At some point, however, an encounter with the state or the economy becomes unavoidable as one or the other becomes a barrier to movement ideals. The fantasy of a politics capable of remaining focused on authentic social relations, a revolution in personal life, and flourishing cultural experiments occludes the legal and

5   Alain Badiou, *The Communist Hypothesis*, London: Verso, 2010, 258.
6   Ost, *Solidarity and the Politics of Anti-Politics*, 57.
7   Slavoj Žižek, *The Ticklish Subject*, London: Verso, 1999, 353–54.

economic conditions that either make them possible or prevent their realization.

The crowds, riots, occupations, and revolutions of the early decades of the twenty-first century are demonstrating that the rejection of the party is itself outmoded. As Jason E. Smith rightly points out, "the question of the party-form can only take place with reference to, and indeed from within the dynamics of, contemporary struggles." These struggles pose the organizational question of the party as "they run up against certain impasses that recur with such predictable if dispiriting regularity."[8] Confronting the challenge of generating, concentrating, and sustaining collective energies, political movement itself thrusts the problematic of the party back onto the terrain of left theory and practice. Peter D. Thomas writes,

> it has been practical experience of the contradictory processes of left regroupment on an international scale—from reconfigurations over the last decade on the Latin American left, to the varying success of coalition parties in Europe such as Die Linke in Germany, Izquierda Unida in Spain, Syriza in Greece and the Front de Gauche in France, to the tentative emergence of new political formations across North Africa and the Arab world—that has firmly placed the question of the party back on the contemporary agenda.[9]

Movement actors increasingly recognize the limitations of a politics conceived in terms of issue- and identity-focused activisms, mass demonstrations that for all intents and purposes are essentially one-offs, and the momentary localism of anarchist street fighting. Thus they are asking again the organizational question, reconsidering the political possibilities of the party form.

---

8   Jason E. Smith, "Contemporary Struggles and the Question of the Party: A Reply to Gavin Walker," *Theory and Event* 16: 4, 2013.

9   Peter D. Thomas, "The Communist Hypothesis and the Question of Organization," *Theory & Event* 16: 4, 2013.

This chapter supports contemporary efforts to concentrate and intensify the international Left by offering a theory of the party that emphasizes the psychodynamics of collectivity, the ways that our collectivity works back on us to make us more than many. I take up critiques of the party form contemporaneous with its emergence: the party is too centralized, too authoritarian. It's a form by which the few dominate the many. In contemporary left discussions, such critiques are often voiced as if they were new insights born of recent experience. They aren't. They were present already in the early years of working class political movement. I focus on the most thorough version of the critique of the party as it appears in the work of Robert Michels. Michels's famous "iron law of oligarchy" applies not just to socialist parties. He extends it to democratic and anarchistic political formations as well. Political organization of *any* sort entails a gap between the few and the many. Rather than being constrained by Michels's analysis, I treat it as an account of the enabling conditions of political collectivity, a way to understand the effects of collectivity on the collective. No party, class, or collectivity is identical with itself. Each is ruptured by an irreducible gap. Drawing from Lacan, I use concepts from psychoanalysis to theorize this gap as a social link or space, highlighting the relation of transference. Transference lets us see the dynamic features concentrated in the space of the Other. I close by putting my psychodynamic account of the party to work, illustrating it with examples from the Communist Party of the United States in the 1930s and deploying it in a critique of John Holloway's argument against taking power. My goal in offering a psychodynamic theory of the party is to dissolve the hold that criticism of the party form still has on the Left such that we can accept again the responsibility of political organization.

The Few Dominate the Many

Some current rejections of the party say its time has passed.[10] Maybe at one time such a political form made sense for radical politics, some concede, but now is not that time. This rejection errs when it proceeds as if the critique of the party were something new, a response to objective changes in the mode and relations of production. The mistake is one of omission: left criticism of the party form is in fact coextensive with the emergence of working-class political movement. From the beginning, socialists worried about their organizations becoming centralized and authoritarian, and hence alienated from actual proletarian struggle.

The First International, the International Workingmen's Association, which lasted from 1864 to 1876, split between the followers of Marx and the followers of Bakunin. Bakunin rejected the inclusion of a political plank in the platform of the IWA, specifically the assertion that "the conquest of political power is the first task of the proletariat." *Contra* Marx, Bakunin emphasized the subordination of politics to the struggle for economic emancipation. Solidarity with respect to economic demands had to come first, the federations and sections of the International left free to decide the political question autonomously. On the one hand, Bakunin's argument is pragmatic: because workers were coming together in struggle against capitalism, the insertion of political questions could make unity harder to achieve. On the other, the argument is rooted in a more fundamental rejection of statism. Bakunin rejects Marx's political plank because he associates it with a strong state. In Bakunin's words: "Marx's program is a complete network of political and economic institutions rigidly centralized and highly authoritarian, sanctioned, no doubt, like all despotic institutions in modern society, by universal suffrage, but nevertheless subordinate

---

10   For example, Badiou, *The Communist Hypothesis*; and Joshua Clover and Aaron Benanav, "Can Dialectics Break BRICS," *South Atlantic Quarterly* 113: 4, Fall 2014, 743–59.

to a *very strong* government—to quote Engels, Marx's alter ego, the autocrat's confidant."[11] Bakunin views the revolutionary dictatorship of the proletariat as no different from any other statism under which the few would dominate the many.[12] For him, the political struggle, and its organizational form, is at best subordinate and at worst antithetical to the economic struggle of the working class.

Rosa Luxemburg transfers to Lenin the criticisms of centralism and authoritarianism that Bakunin levels at Marx.[13] For Luxemburg, the problem is not with the party or the political struggle. Although she is celebrated for the mass strike and although she well understood the ways workers' spontaneous initiatives could surge past their party's capacity for action, Luxemburg always presumes that the energy of the masses needs to be directed. The energy of the masses can swell and grow, but they can only avail themselves of their power through leaders, "the executive organs of their will."[14] Even when critical of the party for failing to keep up with the masses, Luxemburg remains committed to the party as the form for concentrating and organizing political power. Moreover, Luxemburg assumes the necessity of the division of labor in "every socialist concern" for technical reasons of efficiency, discipline, and order. "Technical managers who know exactly what they are doing and give directions so that everything runs smoothly" are indispensible to the socialist economy.[15] So Luxemburg rejects neither leaders nor the party. She rejects what she saw as Lenin's particular version of the party.

---

11   Mikhail Bakunin, "On the International Workingmen's Association and Karl Marx," 1872. Available at marxists.org.

12   Mikhail Bakunin, "Critique of the Marxist Theory of the State," 1873. Available at marxists.org.

13   Rosa Luxemburg, "Organizational Questions of the Russian Social Democracy," 1904. Available at marxists.org.

14   Rosa Luxemburg, "What Are the Leaders Doing?" 1919. Available at marxists.org.

15   Rosa Luxemburg, "The Socialisation of Society," 1918. Available at marxists.org.

Writing in 1904, Luxemburg observes that the conditions of a highly developed bourgeois society that made the German Social Democratic Party organizationally possible are absent in Russia. Russia lacks the formal guarantees of assembly and press through which the masses can acquire political experience via participation in public life. Luxemburg points out that Social Democracy grew because Germany's bourgeois democratic conditions allowed for the direct and independent actions of the masses. A class-conscious proletarian vanguard capable of organizing itself into a party, the heart of the German Social Democratic experience, is simply not present in Russia. Russian proletarians are atomized and isolated, not yet having educated themselves through class struggle. The problem with Lenin, Luxemburg argues, is that he proceeds as if he could simply command a vanguard into being by concentrating all party authority in the Central Committee. Rather than grasping the ways proletarian consciousness changes in the course of struggle, Lenin "mechanically subordinates" the class to the party and the party to the Central Committee. The Central Committee thinks and decides and everyone else carries out its commands. The few dominate the many.

Continuously repeated today, the charges of centralism and authoritarianism, the domination of the many by the few, are damning, striking at the very heart of people's struggle. If the few dominate the many, then working-class struggle merely replaces one set of oppressors with another. The very organization indispensable to people's political struggle stifles and deforms it.

Charges of centralism and authoritarianism, however, have not been confined to socialist and communist parties or even to the party form as such. Already at the beginning of the twentieth century, Michels levels these charges against democratic political participation most broadly: democracy itself leads to oligarchy. The conditions that make democracy possible also make it impossible, whether one is talking about a polity, a party, a union, or a council (syndicate or soviet). Michels's analysis, which I consider in detail below, reminds us that it is a mistake to proceed as if critiques such as Bakunin's and Luxemburg's, critiques repeated *ad nauseum* on the Left, identify problems unique to Marxism or the party. On the contrary, we need to recognize them as attacks on mass, democratic, and people's politics more generally. The charge of the few dominating the many thrown about so vigorously on the Left illuminates *nothing* specific to Marxism, Marxism–Leninism, socialism, or communism. Rather, it points to the challenges of organization, duration, and extension that persist after the dissipation of the crowd. The gap of politics is unavoidable. Repeating the critique of centralism and authoritarianism time after time, in setting after setting, reinscribes fantasies of a politics without politics, fantasies of a beautiful moment when the many immediately know and realize their desire. To the extent that the Left fails to recognize and take responsibility for the enabling condition of political collectivity, it will remain trapped in its own self-critique, unable to build or seize the organizations it needs.

The Iron Law of Oligarchy

The best-known version of the argument that democracy leads to oligarchy comes from Robert Michels's *Political Parties*, originally published in 1911.[16] A student of Max Weber's, Michels taught in Germany, Italy, and Switzerland; he was a member of the German Social Democratic Party, the Italian Socialist Party, and, later, Mussolini's Fascist Party.[17] Lenin dismissed him as "the garrulous

---

16   Robert Michels, *Political Parties: A Sociological Study of the Oligarchical Tendencies of Modern Democracy*, trans. Eden and Cedar Paul (1911), Kitchener, Ontario: Batoche Books, 2001.

17   Juan Linz, "Robert Michels," *International Encyclopedia of the Social Sciences*, New York: Macmillan and Free Press, 1968, vol. X, 265–71. See also Juan Linz, *Robert Michels, Political Sociology, and the Future of Democracy*, London: Transaction Publishers: 2006. Equating psychology with the

Michels," disparaging Michels's *Italian Imperialism* as just as super-ficial as his other writings.[18] Social science treats *Political Parties* as a classic, even "one of the twentieth century's most influential books."[19]

Political Parties explores the "nature of the party." Michels deduces the nature of the party via an analysis of the "nature of the human individual," the "nature of political struggle," and the "nature of political organization." On the basis of this analysis, he posits an "iron law of oligarchy" or rule of the few. Unlike ancient Greek visions of democracy as the *response* of the people against oligarchy's owners of property, Michels construes oligarchy as *intrinsic* to democracy. Democracy, *of any kind*, tends to oligarchy. Democracy "necessarily contains an oligarchical nucleus."[20] So while *Political Parties* concentrates primarily on socialist parties, particularly the German Social Democratic Party, Michels's argu-ment is broader, a political version of the Pareto principle or 80/20 rule: in any human association, the few will have more—whether this "more" is of goods, influence, or power—than the many.[21] Parties one might most expect to incorporate rule by the workers in their basic structure, organizations animated by ideals of dem-ocratic participation, even groups with aspirations to anarchism, all ultimately take on a whole slew of oligarchical characteristics.

individual psychology of leaders, Linz overestimates the technical dimensions of organizational needs, paying little attention to group dynamics.

18   Lenin, "Imperialism and Socialism in Italy," *Kommunist* 1–2, 1915; *Lenin's Collected Works*, Moscow: Progress Publishers, 1974, vol. 21, 357–66. Available at the Lenin Internet Archive, marxists.org.

19   Seymour Martin Lipset, "Michels' Theory of Political Parties," *Insti-tute of Industrial Relations*, Reprint No. 185, Berkeley, CA: 1962, 21–22.

20   Michels, *Political Parties*, 6.

21   Michels refers to Pareto several times in *Political Parties*, although not explicitly on this point. For an overview of debates over *Political Parties* see Philip J. Cook, "Robert Michels's Political Parties in Perspective," *Journal of Politics* 33: 3, August 1971, 773–96. Cook points out the mistaken tendency to read Michels as a critic of socialism when his target is actually syndicalism.

Rule by the few is unavoidable. Michels surmises: "the appearance of oligarchical phenomena in the very bosom of the revolutionary parties is a conclusive proof of the existence of immanent oligarchical tendencies in every kind of human organization which strives for the attainment of definite ends."[22] Socialist parties and working-class organizations are not unique. They are representative, clear instances where oligarchical tendencies can be isolated and observed precisely because they conflict with party ideology. If democracy means rule by the many, democracy is impossible.

Michels presents tendencies to oligarchy as technical and psychological. Technical tendencies concern the indispensability of leadership in groups. Psychological tendencies involve people's responses to leadership. They are effects of the fact of leaders back on the people. So there are tasks, means of accomplishment, and there are feelings about, responses to, and interpretations of these means of accomplishment. Both connect the party to the crowd. And both are matters of number: the problem and force of many, the complexity of mass organization, and the prestige accompanying that to which many adhere.[23]

Michels orients his account of the inevitability of oligarchy in a theory of the crowd reminiscent of Le Bon's. The crowd is suggestible, incapable of serious discussion or thoughtful deliberation, and susceptible to the influence of orators. Michels finds evidence of the crowd's incapacity in the fact that most people avoid going to meetings unless the event promises some kind of spectacle or someone famous is speaking. De-individuation is likewise a primary feature of Michels's version of the crowd: "The individual disappears in the multitude, and therewith disappears also personality and sense of responsibility."[24] And as we already learned from Le Bon, a crowd can go off in a panic or a flight

---

22   Michels, *Political Parties*, 13.

23   Lipset emphasizes the technical tendencies but neglects the psychological ones.

24   Michels, *Political Parties*, 21.

of "unreflective enthusiasm." It can be easily dominated, hypnotized, and intoxicated. Conversely, the crowd may be politically indifferent, hard to arouse, and a barrier to action. Number itself undermines direct democracy: thirty-four million people cannot "carry on their affairs without accepting what the pettiest man of business finds necessary, the intermediation of representatives." The crowd, Michels argues, needs "someone to point out the way and to issue orders."[25] Tens of thousands of people can't deliberate together directly and immediately. Basic considerations of space, amplification, and the time, duration, and frequency of meetings, not to mention preparing the agenda and carrying out decisions, point to the unavoidability of delegation.[26] So the crowd's very nature makes it vulnerable to oligarchy. Not only can it not protect itself from bold power-seekers, but it relies on them. It needs leaders to get things done. It even enjoys them.

Michels narrates the slide into oligarchy as an ersatz "story of the Fall" as technical tendencies to oligarchy come to dominance in a group. This story applies to "every organization," whether party, union, or other kind of association. From an initial equality, wherein delegates are chosen by lot or rotation, gradual change sets in as delegates' responsibilities become more complicated:

> some individual ability becomes essential, a certain oratorical gift and a considerable amount of objective knowledge. It thus becomes impossible to trust to blind chance, to the fortune of alphabetic succession, or to the order of priority, in the choice of a delegation whose members must possess certain peculiar personal aptitudes if they are to discharge their mission to the general advantage.[27]

---

25   Ibid., 39.

26   See L. A. Kauffman's critique of contemporary activist practices such as those used in Occupy Wall Street, "The Theology of Consensus," *Berkeley Journal of Sociology*, May 26, 2015.

27   Michels, *Political Parties*, 23.

Demands arise for "a sort of official consecration for the leaders." Leaders need to be vetted and trained, their expertise established. Accordingly, a system of examinations, and hence courses and schools, emerge. Educational associations produce elites with both skills for and aspirations to office. Michels concludes, "Without wishing it, there is thus effected a continuous enlargement of the gulf which divides the leaders from the masses."[28] Even leaders originating from the masses become separated from them in the course of their acquisition of expertise, validation, responsibility, and experience.

Although the division of the leaders from the masses is particularly vexing to socialist parties, syndicalism and anarchism encounter similar problems with oligarchy, again, for technical reasons. By syndicalism, Michels means that socialist current which would replace the duality of party and trade union with "a completer organism" synthesizing political and economic functions.[29] This "completer organism" is the trade union reconceived as a revolutionary association aimed toward abolishing capitalism and establishing socialism. Syndicalists had been vociferous in their critique of the demagogic tendencies of democracy, whether in the German Social Democratic Party or in the trade union bureaucracy. Nonetheless, Michels argues, they also fall prey to the iron law of oligarchy. Leaders of any group can betray or deceive the rank and file, particularly in actions that involve secrecy and conspiracy. Strikes, whether economic or political, offer "to men with a taste for political life, excellent opportunities for the display of their faculty for organization and their aptitude for command." The strike, "instead of being a field of activity for the uniform and compact masses," facilitates the process of differentiation and favors the formation of an *elite* of leaders.[30] In effect, syndicalists have an even greater technical need for leaders than socialists do.

---

28   Ibid., 25.
29   Ibid., 208.
30   Ibid., 210.

Anarchism, eschewing any form of stable or enduring political organization, would seemingly be immune from the problem of oligarchy insofar as there is no party hierarchy to climb or electoral office to seek. Not so, according to Michels. Three features of anarchism bring it under the "iron law." First, like the syndicalists, anarchists favor direct action, which favors the heroic self-assertion of the few. Second, anarchists recognize the necessity of administrative work, "technical guidance of the masses," in the administrative sphere. Federations of councils and communes, even when comprised of purely voluntary associations, would acquire authority over time, thereby falling into oligarchy. Third, anarchist leaders have their own "means of dominion," the same means employed by the "apostle and the orator": "the flaming power of thought, greatness of self-sacrifice, profundity of conviction. Their dominion is exercised, not over the organization, but over minds; it is the outcome, not of technical indispensability, but of intellectual ascendancy and moral superiority."[31] Michels's point is not that there is something wrong with this dominion. It's that anarchism does not escape the iron law of oligarchy. The few are still more authoritative than the many.

The larger the organization, the more powerful the leaders. For Michels, this is in part a technical tendency toward oligarchy, the challenge of organizing many. But it includes a corresponding psychological tendency as well, the psychic effects on collectivities of the fact of leadership. As we saw in Michels's "story of the Fall," a division of labor comes along with "modern civilized society." In larger organizations, tasks become increasingly differentiated. Integrating them becomes complicated. Seeing the "big picture" becomes harder and harder. At the same time, voluntary organizations like unions and parties encounter constant turnover among their members. Members come and go depending on their stage of life—are they young and more interested in love and adventure?

31   Ibid., 215.

Old, jaded, and burned out? Most people have what feels to them as better things to do than spend their free time in political struggle. But not all: some, for varying reasons, attach themselves to organizational work. Some, particularly those who are paid and have acquired a vested interest in the organization, are more constant in their attentions to the group than are others. Those who are more constant and attached start to function as leaders. More than those whose engagement is temporary or sporadic, they know what the organization has done and is doing. They are the repository of organizational history, practice, and knowledge. Leadership can be less a matter of office than of the influence exercised by the regulars.

As leaders emerge, the rank and file become less able to conduct or supervise the organization's affairs. They have to trust those to whom they've delegated the various tasks, perhaps instructing them to provide reports on the work of the group. Generally speaking, most people like it that way. Michels notes that the majority rarely participate. They leave meetings and discussions and organizational tasks to others. "Though it grumbles occasionally," he writes, "the majority is really delighted to find persons who will take the trouble to look after its affairs."[32] This delight is an affective response, a shared sensibility, what we might call relief in delegation or the pleasure that arises from pawning tasks onto others. What matters for my argument here is the flow from the technical to the psychological tendency to oligarchy. Michels argues that the majority reveres or even adores their leaders. Accompanying the crowd's need for direction and guidance is "a genuine cult for the leaders, who are regarded as heroes." So not only does the crowd need leaders for technical reasons, it is also affectively attached to them.

Michels's account of this attachment is more suggestive than precise. But a decade before Freud, likely due to the influence of

---

32   Ibid., 38.

Le Bon and Tarde (he cites both), Michels anticipates key elements of Freud's crowd psychology. The first is a primitive love. Michels attributes to the crowd the lofty moral quality of gratitude to the leaders for working on its behalf. He observes that leaders ask for gratitude as their reward for service and that the mass regards gratitude "as a sacred duty."[33] Reelection or long-term support for party leaders displays this gratitude. At the same time, Michels describes an attachment to leaders exceeding the "sense of obligation for services rendered."[34] This attachment is "an atavistic survival of primitive psychology." Invoking the British anthropologist James George Frazer on myth and political power, Michels finds a latent "superstitious reverence" even for socialist leaders: "It reveals itself by signs that are barely perceptible, such as the tone of veneration in which the idol's name is pronounced, the perfect docility with which the least of his signs is obeyed, and the indignation which is aroused by any critical attack upon his personality."[35] He gives the example of Ferdinand Lassalle's appearance in the Rhineland in 1864. Lassalle was received "like a god." Garlands bedecked the streets; maidens threw flowers; the crowd overflowed with "irresistible enthusiasm" and "frenzied applause"—"Nothing was lacking."[36] Michels notes that this fanatical devotion is not unique. Masses everywhere, in industrial as well as agricultural regions, England as well as Italy, "need to pay adoring worship."[37] They exhibit, Freud might say, a horde mentality. At times the masses' veneration of their leaders takes the form of an "imitative mania" that can grow into "absolute idolatry."[38]

Gratitude and reverence are not the only feelings that adhere the crowd to its leaders. The crowd's admiration also stems from

33 Ibid., 42.
34 Ibid., 44.
35 Ibid., 42.
36 Ibid., 43.
37 Ibid., 45.
38 Ibid., 127.

prestige and identification. The prestige of celebrity influences the crowd. Michels invokes Tarde, noting the way fame impresses with the number of admirers. Prestige is like fame insofar as it incorporates the views of many. It's a matter less of talent than of the esteem held by the crowd. Even as the crowd responds enthusiastically to great orators, it responds even more to the enthusiasm of others, to others' feelings and responses. These responses indicate the greatness of the oratory, not its content. People adhere with and to others in common admiration. One admires the leader because others do. When celebrity influences us, Michels explains with a quote from Tarde, "it is with the collaboration of many other minds through whom we see it, and whose opinion, without our knowledge, is reflected in our own."[39] Unconsciously, we see through others. We take the perspective of the many. Our seeing is collective.

This seeing through others gives us a way to understand "imitative mania." The object being imitated is not a specific person but prestige itself, the press and presence of the many, crowd, or mass. Lacan reminds us, "Whenever we are dealing with imitation, we should be careful not to think too quickly of the other who is being imitated."[40] Imitating a leader or celebrity, the many act for each other, showing themselves in their admiring enthusiasm to themselves, making themselves the objects of their own collective gaze. When fans dress up as characters in a movie to attend a movie's opening (as with the *Harry Potter* or *Star Wars* movies) or when they go in costume to fan conventions, they are doing it for each other. As they see themselves seeing themselves, they demonstrate the contingency and replaceability of the revered leader: any one of those imitatively adopting the leader's characteristics is in the leader's place.

---

39   Ibid., 47.

40   Jacques Lacan, *The Four Fundamental Concepts of Psychoanalysis*, Seminar XI, ed. Jacques-Alain Miller, trans. Alan Sheridan, New York: Norton, 1998, 100.

Imitative mania, then, demonstrates the collectivity distorted in the pathology of "absolute idolatry."[41] The point of imitation is not the adoration of one, of a leader or celebrity. It is that the one is nothing but the thing enabling the many to experience its collective force. Enthusiasm arises out of this experience of collective imitation because the collective feels itself amplified, strengthened. Enthusiasm is *nothing but* this collective sense of collective power. In imitative mania, what is being imitated is not a person; it is prestige, the regard of the collective.

Identification is similarly unconscious. Michels observes that a powerful speaker can hypnotize the crowd "to such a degree that for long periods to come they see in him a magnified image of their own ego ... In responding to the appeal of the great orator, the mass is unconsciously influenced by its own egoism."[42] Michels is ambiguous here, eliding the distinction between individual and crowd. Is his point that each individual separately identifies with the leader or that the crowd *qua* mass exhibits its own egoism? If the former, Michels loses the ability to say something about the crowd. If the latter, the speaker would be a vehicle for generating this other ego, this perspective capable of enduring, unconsciously, after the speech ends. The ambiguity, the slippage, affirms the latter point insofar as the speaker becomes an opportunity for collective force to exert itself.

Just as the distinctions between technical and psychological tendencies to oligarchy blur into and reinforce one another, so do the distinctions between crowd and leader, mass and party. Each twists into the other. Each ruptures the other from within, preventing it from achieving self-identity. For example, Michels emphasizes the importance of detachments from the bourgeoisie aligning themselves with the proletariat and animating its class consciousness.

---

41   For a nuanced discussion of idolatry, see James R. Martel, *The One and Only Law: Walter Benjamin and the Second Commandment*, Ann Arbor, MI: University of Michigan Press, 2014.

42   Michels, *Political Parties*, 47.

These members of the bourgeoisie—"philosophers, economists, sociologists, and historians"—help transform instinctive, unconscious rebellion into clear, conscious aspiration. Michels writes,

> Great class movements have hitherto been initiated in history solely by the simple reflection: it is not we alone, belonging to the masses without education and without legal rights, who believe ourselves to be oppressed, but that belief as to our condition is shared by those who have a better knowledge of the social mechanism and who are therefore better able to judge; since the cultured people of the upper classes have also conceived the ideal of our emancipation, that ideal is not mere chimera.[43]

Bourgeois detachments, as a matter of fact comprising the majority of European socialist leaders, serve psychological as much as technical purposes: they enable workers to reflect on themselves; they provide a standpoint from outside the workers that workers can take toward their own condition.

This perspective that comes from without is also generated within the workers' movement. Leaders come from among the workers, pushed up involuntarily by chance and circumstance. Michels quotes Le Bon, "The leader has usually been at one time the led." Party work can separate the worker from the class to the extent that party functionaries are paid (and hence have a new source of income), to the extent that they acquire goals specific to the activities of the party, and to the extent that prestige attaches to leaders—the functionary is felt to stand for the many. Michels uses the party newspaper to illustrate the point: "the editorial 'we,' uttered in the name of a huge party, has a much greater effect than even the most distinguished name."[44] The article or editorial is no longer linked to a single person. It is backed by the force of a collective to which it gives voice.

43 Ibid., 143.
44 Ibid., 85.

Michels concludes, "who says organization, says oligarchy."
Political enthusiasm—the joy of self-sacrifice, the thrill of struggle
—inspires the crowd, but it can't endure. The crowd disperses and
people go home. Keeping the fight alive requires dedicated, professional cadre, a few who devote themselves to the cause. This
very requirement separates the few from the many.

The socialist party is not identical with the working class.
Workers are not automatically socialists and socialists are not necessarily workers. The party can have bourgeois and working class
members (not to mention other classes). These members may
be active or not, leaders or led. The class fragments into various
interests, personal as well as political. Michels writes, "The party,
regarded as an entity, as a piece of mechanism, is not necessarily
identifiable with the totality of its members, and still less so with
the class to which these belong."[45] The party is more than the sum
of the particular interests of its members. The very non-identity
of class and party, the gap between few and many, produces something new.

We have hints about this "something new" in the ideas of prestige, identification, and that exterior point from which the working
class can reflect back on itself. These ideas suggest that the party is
a psychic space irreducible to its members and excreted out of the
technical needs it fulfills. Michels recognizes this space, marking it
with the party program. He writes, "A party is neither a social unity
nor an economic unity. It is based upon its political program."[46]
The program sets out the party's principles, ostensibly providing
the missing point of unity in the "idea" of the working class. To be
sure, this theoretical unity cannot eliminate the more fundamental
class conflicts that express themselves in the party. "In practice,"
Michels observes, "the acceptance of the program does not suffice
to abolish the conflict of interests between capital and labor." Put
more broadly, the collectivity incorporated in the party will always

45 Ibid., 232.
46 Ibid., 231.

be in excess of, never fully reconcilable with, a particular interest. A degree of alienation, of non-identity, is ineliminable. The very fact of a party—or any few carrying out some kind of organizational work—exerts a force counter to personal desire. If personal desire were enough, if it could simply be aggregated into happy outcomes, if the crowd had the capacity to know and get what it wanted, leaders wouldn't emerge. But the gap is irreducible, a repetition in the party of the antagonism rupturing society.

Mind the Gap

Psychoanalysis helps us understand this gap. It can let us see why the division between few and many should not be solidified as a division between real and ideal, pragmatic and utopian, but acknowledged instead as a constitutive, enabling split: impossibility is the condition of possibility for communist politics. The non-identity between people and party is what enables each to be more and less than what they are, for each to enable, rupture, and exceed the other. Michels specifies this gap as the crowd's missing capacity supplied by the leader and the working class's missing consciousness supplied by the bourgeois deserters. Acknowledging that these technical provisions remain incomplete, that organization is more than an instrument, he supplements them by attending to the psychological tendencies of crowds. As gratitude, prestige, imitation, and identification demonstrate, leaders are means through which the crowd can feel and enjoy itself. Michels's own gestures to the unconscious thus provide an entry point for psychoanalysis.

Lacan associates the Freudian unconscious with a gap, a gap where something happens but remains unrealized.[47] It's not that this something is or is not there, that it exists or doesn't exist.

---

47   Lacan, *The Four Fundamental Concepts of Psychoanalysis*, 22.

Rather, the unrealized makes itself felt; it exerts a pressure. The communist party is a political form for the press of the unrealized struggles of the people, enabling the concentrating and directing of this press in one way rather than another.

That the subject of politics is collective means that its actions cannot be reduced to those associated with individual agency, actions like choice or decision. Instead, as chapter three argues, the collective subject impresses itself through ruptures and breaks and the retroactive attribution of these breaks to the subject they expressed. The punctuality of the subject could suggest that it is only evental, only disruptive, utterly disconnected from any body, creation, institution, or advance and thus without substance or content. But this would ignore the persistence of the subject in the press of the unrealized. This persistence needs a body, a carrier. Without a carrier, it dissipates into the manifold of potentiality. Nevertheless, with a carrier some potentiality is diminished. Some possibility is eliminated. Some closure is effected. This loss is the subject's condition of possibility, the division constitutive of subjectivity. Political forms—parties, states, guerrilla armies, even leaders—situate themselves within this division. Although they can be and often are fetishized (positioned so as to obscure the loss or perfectly remedy it), the fact of fetishization should not deflect from the prior condition of the gap and its occupation.

The psychoanalytic concept of "transference" depends on and expresses this gap. In clinical practice, the transference involves the relation between the analyst and the analysand. What sort of feelings and affects are mobilized in analysis and to what kind of structure do they attest? For example, does the analysand want the analyst's approval? Does she want to seduce him, fight with him, obliterate him? Lacan acknowledges multiple ways of conceiving the transference, but rejects the idea that analysis proceeds via an alliance between the analyst and the healthy part of the subject's ego (an idea found in some American versions of psychoanalysis). "This is a thesis," Lacan writes, "that subverts what it is all about, namely the bringing to awareness of this split in the subject, realized here, in fact, in presence."[48] The function of the trans- ference in analysis is forcing the gap. Through the transference different unconscious agencies in the subject become manifest. As the analysand learns to attend to the transference, she can come to recognize and address the Other within, the way, for example, a parental or social other has configured her desire.

The transference is important for a theory of the party because of its function "as a mode of access to what is hidden in the unconscious."[49] The transference registers the effects of an Other beyond analyst and analysand: the analytic relation is not reduc- ible to the interaction between them; it is the site of the appearance of an Other. Transference contributes to a theory of the party in this precise sense of a "mode of access to what is hidden in the unconscious." The party is a form that accesses the discharge that has ended, the crowd that has gone home, the people who are not there but exert a force nonetheless. It is thus a site of transferential relations.

Of course, the party is not an analytical session. Leaders and cadre are not psychoanalysts. This does not mean, however, that something like transference is not at work in the relation between crowd and party. In fact, Michels's emphasis on gratitude points to a transference effect, a love that, counterintuitively, underpins people's adherence to the leaders of an organization. Michels argues that those who have felt like no one was fighting on their behalf generally feel gratitude toward their champions. We could add here the way that people in a group are often grateful to those who step up, do the work, and take responsibility onto themselves. The feeling of gratitude makes leadership appear like a kind of gift, but one different from that which the king bestows on the people. Rather, insofar as he is focused on leadership in democ- racies, Michels suggests a leadership that the crowd produces

48   Ibid., 131.
49   Ibid., 143.

contingently out of itself to give to itself. These are the leaders toward whom people feel gratitude.

Even a gift the crowd gives itself is not without cost. Žižek notes that for Lacan language is a dangerous gift: "it offers itself to our use free of charge, but once we accept it, it colonizes us."[50] The gift establishes a link between giver and receiver. Acceptance creates a bond. It binds the receiver to the giver. "Gratitude" signals the binding power of the link, the felt force of the relation between giver and receiver, the pressure that renders a gift more than an exchange. What matters, then, is this link that is an effect of the gift and the force that it exerts. The gift constitutes a sociality that itself makes demands on us over and apart from those of the giver.

Lacan refers to this sociality as the Other or the symbolic. The transference reveals various components of it, unconscious processes and perspectives contained within the Other. The space of the Other is a crowded, heterogeneous space, a mix of shifting feelings, pressures, and attachments. It has structural features, dynamic features, processes that advance and recede, flow into one another and shift in importance. Multiple, different figures inhabit and en-form these structures and processes.

Features of this Other space that Lacan highlights include the ideal ego, the ego ideal, and the superego. As Žižek explains, Lacan gives a very precise inflection to these Freudian terms:

"ideal" ego stands for the idealized self-image of the subject (the way I would like to be, the way I would like others to see me); Ego-Ideal is the agency whose gaze I try to impress with my ego image, the big Other who watches over me and impels me to give my best, the ideal I try to follow and actualize; and superego is this same agency in its vengeful, sadistic, punishing aspect.[51]

---

50   Slavoj Žižek, *How to Read Lacan*, New York: Norton, 2006, 11–12.
51   Ibid., 80.

The ideal ego is how the subject imagines itself. The ego ideal is the point from which the subject looks at itself. And the superego is the judge that torments the subject as it points out its inevitable, unavoidable failure to achieve either of these ideals. These three points are tied together: the ego ideal verifies the image of the subject. Since the ego ideal is supposed to provide this verification, the subject has certain investments in it. The subject needs the ego ideal for its stability or sense of autonomy. Because of this need, it is resistant to recognizing that the ego ideal is nothing but a structural effect and resentful of the ego ideal's simultaneous power and inadequacy. Moreover, in trying to live up to the expectations of the ego ideal, the subject may compromise its own desire. It may give up too much, which explains why the superego can exert such an extreme, unrelenting force: it is punishing the subject for this betrayal.[52]

While these features of the space of the Other may appear individual, this appearing is nothing but a Freudian residuum. Not only are the features common, but they attest to the workings of collectivity that Freud encloses in the individual psyche. Such features operate in all collectives as groups compete with other groups as well as look at themselves from the perspective of other groups. Cities and nations, schools and parties all have self-conceptions formatted via the processes and perspectives of the Other.

The transference that takes place in psychoanalysis reveals two additional features of the Other space: the subject supposed to know and the subject supposed to believe.[53] These elements are configuring suppositions within the subject, structural features that the subject posits as supports for its desire. The subject supposed to know is the figure that holds the secret to desire. It knows the truth. God, Socrates, and Freud as well as institutional roles such as parent, teacher, expert, and priest can function as such a

---

52   Ibid., 81. See also my discussion in chapter five of *The Communist Horizon*, London: Verso, 2012.
53   Ibid., 28–29.

locus of knowledge for and of a subject. Consider, for example, the opening of an editorial in the *Guardian* by left journalist Paul Mason:

> One of the upsides of having a global elite is that at least they know what's going on. We, the deluded masses, may have to wait for decades to find out who the paedophiles in high places are; and which banks are criminal, or bust. But the elite are supposed to know in real time—and on that basis to make accurate predictions.[54]

Mason literally presents the global elite as the subject supposed to know. Not only does the elite know the obscene truths of paedophilia and expropriation, but they know them as they happen, "in real time," while the rest of us remain deluded. In fact, a persistent question following the economic crisis of 2007–08 was why didn't the elite know. How come no one saw the crisis coming?

Lacan writes, "As soon as the subject who is supposed to know exists somewhere … there is transference."[55] Analysis depends on transference: the analyst has to function for the analysand as the subject supposed to know. The analysand starts talking about her symptoms, doing the work of analysis, because she thinks that the analyst knows the truth, when in actuality it's her work that produces the truth. Analysis can end as the subject recognizes that the analyst doesn't know after all.

Žižek introduces the subject supposed to believe as a more fundamental version of the subject supposed to know.[56] He explains:

---

54   Paul Mason, "The Best of Capitalism Is Over for Rich Countries—and for the Poor Ones It Will Be Over by 2060," *Guardian*, July 7, 2014.

55   Lacan, *The Four Fundamental Concepts of Psychoanalysis*, 232.

56   Slavoj Žižek, *The Sublime Object of Ideology*, London: Verso, 1989, 185. Elsewhere Žižek treats the subject supposed to believe "as the fundamental, constitutive feature of the symbolic order," *The Plague of Fantasies*, London: Verso, 1997, 106.

there is no immediate, self-present living subjectivity to whom the belief embodied in "social things" can be attributed, and who is then dispossessed of it. There are some beliefs, the most fundamental ones, which are from the very outset "decentered" beliefs of the Other; the phenomenon of the "subject supposed to believe" is thus universal and structurally necessary.[57]

The subject supposed to believe refers to this unavoidable displacement of belief on to some other. Concrete versions include the maintenance of the fiction of Santa Claus for the sake of children or the positing of some ordinary person who believes in community values. Michels's description of those detachments of the bourgeoisie who join the proletariat provides another example. Through them, the proletariat believes that their situation is not just unfortunate. It is profoundly unjust.

Žižek emphasizes the asymmetry between the subject supposed to know and the subject supposed to believe. Belief is reflective, a belief that another believes. He writes: "'I still believe in Communism' is the equivalent of saying 'I believe there are still people who believe in Communism.'"[58] Because belief is belief in the belief of the other, one can believe through another. Someone else can believe for us. Knowledge is different. That the other knows does not mean that I know. I can only know for myself. No wonder, then, that a frequent refrain in contemporary capitalist ideology is that each should find out for herself. Capitalism relies on our separation from one another so it does its best to separate and individuate us at every turn.

Institutions are symbolic arrangements that organize and concentrate the social space. They "fix" an Other, not in the sense of immobilizing it but in the sense of putting in relation the emergent effects of sociality. This "putting in relation" substantializes the link, giving it its force, enabling it to exert its pressure. A party

57   Ibid., 106.
58   Ibid., 107.

is an organization and concentration of sociality in behalf of a certain politics. For communists this is a politics of and for the working class, the producers, the oppressed, the people as the rest of us. "Party" knots together effects of ideal ego, ego ideal, super-ego, subject supposed to know, and subject supposed to believe. The particular content of any of these component effects changes over time and place even as the operations they designate remain as features of the party form.

The ideal ego in communist parties is typically imagined in terms of the good comrade. The good comrade may be a brave militant, skilled organizer, accomplished orator, or loyal function-ary. In contrast, the ego ideal is the point from which comradeship is assessed: how and to what end is bravery, skill, accomplishment, and loyalty counted? The party superego incessantly charges us for failing on all fronts, *we never do enough*, even as it taunts us with the sacrifices we make for the sake of the party, *we have always done too much*. Each of these positions can be varyingly open and closed, coherent or contradictory. Insofar as the party is situated in an antagonistic field, insofar as it is not the state but is a part, other ideals and injunctions enter the mix: this is class struggle within the party, the challenge presented by capitalist consciousness. At the same time, the situatedness of the party means that the space it provides necessarily exerts effects beyond party members, provid-ing images and reference points for those who might join, for allies and fellow travelers, as well as for former members or enemies.

The ideas of subject supposed to believe and know are particu-larly useful for thinking about these effects beyond party members. Critics of the communist party chastise the party for claiming to know, for functioning as a location of scientific or revolutionary knowledge. This ostensible expertise has been derided not only as monopolistic but also as false: the knowledge of living with, responding to, and fighting against oppressive power belongs to the people and cannot be confined into a set of iron laws of historical development. Given this critique, which came to be widely shared on the Left in the wake of '68, it's surprising that the collapse of the Soviet Union dealt such a mortal blow to communist and socialist organizing in the US, UK, and Europe. By 1989, only a tiny few defended the Soviet Union anymore. Most agreed that its bureaucracy was moribund and that it needed to institute market reforms. Why, then, did its collapse have such an effect? The "subject supposed to believe" helps make sense of this strange reaction. What was lost when the USSR fell apart was the subject onto whom belief was transposed, the subject through whom others believed. Once this believing subject was gone, it really appeared that communism was ideologically defeated. As a further example, we might consider the prototypical accounts of Communist Party officials with their dachas and privileges. These functioned less as factual exposes than as attacks on the subject supposed to believe: not even the Party believes in Communism. Where the attacks failed, however, is in the fact that they were waged at all. Insofar as they had a target, they affirmed its ongoing function as the subject supposed to believe. The flawed, dessicated Party could still believe for us. Once it utterly collapsed, we lost the other through whom we could believe.

The Party Organizer

Writings from the 1930s in the *Party Organizer*, a publication of the Communist Party of the United States for the internal use of unit and district organizers, display the array of dynamic and structural effects knotted together in the party.

A first example illustrates the intertwining of ideal ego and ego ideal in the Party. The writer vividly narrates how his CP-organized block committee fought to get food relief for a needy woman and her children. As he tells it, the workers "stood up like a solid wall, demanding food." The cowardly relief supervisor, "a capi-
'st tool," called the police, who rushed in and grabbed the CP

organizer. "But the roar from the workers and my determination to fight back put fear into the hearts of the police." The police called for reinforcements and brought "the big fat Judge Mendriski" with them. With a heroic image of himself, workers, and Party standing up to the capitalist relief supervisor, police, and judge and fighting to keep a woman and her children from starving, the organizer recounts, "I looked right at him and said: 'What the hell are you here for, to help this serpent deny this mother with her three children? You don't care ... you with your belly packed with steak.'" The judge orders the police to lock up the organizer. But the police, "seeing the determination of the workers," are forced to let him go.[59] The workers appear as a crowd, a roaring steadfast wall. Their appearing compels the police to take the perspective of the CP and recognize that the united workers are stronger than any judge and his order.

A second example brings out the superegoic dimension of the Party. In the early 1930s, the *Party Organizer* filled itself with articles on how to recruit and retain new members. Month after month, the writers—many anonymous, many district-level organizers—express excitement about gains in new members and dismay over the party's failure to retain them. They worry that their meetings are too long, that they don't start and finish on time, that they aren't "snappy enough."[60] They advise one another on the best design for a party meeting: no more than two hours, not to exceed two and half hours, three hours at the absolute limit. District organizers are advised to pick up members at their houses and bring them to meetings. Members are reminded to talk to new recruits. The CP organizers writing in the magazine sense the "enthusiasm and earnest desire of the workers," but blame themselves for the fact that the workers drop out:

59 "Organized Struggles Defeat Police Terror," *Party Organizer* 6: 1, January 1933, 8–11.

60 "Retaining and Developing New Members of the Party," *Party Organizer* 14: 10, November 1931, 16–19, 18.

The recruit comes into the average unit of the Party and finds there a group of strangers speaking a jargon which he does not understand. No one pays much attention to him and he is therefore left very much to himself ... enthusiasm cools, he becomes discouraged, loses his enthusiasm and finally drops out of the Party.[61]

"Jargon" is a symptom of the problem. "Jargon" means that the people and the Party are not speaking the same language. It marks a division between workers and Party members, even when Party members are workers. The language that members share, the ideas that enable them to see the world in terms other to capitalism's, enhance and hinder belonging at the same time. The very activities they pursue as communists—reading, discussing, meeting, leafleting, organizing, training—separate them from the workers. What makes them communists, what separates them from capitalism's constraints as it provides them with political capacity and conviction, inscribes a gap in the givenness of economic belonging. They are not just economic producers. They are political producers creating not commodities but collective power.

One recommendation for overcoming this division is imagining oneself as a comrade, not a professor.[62] Organizers are advised to speak "not as a soap boxer or a seasoned Communist theorist" but just to "be one of the workers, which indeed you are."[63] Other recommendations include better development of cadres, more effort at education. Still others highlight a kind of transferential relation that can arise from "visiting the workers at least two or three times a week, getting to know them by name and their individual problems, and have them call you by name and feel you are one of them."[64] Imagining oneself as a comrade, particularly when

---

61   Ibid., 17.

62   Ibid., 18.

63   S. V. V., "Examine Our Factory Work," *Party Organizer* 4: 5, June 1931, 19.

64   Sylvia Tate, "Experiences of Neighborhood Concentration," *Party

accompanied by instructions to do what one would normally do, involves a reflexive turn onto the everyday as one looks at what one does from the Party perspective.

The same desire that leads people to join the Party separates them from the crowd. Once they have become communists, they see themselves and the world from the perspective opened up by the Party. They look at the world differently from how they did before. Yet they also have to continue to imagine themselves as the workers they are, bound to the economic struggle. Hence the advice: "Little by little from the conditions in the shops go on to the speed up, wage cuts, unemployment and then to the need for organization. Don't appear too insistent at first."[65] The organizer has to begin from the perspective of the worker and guide the worker to a shift in perspective, to seeing from a different place. The superegoic dimension of the Party is inseparable from its capacity to provide an ideal ego and ego ideal.

The internal criticisms that the *Party Organizer* raises are unrelenting. For every success in increasing membership, there is an injunction to do more, to do better. One article will take up the ways problems are being addressed. The next will hammer home the problems that persist. The demands they place on themselves never let up—another membership drive, more focus on the trade unions, intensification of reading, more thorough reporting. They acknowledge small victories, but every victory—in true superegoic fashion—inspires yet more self-criticism. One writes, "Our influence among workers has increased ten-fold within the last few years, but the membership of our Party has remained practically stationary. Why do the workers come and leave our ranks? What is wrong with us?"[66]

Throughout 1932, the conversation in the *Party Organizer*,

Organizer 5: 8, August 1932, 6–7.

65 "Examine Our Factory Work," 19.

66 J. A., "The Deadly Routine Which Must Be Overcome," *Party Organizer* 6: 3–4, March–April 1933, 22–23, 22.

particularly in the section on mass work, centers on "concentration"—concentration in the shops, concentration in the neighborhoods, concentration in the stockyards of Chicago. "Concentration" is approached from different angles, the emphasis on subjective factors explained in light of objective factors.[67] By February 1933, critical reflection turns round upon "concentration." In "Concentration—A Means of Winning the Workers in the Key Industries," J. P. observes that "concentration" has become a Party term: "we concentrate feverishly."[68] But the formality and sectarianism of the approach to concentration has become itself the problem, the actual barrier to growth and increase. The Party has had the wrong conception of "concentration." What is necessary is more intimate contact with the workers. Six months later a disgusted Party member laments, "we have never taken concentration seriously."[69]

The *Party Organizer* reveals a party in the process of exerting pressure on itself, of imagining itself and struggling as it produces a place from which to see itself. This place is in flux, unstable, sometimes occupied by idealized revolutionary workers and sometimes the place from which workers are idealized. The stronger the Party feels itself becoming, the fiercer and more intense the demands it puts on itself. A letter from an active Party comrade in Chicago expresses the pressure of the relentless injunction to do more:

I will be criticized next Tuesday night at the organizers meeting because the unit is not larger; because I have not done more; because I did not attend some meeting or other … I do the best I can. However, no matter how much I do, I always hate to show my face

---

67   "How Are We Going to Concentrate on Shops?" *Party Organizer* 5: 7, July 1932, 9–10, 10.

68   J. P., "Concentration—A Means of Winning the Workers in the Key Industries," *Party Organizer* 6: 2, February 1933, 5–10, 5.

69   Charles Krumbein, "How and Where to Concentrate," *Party Organizer* 6: 8–9, August–September 1933, 24–27, 24.

because there are things I do not do that I was told to do. Directives, directives, directives. An organization letter sometimes of three pages. Hell, I could not do one tenth of it. I am getting tired. I am just as much a Communist as ever, but I am not 10 communists.[70]

Žižek observes that the symbolic space of the Other "operates like a yardstick against which I can measure myself."[71] The communists appearing in the *Party Organizer* measure themselves as many. The desire that expresses itself in the urgent demands they make on themselves is collective—ten communists—even as it is felt as impossible superegoic command.

Political Organization and its Discontents

Thus far I've emphasized the psychodynamics of collectivity. Whereas critics of the party tend to fault the form itself for its centralism and authoritarianism, I've used Michels's discussion of the technical and psychological tendencies to oligarchy in *any* political group to assert the unavoidability of a gap between few and many. Organizing crowds involves division, delegation, and distribution. Number—being many—has affective force, as we see in prestige, imitation, and identification. Further, I've drawn from psychoanalysis to theorize the gap as a link, a social space knotting together unconscious processes and perspectives. Inserting the party in this gap, I've shown collectivity's work back upon its members. Their very association alienates them from their setting, opening up the possibility of another perspective on it and separating them from how they are given under capitalism.

To be sure, that political organization means a gap between many and few is unavoidable does not imply that the same people should be on one side or the other of it. The history of people's

---

70   "Give More Personal Guidance," *Party Organizer* 6: 1, January 1933, 22.

71   Žižek, *How to Read Lacan*, 9.

struggles (anti-racism, anti-sexism, anti-homophobia, etc.) demonstrates profound and ongoing mobilization on precisely this
point. Likewise, that the gap is unavoidable does not imply that
any given instantiation of the gap is permanent or justified. There
are better and worse parties and leaders. Some are more faithful to
the crowd's egalitarian discharge than others. And Michels's own
discussion brings out the torsion between many and few as power
shifts and folds between them: what appears as an idolized leader
is a refraction of the crowd's enjoyment of the power of number.
Finally, that the gap between many and few is unavoidable does
not mean that gaps should line up with each other: doing more
work should not imply garnering more material benefit. In sum,
the crucial point that follows from the unavoidable gap between
few and many is that the charges of centralism and authoritarianism leveled at the communist party from its inception in fact apply
to politics as such. If we are to engage politically, we cannot avoid
the effects—and affects—of number. To think that we can is to
persist in the fantasy of the beautiful moment.

The utility of my psychodynamic approach to the party
becomes clear in contrast with John Holloway's well-known
attempt to imagine a revolutionary politics aimed at abolishing
power altogether, an aim shared by most anarchists. Published at
the beginning of the twenty-first century, Holloway's influential
account anticipates the post-anarchist converging of post-structuralism and anarchism.[72] It also repeats century-old criticisms
of the party form, updating and distilling these criticisms into a
concentrated rejection of power per se. Variations on Holloway's
arguments against the party for its state-centrism and externality to the working class appear today as a kind of common sense
throughout the radical Left.

Holloway orients his vision of politics in a notion of "doing"
as "the movement of practical negativity." Doing, for Holloway,

72   See the contributions to *Post-Anarchism: A Reader*, eds. Duane Rousselle and Süreyyya Evren, London: Pluto Press, 2011.

goes beyond the given, and hence is akin to the gap I associate
with the work of collectivity back on itself. Embedded in the flow
of human movement, Holloway's doing is likewise necessarily
social: "there is a community of doing, a collective of doers, a flow
through time and space."[73] But insofar as his collective doers are
nothing but flows through time and space, their collectivity exerts
no effect back upon them as a collective. Holloway's collective is
at best a crowd. At worst it is nothing more than mobile social substance. It can split a field, produce a gap, but it has no place from
which it looks at itself.

Lacking reflexivity, the sociality Holloway describes is a sociality
without sociality. He comes close to acknowledging this omission
when he says that "this collective doing involves, if the collective
flow of doing is recognized, a mutual recognition of one another
as doers, as active subjects. Our individual doing receives its
social validation from its recognition as part of the social flow."[74]
People recognize one another, in relations imagined as multiple
dyads, exchanges of recognition. Yet the role of the Other as the
field of social validation remains unremarked. It has no effects or
dynamics of its own, no impact apart from the acknowledgment of
individuals. Holloway's flow of doing, in other words, omits the
function of the space of the Other.

Holloway nevertheless presupposes such an Other space when
he criticizes the party for its externality to the working class. In
the Marxist tradition, he argues, the failure of workers to revolt
is explained with notions of ideology, hegemony, and false consciousness. All three are "accompanied by an assumption that the
working class is a 'they.'"[75] Holloway claims that the problem of
communist organization is "how can we make them see?" "We"
see clearly. "They" do not. Holloway's mistake consists in the

---

73   John Holloway, *Change the World Without Taking Power*, London:
Pluto Press, 2002, 42.
74   Ibid., 43.
75   Ibid., 87.

way he presents division as if it were a division between groups—workers on one side, party on another—rather than a division constitutive of political subjectivity (of the gap necessary for the subject to appear). Seeing differently involves a reflective twist, a different perspective on where one is. Where one is has to appear other than how it was. There has to be a gap between the social flow, to use Holloway's term, and the political assertion of this flow. The problem is not externality, as if the party or the state were separate from and unaffected by society. The problem is the perspective from which something appears differently. A strike can be a matter for the workers in a specific factory. It can also be politicized as a component of a larger struggle. Is a particular strike simply for higher wages so that individual workers can increase their capacities to consume? Or does it incorporate claims of fairness, equality, and right? Does it link itself to other such actions so that it appears as the struggle of a class?

Holloway's critique of externality repeats the old charge of vanguardism leveled at the Leninist party. Holloway attributes to Lenin the view that the party is necessary because class consciousness can only come to workers from "without." Lenin's ostensible error here is one of elitism. It comes from validating intellectuals over workers: workers on their own lack the capacity to develop class consciousness; intellectuals, however, have the requisite knowledge and skills. Daniel Bensaïd demonstrates that this argument is misplaced.[76] Lenin's point is that political consciousness comes from outside the *economic* struggle, not the class struggle. The economic struggle takes place between particular interests within the field of capital. The terms of the struggle are set by capitalism. The political struggle—for communists—is over the field itself. When "we" is used as the designator for the subject of a politics it asserts more than a collective will. It announces a will to collectivity, a will to fight together on terms that challenge rather

---

76   Daniel Bensaïd, "Leaps, Leaps, Leaps," *International Socialism* 2: 95, 2002.

than accept the given. Class consciousness is not spontaneous. As Žižek emphasizes, what is spontaneous is misperception—the perception that one is alone or that one's circumstances are unique.[77] The political "we" of the party ruptures this immediate consciousness to assert a collective one in its place.

Holloway extends his critique of the externality of the party to Georg Lukács. He charges Lukács with failing to explain how the party can adopt the perspective of totality. This charge, too, misses its mark. The party doesn't adopt the perspective of totality in the sense that it can and does see everything. Rather, the party tries to establish the space for a perspective on the totality, a perspective that is not determined completely by the setting in which it finds itself as if it had no impact on this setting. The party works to create the condition of possibility for a perspective that, empirically impossible, ruptures the openness of the capitalist manifold from within.

Holloway takes direct aim at a Marxism viewed as a source of objective, scientific knowledge:

> If Marxism is understood as the correct, objective, scientific knowledge of history, then this begs the question, "who says so?" Who holds the correct knowledge and how did they gain that knowledge? Who is the subject of the knowledge? The notion of Marxism as "science" implies a distinction between those who know and those who do not know, a distinction between those who have true consciousness and those who have false consciousness.[78]

The subject supposed to know is a structural position. The party doesn't know. It organizes a transferential space offering the position of the subject supposed to know. In Žižek's words, "the authority of the Party is not that of determinate positive knowledge, but that of the form of knowledge, of a new type of

---

77   Slavoj Žižek, *Revolution at the Gates*, London: Verso, 2002, 189.

78   Holloway, *Change the World Without Taking Power*, 168.

knowledge linked to a collective political subject."[79] This form is that of a shift in perspective, a collective political position on a situation that had appeared limited and determined by capitalism. The perspective of the party comes not from religion, law, or individual insight but rather from the fact of collectivity, as I've been arguing here, from fidelity to the equality of the crowd discharge.

Holloway asks how we can ever know whether those in the know are correct, how it is even possible for them to know. He is right to suggest that we cannot know this: there is no Other who knows. His questions thus voice the end of a transferential relation to the party. In Holloway's case, however, the end of that relation to the party does not mean the end of transference. He mourns that "the Leninists know, or used to know ... the knowing of the revolutionaries of the last century has been defeated."[80] Of course, Lenin didn't know. Lenin famously shifted positions and courses, "bending the stick" and responding to the movement of the revolution. Holloway's inability to acknowledge that Lenin was lucky, that he erred, that he changed his mind, that he did not know tells us that he, Holloway, remains attached to a position he can't not presuppose. The position is there, but loosened from the ties that inspired it, disconnected from the victories of people's struggles, pushed into the past as something left behind but exerting a force.

On the one hand, Holloway recognizes that there is no Other of the Other, no guarantor of political knowledge. Political knowledge arises through practice, over time, in ways that remain unfixed and contingent. On the other hand, insofar as the position of the Other remains, Holloway fights to keep it empty, to doubt any and all who might occupy it. Abandoning any connection between the substance of emancipatory egalitarian political struggle and the perspective this struggle creates, he insists on the "not-knowing of those who are historically lost," the not-knowing of the defeated, as if nothing had been learned, as if there were no trace of past

---

79 Žižek, *Revolution at the Gates*, 189.
80 Holloway, *Change the World Without Taking Power*, 308.

victories and achievements.[81] Trusting none to bear the knowledge necessary for revolution, he asserts non-knowledge even as he resorts implicitly to vague supports such as the knowledge of intellectuals. What Holloway can't acknowledge is that the erasure of past victories and achievements is an effect of his own disavowal of the body that carries them, the party, a disavowal in turn of revolutionary power.

Ultimately, Holloway's critique of the party follows from his rejection of the state. Reformist and revolutionary Marxists alike treat the state as the means through which society can be transformed. Holloway calls this an "instrumental" view of the state premised on the "fetishistic" idea that the state is separate from and external to society. Armed by this instrumental and fetishistic vision of state power, Marxists concentrate and direct radical energies toward its conquest. The party is the organizational form of this state fetishism insofar as it is abstracted from all other social relationships to appear as the primary object of political circulation. The party disciplines and impoverishes class struggle, subordinating its myriad forms to "the over-riding aim of gaining control of the state." [82] When politics is channeled through the party form, political feelings, experiences, and relations failing to contribute directly to the conquest of state power are deprioritized, subordinated, rendered as lesser than.

Holloway is right to say that the party is a form for disciplining class struggle, but he fails to consider what discipline means. For communists, discipline involves building solidarity, strengthening collectivity, and sustaining courage in the face of capitalism's efforts to isolate us in self-interest and fear. The "instrumentalist impoverishment" of which Holloway accuses Marxists is Holloway's own, apparent in his omission of the abundant lifeworld of practices organized by communist parties everywhere. It prevents him from acknowledging the diverse activities involved

81   Ibid.
82   Ibid., 27.

in communist party organizing, activities such as establishing newspapers and literary journals, forming youth leagues and sports teams, building support networks for women's groups and racialized minorities. Once these multiple and varied activities are included in our conception of discipline, we see again the party as a social link, one that interrupts the imaginary and symbolic order of the bourgeoisie to insert egalitarian ideals and collectivist perspectives. Understood most generally, party discipline is nothing but establishing and maintaining this link.

Bensaïd observes that Holloway reduces "the luxuriant history of the workers' movement, its experiences and controversies to a single line of march of statism through the ages, as if very different theoretical and strategic conceptions had not been constantly battling with each other."[83] What Holloway refers to as the subordination of myriad forms of class struggle to the goal of gaining control of the state has historically included an array of tactics and been carried out in multiple time frames. Tactics for winning the state span a wide range: from securing an electoral majority and participating in governing coalitions to organizing factories and neighborhoods into a counterforce; stretching the resources of the state until it collapses; subverting the state from within; violently overthrowing it and militarily invading it. These different tactics fold into one another, operating along different time frames with short-term and long-range goals and cutting across national and regional borders in fronts, alliances, rings, and pacts. Nothing about communist organizing presumes the externality of the state to society much less the autonomy of the state from international political, economic, social, cultural, and environmental forces.

A less reductive treatment of the communist revolutionary legacy would note how communist visions of the party as a means of waging revolution explicitly state, time and again, that

---

83   Daniel Bensaïd, "On a recent book by John Holloway," trans. Peter Drucker, *Historical Materialism* 13: 4, 2005.

revolution requires changing people, beliefs, and practices. Even crude treatments of historical communism admit as much when they attack as totalitarian twentieth-century efforts to create the new socialist man or a new type of human being. The focus on the revolutionary goal does not distance the party from everyday practice, as Holloway implies. On the contrary, revolution is an effect of shared purpose. The goal is an instrument of its realization: a collective that has a goal and works to achieve it exerts power over itself. The production of the collective space of the party as a knot of transferential effects is the way people are changed through struggle, the way they induce a gap in capitalism where another perspective becomes possible. Members look at themselves and their interactions from the perspective of the association they create through their association, the party. The goal of revolution lets us see the reflective dimension of the instrument of revolution in terms of its effects back on those out of whom it arises. The party affects members, fellow travelers, opponents, and the general setting insofar as its knotting together of elements of the Other consolidates the space of a politics, establishing a place from which a collective can look at itself.

The Party Opening

Holloway claims that the party "is historically closed to us now." He writes,

> Whether or not it ever made sense to think of revolutionary change in terms of the "Party," it is no longer even open to us to pose the questions in those terms. To say now that the Party is the bearer of the class consciousness of the proletariat no longer makes any sense at all. What Party? There no longer exists even the social basis for creating such a "Party."[84]

---

84   Holloway, *Change the World Without Taking Power*, 131.

Some on the Left have become convinced of this point. They repeat it as if it were an obvious truth. It's not.

What does it even mean to say that there is no social basis for the party? Some argue that changes in the social composition of labor and the capitalist mode of production have eliminated the industrial workforce necessary for a politics of the proletariat in the North and/or the West. Rather than acknowledging the historical importance of the peasantry in communist revolutions and parties, they presume a seemingly organic link between industrial worker and party as if factory organization automatically generated party organization or as if workers were naturally solidaristic. Part of the oddity of the claim that there is no social basis for the party is the way it inverts previous explanations for party identification. These explanations held that people join together in parties not because they already feel connected to others but because they don't. Individualism, isolation, and the need to belong motivate people to join together.[85] The same effect—party belonging—is thus attributed to connectedness *and* isolation, a prior solidarity *and* a prior individualism. When critics of the party use socio-economic factors to support their claims for the obsolescence of the party form they treat isolation, fragmentation, and individualism as explanations for their own continuation. Previous analyses, however, understood these as problems party belonging redressed.

Nevertheless, something about Holloway's claim rings true. After all, if the party form were compelling now, wouldn't we see something like a party exerting a force on the contemporary Left? His point that the idea of the party as the bearer of working-class consciousness no longer makes any sense at all has an element of truth. But what is this element?

---

85   Seymour Martin Lipsett, "Introduction: Ostrogorski and the Analytic Approach to the Comparative Study of Political Parties," in Moisei Ostrogorski, *Democracy and the Organization of Political Parties*, vol. II, London: Transaction Books, 1982, xxix.

As he positions Leninists as the subject supposed to know, Holloway implies that there was a time when the Party *was* the bearer of working-class consciousness. There was a time when people—workers, peasants, intellectuals, even capitalists—*believed* that the Communist Party was the bearer of working-class consciousness. More precisely, they believed that others *believed* that the Communist Party was the bearer of working-class consciousness. In the second half of the twentieth century, this belief collapsed. The slogan from the Cultural Revolution makes the point most powerfully: "the bourgeoisie is in the Communist Party." This is the element of truth in Holloway's claim that it no longer makes sense to think in terms of the party. Few today believe that the Communist Party is vanguard of a revolutionary working class.

The assumption that revolutionaries *used to know*, however, points to the continuation of transference: Holloway doesn't say that they never knew. He doesn't say that the party *never* was a bearer of working-class consciousness. The space opened up and held by the party remains. It's as if the party's form as "enigmatic subject support" persists even as the working class no longer appears as a revolutionary subject.[86] Such a support continues to exert an effect even in the claim that "the bourgeoisie is in the Communist Party." The claim is reflexive. It is the party itself that opens the space for this criticism of itself. The party holds up the subject making this criticism, a point Holloway attempts to disavow but cannot not presuppose. He is right to say the party is not the bearer of working-class consciousness. In fact it never could be the bearer of such a fiction, the efforts of German Social Democracy to present it otherwise notwithstanding. The party is the support for the subject of communism. This subject has been variously figured as proletariat, peasantry, and divided people.

---

86   For a more detailed discussion of this point see *The Communist Horizon*, chapter three. "Enigmatic subject support" comes from Alain Badiou, *Theory of the Subject*, trans. Bruno Bosteels, London: Continuum, 2009, 189.

The party operates as the support for the subject of communism by holding open the gap between the people and their setting in capitalism. The more the gap appears, the more the need for and perhaps even sense of a party impresses itself. This gap isn't a void. It's a knot of processes that organize the persistence of the unrealized in a set of structural effects: ideal ego, ego ideal, superego, subject supposed to know and believe—the party as the Other space. This Other space doesn't have its own interest, a correct line, or an objective science that tells it the truth of history. It is instead a rupture within the people dividing them from the givenness of their setting, a rupture that is an effect of their collectivity, the way their belonging works back upon them.

Political experience shows that radical movements cannot simply avoid the state—the state won't let them. It actively infiltrates, polices, and subverts them. To the extent that movements pose a serious challenge to state power, they encounter its reactive counterforce. That society can seize itself is a myth that has outlived whatever usefulness it might have had for the Left and become visible as the instrument of the expansion of capitalism.[87] Gaining political control of the state thus remains an important goal because the state presents a barrier to political change. As the political instrument of capitalist class rule, the state enforces order in the interest of capital as a class, doing all it can to prevent, redirect, and smash opposition. In the face of militarized policing, not to mention the evisceration of the social gains of working-class movement, does it make sense to envision a political revolution that ignores the state, allowing the state to go on exercising its policing, repressive, and legal functions? If we do not think that the state should remain in the hands that it is in, then we lapse into the politics of the beautiful moment when we fail to factor it into our political perspective.

---

87   Writing in 1984, Félix Guattari announced: "The only acceptable objective now is the seizing of society by itself," *New Lines of Alliance, New Spaces of Liberty*, 126.

One might object that contemporary decentered, federated, and interlinked states are not in anyone's hands and therefore cannot be seized. This objection, however, implicitly endorses a liberal technocratic view of the state. It proceeds as if the systems of laws and assumptions on which states are based are nothing more than neutral protocols. The classic communist ideal of the dictatorship of the proletariat confronts this lie directly. The liberal state is in actuality the dictatorship of capital. Its premises ensure that the benefit of the doubt, "common sense," falls on the side of capitalism, that what feels like the right decision is the one that confirms the bourgeois mindset: protect private property, preserve individual liberties, promote trade and commerce. The goal of gaining control of the state takes aim at this underlying level of laws, practices, and expectations, targeting common sense to make it the sense for and of the common.

Capitalists will not voluntarily reorganize processes of accumulation so as to put an end to proletarianization. They will not simply hand over control and ownership of the means of production. States will not just stop oppressing, arresting, and imprisoning those who resist them. Such fundamental changes will only come about through political struggle, carried out internationally. A Left that eschews organizing for power will remain powerless. This is why we are talking about the party again.

5

The Passional Dynamics
of the Communist Party

It sometimes seems as if people on the Left love revolution, but hate the party. We enthusiastically support transformation, especially *personal* transformation. Yet in the same breath we scoff at institutionalized practices strategically oriented toward the pursuit of radical political change. Many of us thus reject the organizational form that marks the difference between the chaos of revolution and the building of a new political and social order. With this rejection, we shield ourselves from a confrontation with the real of division, luxuriating instead in the fantasy of the beautiful moment.

The party is a political form that compels this confrontation. It claims, occupies, and mobilizes it. This chapter continues the investigation of the psychodynamics of the party introduced in chapter four. Using examples from British and US American communism, I highlight the symbolic space of the party. What enabled the Communist Party to provide a location from which communists in the UK and US could see their actions as valuable and worthwhile? My claim is that the affective infrastructure of the party provided the material support for its symbolic location. Ceaseless practice generated the intensities that members directed onto themselves, letting them push themselves such that they could see themselves as changing the world. They became bigger, able to do more than they could have imagined, and the world became present in the everyday. So instead of considering the communist party in terms of ideology, program, leadership, or organizational structure, I approach it in terms of the dynamics of feeling it generates and mobilizes. More than an instrument for political power, the communist party provides an affective infra-structure that enlarges the world.

The communist party's capacity to enlarge the world comes at a cost. The knot of unconscious processes that holds open the space for communist political subjectivity exerts constant, even unrealiz-able, demands. Bluntly put: seeing yourself as changing the world requires you to look at yourself from a position that makes relent-less demands on you, a position that compels and judges and accepts no excuses. If that's what communists want, and we should, then we have to confront these costs head on. The stronger the political organization we build, the greater will be its—and our—expecta-tions. Organizing us, the party compels us, or, differently put, it is the apparatus through which we compel ourselves to do what we must, to do what has to be done because we cannot, will not, acquiesce to inequality, exploitation, and oppression.

Sometimes You Have to Cook a Few Eggs

I begin with a story from Vivian Gornick's *The Romance of American Communism*. It's about an organizer named Eric Lanzetti and a young party member named Lilly. I like this story because it illustrates the themes of enlargement and courage that the Party perspective provides.

Lanzetti grew up in a West Virginia mining town after fascism pushed his father out of Italy. He attended Brown and Oxford on scholarship. In 1938, having been radicalized by the war in Spain, Lanzetti joined the Communist Party. Within a short time, he was made a section organizer on the Lower East Side of New York City.

In one of the interviews with American Communists at the basis of Gornick's book, Lanzetti tries to convey the reach of the Party on New York's Lower East Side in the thirties, its moral place in the life of the neighborhood. He gives the example of Lilly:

> She wasn't the smartest person in the world, but she was a hard-working, conscientious Communist, with a powerful sense of class. She lived alone with her father on Rivington Street. The old man was an Orthodox Jew who paid absolutely no attention to her or to her politics or anything. She made his breakfast in the morning, went to work, came home, made his dinner, went to a meeting, came home, made him hot milk, and that was it. The old man sat reading the Talmud all day long. Lilly ran the house entirely. If it wasn't for her working, they would have both starved. But he was her father and she was scared shitless of him.[1]

One evening after a meeting, Lanzetti recalls, Lilly wanted to talk to him about something. Hesitantly, she started to tell him about a man with whom she was in love. Lanzetti assumed Lilly wanted to know whether she should sleep with him, so he started to talk about how sex outside of marriage is not a problem. "'Oh no, no, no,' she interrupts me, 'it's nothing like that. Of course, we've been sleeping together. It's that he's Chinese. I'm terrified to tell my father we want to get married.'" Lanzetti recounts that he stared at her, momentarily dumbfounded. Then he replied, "'Look, if you're afraid to tell him alone I'll go with you.' 'You'll go with me?' she says. 'Not only me,' I say, 'we'll take a delegation if that'll make you feel any better.' 'A *delegation?*' she says. 'Sure,' I say, getting into the swing of it, 'we'll take the whole damned Communist Party.'"

A month later, Lilly approached Lanzetti again. He asked her what had happened. She says that it took a while for her to get

---

1   Vivian Gornick, *The Romance of American Communism*, New York: Basic Books, 1977, 123–24. I am indebted to Jon Flanders for the gift of this book.

up the nerve, but then she finally told her father she was getting married. Her father asked, "Is he Jewish?" No, she answered. He's Chinese. Lilly's father was silent for a long time. "I'll kill you," he finally said. Lilly relates that her knees started to buckle:

> Then all of a sudden it was like you were in there in the room with me. I saw you and my branch organizer and all the people I work with and I felt like the whole Communist Party was right there in the room with me. I looked at my father and I said to him: "If you kill me, who'll cook your eggs?"

Lanzetti tells a story of expansion, of becoming many. He describes how he imparted to Lilly the sense that she wasn't alone. There was a crowd standing with her. She was backed by the Party. She could gather confidence from the fact that countless others—*the whole damned Communist Party*—would be right there with her when she confronted her father. And, according to Lanzetti, Lilly felt this, she saw them. Her sense of having the solidarity of the specific people she knew expands into a sense of the whole of the Party standing there with her, supporting her. As she sees the Party right there with her, she becomes stronger, more courageous. A cramped apartment layered in fear transforms into a site of triumph, collective power saturating the everyday in the courage of the cheeky retort, "who'll cook your eggs?"

Lanzetti sees Lilly as a class-conscious communist, someone who works hard, who is at the edge of survival but nonetheless attends meeting after meeting after working both to earn a wage and care for her father. He observes the repetitions of her daily life, how she prepares meal after meal for the silent father she fears. As Lanzetti narrates the story, he stumbles. He mistakenly presumes that, for Lilly, he is a supposed to know a kind of truth about sex: the conditions of its permissibility. Lanzetti slips into imagining himself as one who might validate a young working-class Jewish woman's sexual independence. She wasn't the smartest person in the world, after all. But Lilly doesn't position him as knowing something about sex. She doesn't need this validation. *Of course* she was sleeping with the man she loved. The problem wasn't sex. It was her father as he held the place of family, religion, and race. Lilly was terrified by the prospect of a confrontation with her father, by the challenge of open rejection of his law. Lanzetti recognizes his error. He didn't know. He guessed wrong about what she wanted and in the moment of his guess he confined Lilly to a traditionally gendered expectation beyond which she had already moved. After all, she was a class-conscious communist. Correcting himself, Lanzetti turns to the Party for its solidarity, no longer imagining himself as the one who might authorize Lilly but looking at both of them from the perspective of the Party. He gets into the swing of things, feeling the power that accrues as one becomes more and then many—himself, delegation, the whole damned Party.

Lanzetti's story is about more than Lilly. It's about himself as an organizer and how he transmitted the sense of the Party to Lilly so that she was emboldened openly to reject her father (and not just covertly to transgress the law he embodied). Class consciousness, which Lilly already has, isn't the same as the political confidence or practical optimism that the Party inspires. The life of a neighborhood, as well as the workplace experience, may generate a shared sensibility or even identity. That sensibility nourishes political potential. But it is not sufficient for a politics. It is not yet explicit as a division or a will. To be a communist is to go to meeting after meeting, to work hard, maybe even to remain poor, but it is also to have access to a force strong enough to go up against the law and win, a force neither fully internal nor external, neither reducible to particular organizational features nor separate from them, but rather an affective infrastructure capable of enlarging the world.

The Enduring Crowd

Elias Canetti's study of the crowd is a theory of collective desire. The crowd assembles libidinal and affective intensities into the force of a longing irreducible to the crowd's emotion, to the specific excitement or event that calls it together. Canetti classifies crowds with respect to their prevailing emotion—the baiting crowd out for the kill, the flight crowd in which everyone flees, the prohibition crowd that refuses, the reversal crowd turning against those who command or oppress it, and the feast crowd that enjoys in common. What we might think of as the unconscious structure and processes of the crowd, the crowd's economy of enjoyment, persists through or underneath these different types of crowds. As I discussed in chapter three, this crowd unconscious has four attributes: a desire to grow, a state of absolute equality (which Canetti defines as the "discharge"), a love of density, and a need of direction.

These crowd attributes dynamically generate collective *jouissance*. The desire to increase, expand, accumulate, and extend infuses even the crowd enclosed in an institution. The urge to grow is ineliminable, a primary impulse of the crowd. Crowds can be open or closed, but even spatial limitations can be breached by the crowd's desire to grow. Consider, for example, the odd obviousness of majority rule. The weight of number forces itself as the push of the crowd. It exerts as pressure, no matter whether right or wrong, reasonable or not. Even those who object and resist encounter this pressure. Going against the crowd is hard. The crowd wants to pull everything into itself, to take on more and increase itself. Canetti writes, "the crowd never feels itself saturated."[2]

With the discharge, Canetti offers a view of equality fundamentally different from the psychoanalytic association of equality with

2   Elias Canetti, *Crowds and Power*, trans. Carol Stewart, New York: Farrar, Straus and Giroux, 1984, 22, originally published in German in 1960.

envy. Equality in the crowd is de-differentiation, de-individuation, the momentary release from hierarchy, closure, and separation. "It is for the sake of this equality that people become a crowd and that they tend to overlook anything which might detract from it," Canetti writes. "All demands for justice and all theories of equality ultimately derive their energy from the actual experience of equality familiar to anyone who has been part of a crowd."[3] The press for equality comes not from *ressentiment*. It's not born of weakness or deprivation. It comes from the strength of many as it amplifies itself, reinforces itself, and pushes itself back upon itself. With shouts, exclamations, and noise—the spontaneous "utterance in common"—the crowd expresses the equality that is its substance.

The crowd's density is its indivisibility or degree of solidarity. Understood physiologically, density manifests itself in commonality of feeling, for example, the excitement that passes through the crowd, amplifying and feeding into itself. Close proximity helps here. Canetti pairs equality and density, telling us that in the dancing crowd they coincide. The "skillful enactment of density and equality" engenders the crowd feeling.

The crowd's direction is its goal. When common, the goal "strengthens the feeling of equality." The stronger the common goal is, the weaker the individual goals that threaten the crowd's density. Whereas Le Bon and Freud attribute the crowd's need for direction to its need for a leader, Canetti makes direction into a process internal to the crowd: direction, common cause, subordinates individual preferences. Everyone belonging to a crowd "carries within him a small traitor who wants to eat, drink, make love and be left alone."[4] When the crowd has a direction, when it is moving toward a goal, it can remain dense. Without its goal, the crowd disintegrates into individuals pursuing their own private ends. The goal is outside the crowd, that toward which it is oriented. The goal is not the discharge, although the discharge is the aim.

---

3 Ibid., 29.
4 Ibid., 23.

Canetti's crowd processes resemble psychoanalytic dynamics of desire and drive. Growth and direction point outwards. Equality and density turn back in. Together they form the knot of intensities I am referring to as the crowd unconscious. The crowd isn't structured like a language. It isn't a discursive formation. Rather, it's the dynamic press of many, the force exerted by collectivity. It doesn't have a politics any more than does an anthill, forest, or heap of stones. Canetti's crowds include dancing warriors and swarms of insects, spermatozoa and the dead, production and inflation. The real press of many takes and disrupts multiple forms: material, institutional, imaginary, symbolic. It also occurs in varying temporalities: quick or slow, momentary or enduring. The multiplicity of forms and tempos overlap and intersect, flowing together into a crowd of crowds. What the crowd wants most of all—what it lacks—is endurance.

Canetti writes: "The tendency of all human crowds to become more and more—the blind, reckless, dynamic movement which sacrifices everything to itself and which is always present in a gathering crowd—this tendency is transferable."[5] He doesn't explicate the concept. Instead he gives multiple examples: hunters transfer the growth tendency to their prey, farmers transfer it to their crops, modern Europeans transfer it to money, using the word "million" as the basic unit for counting population and money— "the abstract number has become filled with a crowd-meaning contained by no other number today."[6] The mechanisms of transference matter little to Canetti. He blurs together rituals, symbols, and processes. All enable the transmission or displacement of the crowd's desire to increase from the crowd onto something else. Wheat, mountains, and sea can become crowd symbols because they can carry the desire for increase.

---

5   Ibid., 197.
6   Ibid., 185.

Practical Optimism

Although Canetti doesn't make this point, the party, too, can carry the desire for increase as well as other attributes of the crowd unconscious. As it gathers and generates power, the party, especially the communist party, operates as a transferential object—a symbol and combination of rituals and processes—for the collective action of the many.

The crowd wants to endure. The party provides an apparatus for this endurance. Marxist discussions of the party typically focus on the organizational and ideological aspects of the party apparatus: vanguard versus mass, covert versus legal, revolutionary versus reformist. Left out is the affective infrastructure of the party, its reconfiguration of the crowd unconsciousness into a political form. Gavin Walker shifts discussion toward this reconfiguration. He describes the party as a "material substratum" that "allows the reverberations or 'overtone' of the event to remain at the core of a consistency."[7] As the body that turns the subjectivizing crowd event into a moment in a subjective process of politicizing the people, the party is tasked with transmitting the event's overtone. It can't simply declare an event to be an action of the heroic working class or revolutionary people. The party has to defend this declaration in a hostile setting. Even more, it has to ensure its truth, conducing the affective intensity of the crowd discharge in the wake of its dissipation.

Under contemporary conditions of communicative capitalism, nonstop ubiquitous media offer a never-ending supply of disasters, invasions, shootings, and protests. Scandals and epidemics displace one another as the most important issue of the day, their measure in tweets testimony to their inability to produce a gap in the dominant order. Anyone can issue an interpretation of an event, calling it this or that and attempting to push discussions in

7 Gavin Walker, "The Body of Politics: On the Concept of the Party," *Theory & Event* 16: 4, 2013.

one direction rather than another. Moreover, a certain reflexivity, a self-consciousness about media, is a constitutive feature of communicative capitalism. Hashtags, slogans, memes, images, and phrases or manners of speech that briefly achieve a kind of recognizable currency before becoming outmoded or forgotten all point to the multiple, distributed ways in which communicative acts are less about meaning than circulation, less about use value than exchange value.[8] This setting poses particular problems for left politics: How can acts remain intelligible as acts of a collective subject? How do the people prevent their acts from being absorbed back into communicative capitalism?

The party provides an affective infrastructure that can help address these problems. Rather than ceding the transmission of the overtone to intellectuals, particularly those individualized within academic or journalistic career paths, and instead of requiring fragmented activists working along multiple separate trajectories to produce their alliance event by event, issue by issue, the party is a form for concentration and endurance. In a capitalist setting, the party provides communism with a body—one that is heterogeneous, porous, and polymorphous.

By the end of the twentieth century, this body was present primarily as memory, fear, bureaucracy, or sect, as former necessity and current impossibility. The perspective it provides became so many scattered inclinations to political correctness, no less righteous and insistent for all their fragmentation into weakness. Indeed, the superegoic effects of righteous injunction seem all the more intense precisely because there is no party that can anchor them, no program to which one might appeal for justification and relief. Circulating as insults and directives in social media, these effects rage as an incessant urge to police and punish, whipping the Left into the frenzy of its own failure. The Left can see differences, but no longer pull them together into a politics.

---

8   See my discussion in *Democracy and Other Neoliberal Fantasies*, Durham, NC: Duke University Press, 2009, chapter one.

Concentration and endurance are not the same as agreement. Communist parties—like the Left more broadly—are always sites of debate, argument, factions, and splintering. Put in Lacanese: to think of the party in terms of either agreement or schism is to remain at the level of the imaginary where the party is nothing but a figure of egoism and competition. But the symbolic dimension of the party, its form as a place from which communists assess themselves and their actions, is what matters. Concentration and endurance adhere to the party form at the level of the symbolic.

The everyday experiences of rank-and-file members of CPUSA and CPGB testify to the symbolic effect of the Communist Party. I use examples from these parties because of their weakness. The US and UK were neither party-states nor parliamentary systems where Communists have ever had much electoral success. Even in the 1930s and '40s when the Communist Party was at its strongest in the US and UK, actual political power was out of reach. In the twentieth century, neither country appeared on the brink of proletarian revolution. Instead each encountered a mix of de-radicalizing middle-class prosperity, working-class defeat, and capitalist aggression, not to mention the intense anti-communism of the Cold War. How, then, under conditions even Moscow agreed were far from revolutionarily ripe, did a communist sensibility endure? What enabled the Communist Party to provide a location from which members in the US and UK could see their actions as necessary and important and that even non-members could and would adopt? My claim, as I mention at the outset of this chapter, is that the affective infrastructure of the Party provided the material support for its symbolic location.

Lauren Berlant presents affect theory as "another phase in the history of ideology theory."[9] Common and atmospheric, affect intertwines knowing and doing, infusing each with a feeling-mood-sensibility irreducible to individual emotional dispositions.

9   Lauren Berlant, *Cruel Optimism*, Durham, NC: Duke University Press, 2011, 53.

Attention to affect can open up a register beyond texts and practices, providing access to a domain of attachments and expectations productive of a mode of life. Berlant observes that the Marxist tradition "has offered multiple ways to engage the affective aspects of class antagonism, labor practices, a communally generated feeling that emerges from inhabiting a zone of lived structure."[10] Whether as histories of the working class, analyses of the structure of feeling specific to an historical formation, or readings of a world in terms of its aesthetics, Marxist cultural theory has usefully documented and explored the conditions of class belonging. It generally neglects party belonging. Where class appears in the rich fabric of work and life, in the culture and customs ostensibly inspiring that collective identity mobilized in the party, the party appears as mechanistic and cold. Against the abundance of everyday diversity, the party seems abstract, calculating, instrumental. I want to change this perception of the party.

Berlant herself looks to affect to discern the specificity of the mediation of desire in late neoliberalism. She is concerned with "the attrition of a fantasy, a collectively invested form of life, the good life."[11] In contrast to Berlant's "cruel optimism," I attend to the practical optimism generated through the Party.[12] I consider the building up of hope through the transmission of a communist sensibility in settings characterized by its absence. Rather than tracing diminution and loss, I track intensification and gain, the production of new conviction, as we see with Lilly and Lanzetti. The Communist Party provided an affective infrastructure through which everyday experiences took on meanings separate from those channeled through capitalism. The Party held open a gap in the given through which people could see themselves in collective struggle changing the world.

---

10   Ibid., 64.

11   Ibid., 11.

12   Thanks to Bonnie Honig and James Martel for working out this formulation.

The American Communists speaking in Gornick's book recount their lives in the Party in sensorially vivid terms. The intensity of the felt experience that they invoke cuts through everyday deprivation and frustration, making real the possibility of another world: they can already feel it. Working to build it, to bring it about, they remake their individual experiences of capitalist injustice into moments of collective communist equality. Ben Saltzman, a New York garment worker says, "I had the Party and I had my comrades, and they made me strong, strong on my feet."[13] Joe Preisen, a Brooklyn trade unionist, similarly observes, "History was all around you. You could touch it, smell it, see it. And when a labor organizer who was also a Communist got up to talk you could taste it in your mouth."[14] Belle Rothman, a union organizer, insists,

You don't understand. We had no choice. It's not like today, where the kids think they have the choice to be political or not be political, or be any other damn thing they want to be. We had no choice. We did not choose, we were chosen. Life came in on us, and we were bashed over the head, and we struggled to our knees and to our feet, and when we were standing there was the Communist Party.[15]

Sarah Gordon, who grew up communist in the Bronx, explains how political attachment to the Communist Party "literally negated our deprivation. It was rich, warm, energetic, an exciting thickness in which our lives were wrapped. It nourished us when nothing else nourished us. It not only kept us alive, it made us powerful inside ourselves."[16] By attending to the affective attachments of Communists to their party, I draw out the practical optimism that

---

13   Gornick, *The Romance of American Communism*, 36.
14   Idid., 46.
15   Ibid., 52.
16   Ibid., 32.

enabled the egalitarian intensity and desire of the crowd to endure after the crowds dispersed.

Infrastructure of Feeling

Writing in the 1980s, as *Marxism Today* was reconfiguring British communism for new times, replacing capitalism with Thatcherism as its enemy and communism with progressive modernization as its goal, Raphael Samuel evoked *The Lost World of British Communism*.[17] The proximate occasion for Samuel's evocation was the defeat of the miners' strike and the split in the CPGB, variously rendered as an opposition between a "hard" and a "soft left," "Stalinists" and "Eurocommunists," "Fundamentalists" and "Realists," or *Morning Star* and *Marxism Today*. The more fundamental occasion was the change with which the Left had found itself grappling since 1968: the erosion of collectivity amidst ever-increasing political, economic, and societal emphasis on "personal identity and individual self-assertion."[18] "Collectivity, instead of being the means of realizing the common good," Samuel writes, was coming to be seen "as an instrument of coercion, promoting uniformity rather than diversity, intimidating the individual, and subordinating the minority to the unthinking mass."[19] In the seventies and eighties, all social institutions—particularly those associated with the welfare state—came under attack from left and right. Yet as Samuel explains, those associated with working-class collectivism were particularly vulnerable: "Once the decision to strike becomes a matter of personal decision rather than of obedience to collective discipline, or of upholding collective honour, it is

---

17   Raphael Samuel, *The Lost World of British Communism*, London: Verso, 2006. The book is comprised of three essays originally published in *New Left Review* between 1985 and 1987.

18   Ibid., 7.

19   Ibid., 8.

subject to all those discriminations and cross-currents which make it so difficult to cope with everyday."[20] Samuel writes to refresh and retain the memory of collective power.

In some ways, Samuel gives us a communism resolutely in step with the one its critics describe: a secular religion woven out of ministry, self-sacrifice, faith, and unity. Here communism is "the way, the truth, and the light." Providing an international fellowship, "promise of redemption," and the Soviet Union as the "promised land," the communism of Samuel's childhood exudes rightness and certitude. At the same time, his communism also appears as familial and pedagogic, less a matter of metaphysical conviction than of everyday life. Samuel's mother and most of her relatives were communists, their communism "a bridge by which the children of the ghetto entered the national culture" as well as an educational "surrogate for university."[21] To be recruited into the Party was to enter into a system of education with readings, classes, lectures, and study.

In this setting, class consciousness was developed as a political consciousness. Neither an individual identity, sociological given, or even collective self-awareness, class was used "in a metaphorical rather than a literal sense."[22] It was an outlook on the world, a way of thinking in terms of laws and tendencies and acting in accordance with political allegiance. Samuel rejects the idea that the Communist Party was ever workerist, seeing the "retreat into trade unionism" in the sixties and seventies as a displaced expression of the Party's "disenchantment with itself," a symptom of the accretion of failure, disappointment, and tragedy following Khrushchev's secret speech, the invasion of Hungary, and the Sino-Soviet split.[23] The Party lost the will and capacity to make demands on itself. Those industrial workers who remained in the

---

20   Ibid.
21   Ibid., 67.
22   Ibid., 171.
23   Ibid., 206.

Party turned their focus to factory issues and factory workers turned less to the Party than to their own immediate struggles.

Underpinning these institutional analogies of church, family, and university were the practices through which the Party organized its members. Communists were caught up in "an endless round of activity that left them very little personal time."[24] Treated as a good in itself, activity not only enveloped members deeply and daily in political work but also incited a sense of urgency: what they were doing *had to be done*; it was *vital, necessary, urgent*. Good communists involved themselves in a wide variety of day-to-day struggles. The Party held meetings, rallies, and membership drives. It published and distributed a wide array of literature. It organized demonstrations, mobilized strike support, carried out emergency protests. Committed to direct action and immediate struggle, the CPGB planned campaigns, developing systems and processes for making its actions more efficient, for following up and self-assessment. It worked to concentrate its resources and energies so that it would "seem more powerful than it was." It reviewed tasks, prepared agendas, and drew up committees.

Members were more than members. They had practical positions and responsibilities far beyond those given to them by their place in capitalism. They had specialized roles such that each was always more than him or herself. Each was also someone in the Party: organizer, bureau member, instructor, trainer, branch officer, propagandist, literature seller, delegate, agitator. Related to this, Samuel says, "was a positive mania for reports which served both as an elaborate system of tutelage and as a method of accountability."[25] Reporting installed a practice of looking at activity from the perspective of the Party.

Samuel describes communist organizational passion in detail, treating it as a series of disciplines of the faithful—efficiency in the use of time, solemnity in the conduct of meetings, rhythm and

24 Ibid., 36.
25 Ibid., 106.

symmetry in street marches, statistical precision in the preparation of reports. What comes through in his account is the affective register of organization. Organization is not just a matter of bureaucracy and control. It's a generator of *enthusiasm*, an apparatus of intensification that ruptures the everyday by breaking with spontaneism. Planning is a matter of collective mindfulness. Samuel writes, "To be organized was to be the master rather than the creature of events. In one register it signified regularity, in another strength, in yet another control."[26] Organization produced a shared sense of strength, of a collective with the capacity to carry out its will.

The Party meeting, even at the local and branch level, was conducted with great care. Samuel recounts meetings that his mother's husband, Bill, attended in the early thirties. Ten to fifteen comrades met in the kitchen of a locomotive driver and his wife. The leader was a schoolteacher. The treasurer was a dockworker who hadn't "a political idea in his head but just loved the Party. He was very passionate about funds."[27] Bill remembered the meeting as "solemn." Members would discuss world events but the primary purpose of the meeting was "checking up on decisions," knowing who was going to do what. Later during the war Bill attended meetings of his factory branch in the Three Magpies pub. "*It wasn't exactly formal, but there was a lot of authority there. It wasn't me. It was in the room.*"[28] Bill doesn't mean in the pub. But he doesn't mean not in the pub, either. He is pointing to the sensibility the group meeting generated. The meeting authorized those who met, transforming a group of people having a pint in the pub into the Communist Party. Their words and actions took on an importance far beyond what they would have been absent the Party. They acquired resonance, transferring the force and important of global struggle into the Three Magpies.

26   Ibid., 103.
27   Ibid., 108.
28   Ibid., 109 (italics in the original).

Samuel sets out the specific elements of a meeting. The comrade who opened the meeting made a report. The one who closed it "summed up." Everyone was expected to contribute to discussion, speaking formally by addressing the chair, "Comrade Chairman." Samuel writes:

> The point of a Party meeting was to get things done, to trans-late the events of the day into campaigning issues. The "political report" which opened a meeting (even a disciplinary hearing began with one) started with the international situation before "drawing the lessons" and setting out targets and tasks. If the discussion got bogged down in particulars, there would be someone to "raise the level of the discussion" by reminding us of the seriousness of the situation.[29]

The meeting connected the local, the immediate, with world-historical events (think globally, act locally was communist practice long before it became an activist slogan). Unlike the moves to the personal and political that often disrupt political discussions in an individualist age, comrades drew strength from seeing themselves in a larger setting, from recognizing that rather than being unique they were typical, generic. The particular was a bog, a swampy morass that a group could get stuck in and out of which it would have to be pulled. Lessons could then be learned, conclusions drawn and plans made. Meetings broadened lives by opening them to the political, attaching them to movements and tendencies that took them out of miserable isolation. The world didn't simply happen to them. They fought to shape the world.

Samuel observes that much Party activity was "less instrumental than expressive."[30] Organization had a fantastic dimension, buttressing illusions of control, expressing dreams of power and efficacy as capable of being fulfilled. If weakness was a matter of

---

29   Ibid., 108.
30   Ibid., 120.

failures of organization, then strength would accrue as these were corrected. To the extent that organization enabled members of the CPGB to imagine their Party as shaping the world, they could believe in what they were doing whether or not their rallies and *Daily Worker* headlines corresponded to any actually significant political influence. But even with this observation, Samuel rightly refuses to allow the cynical, dismissive, and defeatist attitude of a contemporary Left that looks at the world from the perspective of capitalism to fill in the gap of possibility British communists were able to maintain. He continues to see from the perspective of the Party. The Party, shortcomings and all, continues to provide an ego ideal or symbolic point from which to view actions as momentous. The Party sustains the perspective it provides such that agitating against imperialism in a colonial society, campaigning against fascism, keeping alive the housing question, and supporting twenty years of Hunger Marches manifest the heroic work of energetic comrades, communism in the actuality of political movement. Multiple activities were not a differentiated pluralism of possibilities but a singular communist politics, envisioned as and from the perspective of the enduring struggle of the masses.

Samuel's account of Party activity isn't unique to CPGB. It resonates with the experiences of American communists. Gornick writes,

> For thousands of Communists, being a Communist meant years of selling the *Daily Worker*, running off mimeographed leaflets, speaking on street corners, canvassing door-to-door for local and national votes, organizing neighborhood groups for tenants' rights or welfare rights or unemployment benefits, raising money for the Party or for legal defenses or bail bonds or union struggles. Only that and nothing more.[31]

---

31   Gornick, *The Romance of American Communism*, 109–10.

What Gornick calls the "grinding ordinariness" of the life of Party members in the US, like that in the UK, involved ceaseless activity. Gornick presents the dream of revolution as external to this activity. I disagree. It wasn't the vision that sustained the activity. The activity was the practical optimism that sustained the vision. Consistent activity—particularly the planning, meetings, and reports—generated the perspective of the Party that enabled it. Consistency made it possible for the everyday to feel momentous, for neighborhood matters to become more than their immediacy, to become vehicles transmitting the sense of the world. Organization concentrated collective sentiment into a form other than the deprivations of capital and state, enabling people to see themselves and the world from the perspective of a gap in the given, a gap of hope and possibility.

Hosea Hudson's experiences as a black communist in the US South support my reversal of the relation between activity and vision. Hudson describes unit meetings, section meetings, and branch meetings; printing and distributing leaflets; reports, check-ups, and criticism; recruiting people one by one. Born in 1898 into a family of Alabama sharecroppers, Hudson worked as a molder at the Stockham foundry in Birmingham in the 1920s. Even before the Depression hit in full force, workers in the gray iron department faced wage cuts, the result of the "stagger system"—they would work two days one week, three the next, and some weeks not at all—that accompanied the introduction of a conveyor and a points system for determining pay. Hudson became aware of the Party in 1930 because of their leafleting: "The people were always putting them around the community, but I didn't know who they was. They'd drop by at night and you'd pick them up in the morning—there'd be a leaflet on your porch."[32] Hudson couldn't read, so he'd get his wife to read the leaflets for him. Early in 1931, his interest in the Party increased because of the Scottsboro case.

32   Nell Irvin Painter, *The Narrative of Hosea Hudson: His Life as a Negro Communist in the South*, Cambridge, MA: Harvard University Press, 1979, 82.

Nine young African American men (one was twelve years old) were accused of raping two white women on a freight train. The Party led the campaign in their defense.

When invited to his first meeting, Hudson was living in a company house, "stoolpigeon row," that is, a block where all the houses were occupied by company people. Hudson was anxious when Al Murphy, a Party member recently fired from the foundry, approached his house in broad daylight with an armful of papers, including the *Liberator*, which argued for Negro self-determination in the Black Belt of the US South. "And here come this guy Murphy they done fired out the shop. He know he been spotted, they know who he is … He brought me papers, come strutting up the street, everybody know him, ain't nowhere to hide, and he come there, leave me a paper."[33] Hudson had known Murphy briefly when Murphy worked in the foundry's coal room. He knew Murphy was involved with an organization defending the Scottsboro boys and that he had been in New York. Hudson had asked Murphy about meetings in Birmingham, but Murphy, suspicious, kept mum. And then he comes by Hudson's house, openly, "strutting up the street." Anyone can see him, and people know who he is. Murphy's not afraid. Hudson says that he himself was "never scared of the Reds," although other people were because of the risk of losing their jobs. Hudson wasn't afraid of that either, having been fired multiple times. When he says that Murphy "come busting up to my house and yard with an armful of papers in broad daylight," he isn't contrasting Murphy's confidence with his own fear. He associates it instead with the damage that people who are inexperienced in the Party can do to someone with a job and living in a company house. Hudson judges Murphy from the Party perspective to which Murphy himself introduced him. It's as if Murphy embodies a set of different breaks and possibilities, breaks between employed and unemployed, housed and homeless,

---

33   Ibid., 86.

open and hidden, literate and illiterate, confident and cautious, developed and inexperienced.

That first meeting Hudson attended was in the small house of another worker from the shop. As Hudson tells it, "I didn't say anything, but I'm a little let down, cause I'm looking for a big something, important people. And here's the guys working in the shop with me, regular guys." In this disappointing, unimportant setting, a small house with regular guys, Murphy outlines the role and program of the Party:

> the Scottsboro case and the unemployed and the Depression and the imperialist war. You had all that he was talking about that night. In the biggest part, I didn't know what he was saying. All I know is about the Scottsboro case. He was explaining about how the Scottsboro case is a part of the whole frame-up of the Negro people in the South—jim crow, frame-up, lynching, all that was part of the system. So I could understand that all right, and how speed-up, the unemployment, and how the unemployed people wouldn't be able to buy back what they make, that they was consumers and that it would put more people in the street … He took the conveyer, up there where we mold, took that and made a pattern, said, "How many men been kicked out in the street after they put that conveyer machine in there?" I could see that.[34]

Hudson understands some of what he hears, but not everything, not even the "biggest part." Murphy's words evoke something bigger that Hudson hears but doesn't understand even as he gets that this bigger something connects with his life, his concerns. Hudson goes to the meeting expecting "a big something" which he doesn't quite find for the biggest part remains what he doesn't know. Important people don't occupy that place. Instead, regular guys, like him, are, like him, there in the small house listening to Murphy and all signing up that night for the Party.

34   Ibid., 87.

Hudson doesn't describe a rousing, inspiring speech. He doesn't say anything about revolution or the mission of the proletariat. Instead, he sees a pattern, a pattern that connects the conveyor in the foundry, unemployment, Jim Crow, and lynching to something bigger. Hudson doesn't say that the Party knows what this something is, but he experiences it as the place of this something, this gap of more to and in the world than what he has already known. He mentions looking on Murphy and another comrade, Ted Horton, as "kind of special." Unlike people who could only talk about what was happening around Birmingham, Horton and Murphy met different people, people coming through from New York and Chattanooga. "They could always talk about a certain meeting over yonder."

The same night Hudson joins the Party he's elected organizer of the Stockham unit. Murphy tells him that it will be his responsibility to meet on Friday nights with other unit organizers from around Birmingham. Hudson's first unit organizers' meeting was much like his first Party meeting. "I was somewhat surprised, to see such a small group of people," he explains. "I was looking for a large group of people."[35] He feels that the Party is something big; he expects it to be bigger. The seven people at that first organizers' meeting—all black, Hudson doesn't meet a white comrade until the next year—are thrilled finally to have an actual industrial worker in their group. They were all from community units and the Party was trying to concentrate on industry, as Hudson would later learn. After he was fired five months later, members of his shop unit were afraid to meet, so he set up neighborhood units, organizing people around unemployment relief.

Leafleting was the primary activity of Hudson's unit. The group would leave pamphlets setting out the Party program and updating readers on the Scottsboro boys' case on porches, gates, and church steps. The units also held classes where they would read and discuss articles from the *Liberator*.

---

35   Ibid., 88.

We would read this paper and this would give us great courage.
We'd compare, we'd talk about the right of self-determination. We
discussed the question of if we established a government, what role
we comrades would play, then about the relationship of the white, of
the poor white, of the farmers, etc. in this area.[36]

In Depression-era Alabama, the space of the Party enabled
Hudson and his comrades to see themselves as possessing constituent power, to imagine themselves as establishing a government,
setting out the principles and processes for a new, liberated, major-
ity-black society. Hudson couldn't read, but he had a practical
optimism sufficient for imagining himself making a new world as
he engaged in the struggles of the day—"the right to vote, against
lynching, police brutality, the right for poor rural Negroes to sell
they products, that was immediate."[37] Hudson had this practical
optimism because of his work in the party.

In one of these meetings on a hot July night Hudson first learned
about democratic rights. Someone asked a white comrade from
New York whether Negroes would ever enjoy democratic rights
under the current system. Hudson stops him, saying "I don't know
what you mean by 'democratic rights.' I hear you all talking about
'democratic,' what *is* 'democratic rights'?" The white comrade,
Hudson says, "Didn't get mad, say 'You ought to know,' or stuff
like that. He stopped and explained it in detail."

In the Party, Hudson learned to read and write well enough to
publish a book. He attended the Party's National Training School.
The Party reinforced his confidence, strengthening his courage:

What the Party was doing was taking this lower class like myself
and making people out of them, took the time and they didn't laugh
at you if you made a mistake. In other words, it made this lower
class feel at home when they sit down in a meeting. If he got up and

---

36   Ibid., 102.
37   Ibid., 103.

tried to talk and he couldn't express hisself, nobody liable to laugh at him. They tried to help him and tell them, "you'll learn." There was always something to bring you forward, to give you courage ... The Party made me know that I was somebody.[38]

Before he joined the Party, Hudson sang with a quartet and attended church. So he had already a kind of confidence, but not the kind that would let him speak easily with the "better class" blacks or with whites.

In part Hudson's insecurity was a matter of his illiteracy. The little primary education he had as a child was traumatizing. To get to school, he had to walk several miles alone through woods and pastures and he was afraid of encountering a snake or mad dog. Once he got to school he chewed his sleeves with nervousness. His grandmother instructed the teacher to whip him till he stopped. As soon as he was big enough, he was pulled from school for spring plowing even as his younger brother was allowed to continue to study. The favored younger brother became a preacher. Until he joined the Party, Hudson was held down in inferiorities that tied him to a world of poverty and violence. The Party brought him up out of it, not just by helping him acquire skills but by imbuing him with collective strength. He came to know he was somebody by experiencing the way the Party made people out of the lower class. Even meetings, perhaps especially meetings, helped instill this sensibility as they made them feel at home. As comrades in the Communist Party, they could see and feel the power their collectivity gave them, the strength that comes from solidarity. Comrades wouldn't laugh at someone having trouble expressing himself. They would support him as one of their own and in that support give him the sense of a world where equality was possible, even when it wasn't easy.[39]

---

38 Ibid., 22.

39 For more comprehensive accounts of the history of African American involvement in and influence on US communism see Robin D. G. Kelley,

Collective Desire

Mid-century British and US American communists experienced the political life structured by the Party as intensely demanding and alive. Its language, meetings, rituals, and reports channeled poverty and hope into practical optimism. The Party perspective made their actions significant, nothing less than the historical struggle of the world's oppressed. Isolated deprivation became collective power, rupturing capitalism's own incessant drumbeat of inferiority and failure. No one had to go it alone, to experience politics as either out of reach or inchoate longing. The Party provided an affective structure that didn't allow people to give in to their shallower desires and, in so doing, brought out the best in them.[40]

This disallowance was a constraint, sometimes experienced as punishing, always felt as a requirement or compulsion, that which must be done. Sarah Gordon describes how she hated selling the *Daily Worker* during her twenty years in the Party.

> But I did it, I did it. I did it because if I didn't do it, I couldn't face my comrades the next day. And we all did it for the same reason: we were accountable to each other. It was each other we'd be betraying if we didn't push down the gagging and go do it. You know, people never understand that. They say to us, "The Communist Party held a whip over you." They don't understand. The whip was inside each of us, we held it over ourselves, not each other.[41]

Hammer and Hoe: Alabama Communists During the Great Depression, Chapel Hill, NC: University of North Carolina Press, 1990; Erik S. McDuffie, *Sojourning for Freedom: Black Women, American Communism, and the Making of Black Left Feminism*, Durham, NC: Duke University Press, 2011; Mark Solomon, *The Cry Was Unity: Communists and African Americans, 1917–1936*, Jackson, MS: University Press of Mississippi, 1998.

40 Gornick, *The Romance of American Communism*, 123.
41 Ibid., 110.

"Party" names a common interior force. Gordon couldn't help but resist it. Its demands went up against her natural inclinations as if shoved down her throat. Her opposition was visceral. Yet the interiorized structure of comradeship would win out. A collective desire for collectivity was stronger than her individual wants. Feeling its strength inside her, she felt the power of the Party. The sense of what she *must* do was the same as the sense of what the Party *could* do.

Hudson recounts how recruiting people into the Party requires patience, nuance, and judgment. Recruiting wasn't just grabbing or pushing. It had to be taught: "We were teaching our comrades all the way down through the units, we'd teach how to approach people, how to recruit." In the early thirties, the Party was concentrating on industrial workers, which meant "contacting individual people, making it a regular responsibility."[42] Steelworkers, railroad porters, schoolteachers, and chauffeurs were all different and had to be approached differently. Hudson evokes the difference by contrasting the feeling of "facing that hot steel" every morning with being someone who "got a party somewhere they going to tonight." Teachers and insurance writers are workers, "but they line all different altogether, big time, big parties, having big outings somewhere. They ain't got time to talk about working class oppression." Industrial workers have time to talk about it because they face it every day. Yet these workers, even though they know all about the mine, all about the plant, when they come out, they "don't have nothing to say."[43] One group of workers can talk but they don't have time. The other has the time because they *have* to have the time. But they don't express themselves. Hudson makes the Party into an instrument for the workers' self-expression, a vehicle for getting that feeling in the mine that they all know up out of the mine and connecting it with the world. Without the Party, working-class oppression would remain underground, unexpressed.

42 Painter, *The Narrative of Hosea Hudson*, 189.
43 Ibid., 190.

Hudson presents the Party's work as like that of a nursing mother; industrial workers are the main baby. "You got to nurse that baby, but you ain't going to let the baby over here go hungry because you are trying to nurse this one." He presents the Party's work as like that of a farmer: "You sow the seed." And he presents it as a moral imperative, compelling because of the way it comes in to take the feeling that workers face every morning in the mine and turn it into something else, a source of strength that the workers feel collectively in themselves. Hudson describes writing leaflets with the industrial workers (his steel plant section published a monthly bulletin, the *Hot Blast*): "You tell what's going on, tell how it's happening, but let the workers help to write it. Don't you write it. Involve them all the way through. Make them believe that they somebody. In other words, make them feel that they doing it, and not you doing it for them."[44]

Practices of reporting and checking amplify the sense of being somebody as they make each accountable to the group—one was somebody because one mattered to the collective. These practices were key to the leafleting system. Hudson's network could cover all of Birmingham in half an hour. He describes a checkup meeting in 1933. Some in the section had talked to people in the community where a John Gordon was supposed to have distributed leaflets. The people hadn't seen any. At the checkup meeting, members made reports about their leafleting. John Gordon talked all about where he put his leaflets, what people had said about them, how they were reading them and then giving them to neighbors. Hudson says to Gordon, "I went through there, and I found ain't nobody know anything about those leaflets. I asked three or four people, nobody ain't seen the leaflets." At this point, Gordon gives in. As Hudson tells it, "You see guys go to sweating then, cause the questions getting too sharp." Gordon "began to scratch and wiggle in his chair." Other comrades pressure him with questions—where did

---

44   Ibid., 191.

he actually put the leaflets? It turns out, he put them down a sewer manhole in the street. "And then we all showed him just how he was helping the bosses against the interest of the oppressed Negro and poor white workers who could not get sufficient food to eat and clothing to keep themselves and their children warm from the cold winter weather."[45] John Gordon mattered. No one was going to do his work for him, just like no one but the communists was seeing after the oppressed Negro and poor white workers. Those ten leaflets down the sewer were ten leaflets that poor Negroes did not get to read, ten missed opportunities for understanding why their children were hungry and how they could do something about it. The opportunities were now lost and exerted the force of their unrealization on the comrades. To be somebody was to be accountable and to be accountable was to feel the moral pressure of the collective. The Party expected members to do what they said they were going to do. It turns out John Gordon had been talking a lot with the Birmingham police. He was kicked out of the Party.

The Party made Hudson feel like somebody. As a Party organizer he sought to let others feel like somebody—which meant seeing themselves from the perspective of the party. The feeling of mattering is a political consciousness, the practical optimism that accompanies an understanding of how things work, the patterns that connect new machinery in the plant with lynching and imperialism. Knowing how things get done flows into a sense of what it takes to get things done—planning, organization, and solidarity—which feeds back in on and is reinforced in the affective space of the Party. The affective intensity of the Party works on its members, making them stronger together than they were apart as it pushes them to act in collective rather than individual interest. Each feels the inner force of their collective strength as a command or duty. This duty is the collective desire impressing itself in the

45 Ibid., 193.

individual comrade. To the extent that the individual is a comrade, is a communist, doing his or her duty isn't a ceding of desire; it's fidelity to it. Betraying the Party is giving way on desire, and the only thing, Lacan would say, of which one can be guilty.

Hudson's wife, Sophie, didn't support his Party work. "By she not being politically developed, not being developed along with me, it just pulled us apart."[46] Hudson learns in the seventies that while he was busy organizing back in the thirties, going to meetings and traveling, Sophie was having sex with another man.

> That's some of the results of the things I had to pay for and sacrifice for, trying to carry out this one thing that was my duty as a Party person. The Party was a political party, and only the most developed, the most developed and class-conscious, the people who's willing to sacrifice, to take the sacrifice, to make the sacrifice and would be willing to accept the discipline of the Party could be members of the Party.[47]

Hudson did not have to be a member of the Communist Party. In fact, he couldn't even just choose to be a member. He had to be chosen. Not just anyone was invited to join. Being chosen meant that he was somebody and the sacrifices he made for the Party confirmed that the Party was right in its choice. He was, in fact, somebody. He was somebody because of his identification with the ego ideal of the Party. From the perspective of the Party he could see himself as doing things that were important.

Samuel, in his account of British communism in the forties and fifties, is not wrong to imply that the CP embodied a secular Calvinism whereby comrades sought to justify their election. "The willingness to make sacrifices, whether in terms of time, comfort, or money, also seems to have been a litmus test of dedication lower down the Party scale: as in some of the Party's successor

---

46   Ibid., 116.
47   Ibid., 119.

organizations of more recent times, there was a relentless pressure on members to be 'active.'"[48] The pressure was the interior force of their own collectivity. They exerted it on themselves. Every sacrifice strengthened it, generating a sense of the more that needed to be done and that could be done if more sacrifices were made. To be "politically developed," as Hudson would say, was to feel a gap open up in the world between the actual and the possible and to see the world from the perspective of that gap.

Samuel reads a CPGB appeal from 1945 as masochistic in its evocation of specific instances of heroic self-sacrifice, the heads on the blocks and nooses around the neck, the starvation, imprisonment, and deprivation endured with steadfast hope. I take "masochistic" to signal not self-punishment or self-inflicted pain but the reflexivity of collective desire as it works backs upon itself. The Party takes the perspective that the situation of the oppressed and exploited is not necessary. It can be changed, redressed, abolished. To the extent that exploitation continues, enough is not being done to stop it. The Party is the collective that makes the force of this realization into its maxim. There is always an answer to Lenin's question "what is to be done?" And that answer is always too much. Too much is to be done and that excess is the force the Party turns on itself. The enthusiasm and solidarity that infuses the Party's commitment to ongoing political action works back on the comrades as an intensity that relentlessly pushes them from within themselves.

Peggy Dennis, a journalist and organizer for CPUSA (her husband served as General Secretary and went to prison under the Smith Act during the McCarthy era), expresses the interior pull of the Party. Dennis was the daughter of Russian Jewish revolutionaries who immigrated to California shortly before the 1905 revolution. Her mother was disappointed when Dennis got pregnant and married. She had taught her daughter "that personal love

---

48   Samuel, *The Lost World of British Communism*, 55.

was not a sufficient singular purpose in life; that for women, no
less than for men, there must be much more to an enriched life.
Conventional marriage was the deadly trap and motherhood was
the snaplock to that trap door."[49]

In 1929, when Dennis's child was first born, her husband was in
jail. He had been arrested during a street meeting in front of the
marine workers' union hall. The unpermitted street meeting, "a
tumultuous assembly," came about because the hall for a planned
protest was denied at the last minute. The protest was around
the "Red Camp Case." The Young Communist League's children's summer camp had been "raided by a posse of American
Legionnaires led by local sheriffs." The children were moved to
juvenile court. The adults were charged with "conspiracy to teach
the tenets of communism."[50] The raid on the camp and subsequent
arrest of communists and militants was part of an ongoing struggle
in Los Angeles as employers and government viewed demands for
"Jobs or Relief" and "Bread or Wages" as "the harbinger of social
revolution." Dennis writes:

> Meanwhile, I was chafing, restlessly. I nursed our infant, scrubbed
> his diapers and carefully observed the rigid schedules prescribed
> in those days by government pamphlets on infant training. But no
> great surge of mother love enveloped me. Mama adored the baby,
> but carefully left me in sole charge ... Gene came home from his
> meetings or jail absences to stand gazing at his sleeping son. Only I
> was an unfeeling monster; except in the silence of the 2 am feeding.
> With the child pulling at my breast and the exciting world outside
> stilled, the small body in my arms and I did communicate. But with
> the morning came the beat of struggle that passed me by.[51]

---

49   Peggy Dennis, *The Autobiography of an American Communist*, Berkeley: Creative Arts Book Company, 1977, 36.
50   Ibid., 40.
51   Ibid., 41.

Dennis feels the Party as the beat of struggle, the pull of solidarity, a longing for the density and equality that comes through collective action. Self-critically she observes her own chafing against the reduction of her world around an infant's demands even as she links these demands to a rigid, coercive government. She judges herself as monstrous for longing for the excitement of the external world. The struggle that matters is outside, the fight "to feed, clothe, or house the millions thrown on the scrap heap of capitalism."

Confined by "the deadly trap of motherhood," Dennis is pulled in different directions by an interior crowd. She writes that she "was under strict orders from everyone" not to get arrested. "Everyone" included her mother, husband, the Young Communist League, and the Party. A crowd was enjoining her to focus on the baby. She was a nursing mother and had to attend to the newborn. Dennis explains, "Not getting arrested meant staying out of street actions or public meetings. I taught classes, wrote leaflets, served on committees that planned actions for others who would get arrested. I felt guilty."[52] As if feeling the avoidance of arrest as a manifestation of what Canetti calls "the traitor within," she judges herself for betraying her comrades, for a failure of courage and solidarity. Dennis subjectivizes an impossibility, turning the barrier to action into an internal barrier, a personal failing. The perspective from which she judges is the perspective of the Party, even when her comrades have told her to stay home and she is still tirelessly doing the work of the Party. The excess that is the Party perspective, the point from which she sees, is the too-much-ness that both gives Party life its intensity and that works back upon the comrades as a superegoic injunction they cannot but give themselves. The gap between possible and enjoined is the gap of communist desire. The Party sustains that gap.

Diana Johnson, a twenty-year member of CPUSA, observes,

---

52 Ibid., 42.

None of us considered the work we did on the "outside" important. Because, after all, we knew it didn't matter what you did out there. You were living in a bourgeois capitalist world where everything was shit, everything fed a single purpose, so what did it matter what you did. Your real life was with the Party, with your comrades, with things you did in meetings and demonstrations.[53]

All the multiple multitudinous activities of living that seem so necessary from the perspective of capitalism fall to the wayside from the perspective of the Party. They don't matter. The Party ruptures the bourgeois world of profit and loss so that another one can appear. No wonder Dennis felt guilty—she had ceded the desire for communism that made life worth living.

The Actuality of the Communist Party

Describing the Communist Party as an awesome structure for concentrating and harnessing inchoate political emotion, Vivian Gornick employs a metaphor Canetti associates with the crowd: a tidal wave. The tidal wave evokes a sweeping force that cannot be contained or channeled. It exceeds all barriers, engulfing everything it encounters. Like the crowd, the tidal wave is natural and unpredictable, indivisible and unchosen, more a dynamic than a structure or thing. The communist party derives its energy from the crowd as it strives to find ways to let the crowd endure, to enable its intensity to be felt even after the crowd has dispersed. It provides a transferential object that can stand in for the crowd, not representing it but pushing the urges it activates in the direction of equality and justice. With meetings and actions, the party produces assemblies of intensity that press comrades into action, involving them in practices and activities through which they are accountable to one another.

---

53   Gornick, *The Romance of American Communism*, 104.

Another assembly of intensity, one the twentieth-century Communist Party shares with other political forms such as the liberal-legal and the religious state, is the trial.

Richard Wright provides a compelling account of the Chicago Party trial of Ross, one of his comrades in the mid-1930s. On a cold Sunday afternoon, a small group of Chicago Communists concentrates the oppression and suffering of the masses of the world into a South Side meeting hall. As they speak, they flood the hall with the needs and struggles of millions upon millions, a sea of workers, a field of peasants, mountains of the unemployed. They transfer a complex array of anger, failure, and longing one to another, building and reinforcing an awareness of what can be done out of what must be done.

At its start, the trial is informal, like a conversation among neighbors over a common problem. Anyone can speak. Underneath the informality, a deeper structure unfolds. Speakers describe the world situation, presenting facts about the rise of fascism and the Soviet Union's struggle to survive as the world's lone workers' state. The logic of this structure is to provide the correct perspective from which to consider Ross's actions. The perspective is like a law, the law enabling communist desire, setting it apart from the capitalist world by holding up and uniting the experiences of the oppressed. It's a law communists give themselves in order to hold themselves together when everything conspires to pull them apart—police repression, fear and paranoia, individual desire and need. In instances where solidarity is at risk of fraying, a standard of common judgment on matters of common concern is necessary. That standard can only come from the struggles of the exploited masses themselves.

Over the course of several hours, party speakers produce "a vivid picture of mankind under oppression." Once world conditions are clear, different speakers talk about the poverty and suffering on Chicago's South Side, specifically, "its Negro population" and the tasks of the Communist Party. They thereby fuse the "world, the national and the local" into "one overwhelming drama of moral struggle." Everyone in the hall participates in it. No one escapes. All are implicated. In the intensity of the trial, the comrades' voices enthrone "a new sense of reality in the hearts of those present, a sense of man on earth. With the exception of the church and its myths and legends, there was no agency in the world so capable of making men feel the earth and the people upon it as the Communist Party.[54]" For those in the hall, the world is not what it was. Reality itself has been ruptured, impressed upon by the weight of the many.

Wright had not wanted to attend the trial and in attending he had vowed not to participate. Yet the passional dynamics the trial sets free sweep over everyone, Wright included. The impossible demands of the many, for which the Party serves as a transferential object, cannot not be betrayed. Confrontation with this guilt unleashes immense, unbearable anxiety. The force of the uncounted many envelopes the hall, becoming more and more, "a gigantic tension" relentless in its commanding need. Turned in on a single person, it is crushing, not in the sense of the density and equality accompanying the discharge but as a more fundamental exclusion that cuts a person off from political subjectivity altogether.

Wright says that the charges against Ross aren't brought until well into the evening. Those that bring them are not Central Committee members or high-level operatives. They're Ross's own friends. When it comes time for Ross to defend himself, he wilts, trembling and unable to talk. He calls no one to speak in his behalf.

> The hall was as still as death. Guilt was written in every poor of his black skin ... His personality, his sense of himself, had been obliterated. Yet he could not have been so humbled unless he had shared

---

54   Richard Wright, *Later Works: Black Boy (American Hunger)*, *The Outsider*, New York: The Library of America, 1991, 354.

and accepted the vision that had crushed him, the common vision that bound us all together.[55]

Ross is guilty because his desire is so great, so magnified and intense, that it cannot not be betrayed. The superegoic force of the Party concentrates collective desire into an impossible, unshakeable desire for collectivity.

Ross confesses. He accepts his guilt, recounts his errors, outlines plans to reform. Wright makes it clear that

> Ross had not been duped; he had been awakened. It was not a fear of the Communist Party that had made him confess, but a fear of the punishment that he would exact of himself that made him tell of his wrong-doings. The Communists had talked to him until they had given him new eyes with which to see his own crime ... He was one with all the members there, regardless of race or color; his heart was theirs and their hearts were his; and when a man reaches that state of kinship with others, that degree of oneness, or when a trial has made him kin after he has been sundered from them by wrongdoing, then he must rise and say, out of a sense of the deepest morality in the world: "I'm guilty. Forgive me."[56]

A ritual assembly for sundering becomes an intense experience of belonging. Even as it concentrates the enormity of global struggle and oppression, the Party provides a structure for relief from that pressure. It gives meaning to suffering. It supplies a vehicle for its redress. Something can be done, but it can only be done together. To insist on one's own way is to do nothing at all because against all of capitalism individual efforts are worthless. In fact, it's even worse: to insist on one's own way is to support capitalism, racism, imperialism, and fascism, to join them in their war against the people. Alone, Ross would be left isolated in his confrontation

---

55   Ibid., 355.
56   Ibid., 356.

with the impossible demands of the people. With his comrades, he could experience the power of these demands in forcing change.

As Wright depicts it, Ross's trial has echoes of Socrates' trial before the Athenians. Charges are brought by friends. The accused does not call on anyone to speak in his behalf. The real trial is before history: Who is actually guilty here? The Athenians? The Party? The difference is that unlike Plato, Wright expresses the ambivalence of collective power. The Chicago comrades were wrong, living blind and limited lives "truncated and impoverished by the oppression they had suffered long before they had ever heard of communism." But a truth appears even through their "corrupted consciousness." The experience of equality across raced division, the discharge Canetti associates with the crowd, cuts through the spectacle of misguided banishment. Seeing with the Party, viewing himself from the same perspective as his accusers, Ross is no Socrates. Where Plato isolates the moral perspective in the figure of Socrates and judges the Athenians from that vantage point, Wright maintains fidelity to the perspective opened by the Party even as it errs, even as it fails to apply this perspective to itself.

Ross wouldn't be going to jail, of course. The Party is a voluntary organization. But the choice goes in both directions: the Party that identifies those made out of "special stuff" also determines who is lacking. It can cut people out, cut them off from the epic struggle of the oppressed, push them out of the crowd and into isolation and anxiety. With language surprisingly evocative of Lacan, Wright confesses that he couldn't escape the feeling that Ross "enjoyed" the trial. "For him, this was perhaps the highlight of an otherwise bleak existence."[57] The trial focused the immense affective apparatus of the Party onto Ross. The enthusiasm and commitment of millions was activated because of him, or at least in those moments he could feel as if it was, he could feel that his

---

57   Ibid., 351.

actions and choices were of world-historical significance. The feeling couldn't endure. He was to be expelled, after all. But at that moment he was conjoined with the world like no other.

Wright describes the trial he witnesses as a spectacle of glory and horror. The ugliness of the Party is the other side of its service as a transferential object, its capacity to make the crowd felt after its dissipation. An engulfing crowd may be frightening. The release from the limits of the everyday may be too much. An apparatus for mobilizing emotional longing and generating affective attachment in the service of struggle, the Party wields power by exerting the force of the collective on its members. It wields this within the members themselves, as their own collective desire for collectivity. How else would the Party maintain a gap within its capitalist setting? Glory and horror are the same arrangement of intensity from two perspectives, the profound feeling of collective strength and the fear such strength can generate. Wright invokes the words of the *Internationale*, "Arise, you pris'ners of salvation!"

The trial exposes the gap of desire as perhaps no other element of Party infrastructure can. Desire is never desire for a specific obtainable object—desire cannot be satisfied. Lacan's famous dictum is that "desire is the desire of the Other." Desire opens up as a gap in the Other, as what the Other lacks. At times desire can become so overwhelming that it becomes concentrated in a singular place, such as a person imagined as a unified individual. The gap is filled in, the dream of justice truncated and distorted. Misdirected, thwarted back in on itself, desire becomes obscene. It pushes beyond need, beyond demand, into the destructive insistence of the drive. The desire for justice turns in on itself in the enjoyment of power.

The actuality of the Communist Party exceeds its errors and betrayals. It encompasses the hopes for justice and aspirations for equality invested in it. To reduce the Party to its excesses fails to recognize its indispensable capacity to generate practical optimism and collective strength. Such a reduction likewise reduces the world, contracting possibility into what can be done instead of forcing the impossibility of what must be done. The Communist Party enlarged the world. Expanding the crowd's egalitarian discharge so that it can endure as the emancipatory push of the people, the party increases the crowd's effects. It gives the crowd its meaning and takes this meaning as its own. The party continues the moment of belonging, intensifying and expanding it in solidary purpose.

"For justice thunders condemnation"

How do and can we imagine political change under the conditions of communicative capitalism? Is political change just aggregated personal transformation, communism as viral outbreak or meme-effect, #fullcommunism? Do we think that autonomous zones of freedom and equality will emerge like so many mushrooms out of the dregs left behind in capital flight and the shrinking of state social provisioning? Or do we optimistically look to democracy, expecting (all evidence to the contrary) that communism, or even upgraded social democracy, will arise out of electoral politics? All these fantasies imagine that political change can come about without political struggle. Each pushes away the fact of antagonism, division, and class struggle as if late neoliberalism were not already characterized by extreme inequality, violence, and exploitation, as if the ruling class did not already use military force, police force, legal force, and illegal force to maintain its position. Politics is a struggle over power. Capital uses every resource—state, non-state, interstate—to advance its position. A Left that refuses to organize itself in recognition of this fact will never be able to combat it.

In communicative capitalism, individual acts of resistance, subversion, cultural production, and opinion expression, no matter how courageous, are easily absorbed into the circulatory content of global personal media networks. Alone, they don't amplify; they can't endure. They are easily forgotten as new content rushes into and through our feeds. We indulge in fantasies of the freedom of our expression, our critical edge and wit, disavowing the way such individuated freedom is the form of collective incapacity. Against states and alliances wielded in the service of capital as a class, diverse and separate struggles are so many isolated resistances, refusals to undertake the political work of pulling together in organized, strategic, long-term struggle. The constant churn of demands on our *awareness* disperses our efforts and attention. What the Left should be doing is coordinating, consolidating, and linking its efforts so that they can amplify each other. We don't need multiple, different campaigns. We need an organized struggle against capitalism capable of operating along multiple issues in diverse locations.

Crowds push back. From the perspective of the party, we see them as the insistent people. Fidelity to the insistence of the egalitarian discharge demands that we build the infrastructure capable of maintaining the gap of their desire. The more powerful the affective infrastructure we create, the more we will feel its force, interiorizing the perspective of the many into the ego-ideal that affirms our practices and activities and pushes us to do more than we think we can. Radical pluralists and participatory democrats sometimes imply that there can be a left politics without judgment, condemnation, exclusion, and discipline. Denying the way that collective power works back on those who generate it, they suggest we can have the benefits of collectivity without its effects. But "working back" is an inextricable dimension of collectivity's capacity to cut through the self-interest of individual needs and produce enduring bonds of solidarity. Collective activities always have effects in excess of their immediate goals. Rather than fearing these effects, rather than remaining stuck in the fantasy that an individual can change the world, and rather than remaining so gripped by fears of power that we fantasize a politics that can abolish it, we should confront the force of collectivity directly and take responsibility for generating it and using it. The party capable of building an affective infrastructure that can cut through the barriers of capitalist expectation will err. It is not, cannot be, and should not be believed to be infallible. Sometimes it may turn its immense energies on itself. If we can't bear it, we aren't the Left, the communists, we need.

Anyone who is unwilling to talk about the party should not talk about political transformation.

Conclusion

For over thirty years, the party has been extracted from the aspirations and accomplishments it enabled. Even as "dogma" has been uniformly qualified with "party," dispersed yet ubiquitous left dogmatism has turned the so-called obsolescence of the party form into the primary tenet of its catechism. Every other mode of political association may be revised, renewed, rethought, reimagined—except for the communist party. It's time to put this nursery tale aside and take up the challenge of actively constructing the political collectivity with the will and capacity to bring an egalitarian world into being. The party holds open the space for the emergence of such a will. It doesn't prefigure a new world, but impresses upon us the gap between the world we have and the world we desire.

The innovation of Marxism was linking the political battle for socialism to workers' economic struggles. Social democratic parties sought to expand democratic rights and use parliamentary processes to win political power for the working class. But bourgeois, liberal, and parliamentary democracy stood in the way of working-class power. As the political form of capitalist order, liberal democracy secures this order through principles and processes designed to individualize, disperse, and displace class

antagonism. Encountering the incompatibility between capitalism and the people, revolutionary socialist and communist parties
extended the political struggle beyond its electoral confines and
pursued a wider range of tactics. Social democracy, nearly completely dismantled by neoliberalism and now confined to a certain
fantasy of Sweden, proceeds by way of managing class antagonism. It denies the incompatibility of capitalism and the people
as it finds ways to secure the compliance of the working class. In
contrast, the promise of communism is the abolition of class and
capitalism. The communist party pursues this abolition as a political struggle.

For Marx, "proletariat" names capitalism's self-creation of what
destroys it. This "what" that destroys capitalism is a collective
subject, a force no longer dispersed in individual and local acts
of smashing, sabotage, and disruption, but concentrated in solidarity. Of course, economic destruction alone is insufficient for
the abolition of capitalism. The normal operation of the capitalist
system is characterized by "uncertainty and instability," "a series
of periods of moderate activity, prosperity, over-production,
crisis and stagnation."[1] Contemporary capitalism has refined its
capacity for wealth destruction: over thirty-four trillion dollars of
market value was lost in the financial crisis of 2008. In the course
of the recession that followed, the rich got richer and the poor got
poorer: the top 1 percent captured 121 percent of the income gains
made between 2009 and 2011.[2] Not only was the 1 percent better
able to weather the crisis than the rest of us, but it was also able
to increase its share. So it's not just economic destruction that's
at stake. It's bringing to an end the capitalist cycle of creative
destructive—the destruction of destruction. And *this* political

1   Karl Marx, *Capital*, abridged edition, ed. David McLellan, Oxford:
Oxford University Press, 1995, 275.
2   Bonnie Kavoussi, "Top One Percent Captured 121 Percent of
All Income Gains During Recovery's First Years: Study," *Huffington Post*,
February 2, 2013.

destruction is brought to an end by the proletariat. It is not the task of the working class organized as *workers*. They are already organized as workers in the factory, which enables them to become conscious of their material conditions and the need to combine into unions. The abolition of capitalism depends on the organization of the proletariat as a *party*, a solidary political association that cuts across workplace, sector, region, and nation. The working class *as a class* is implicated in the success or stability of capitalism. Capitalism configures the working class's struggles with the bourgeoisie. In contrast, the party takes as *its* horizon capitalism's supercession in communism. For Marx, the party is necessary because class struggle is not simply economic struggle. It's political struggle.

Consider the famous passage from *The German Ideology*: "We call communism the *real* movement which abolishes the present state of affairs." How should we understand this? Not as immediate insurrection or as prefiguration but rather as *the expansion of voluntary cooperation*. I say this because Marx explains that "the conditions of this movement [we call communism] result from premises now in existence." The premises he is discussing involve the multiplication of productive force through the cooperation of different individuals as this cooperation is determined by the division of labor and not as an effect of people's own united power. Abolishing determination by the division of labor is a matter of *self-conscious collective action* wherein cooperation isn't forced, isn't out of our control, but is instead willed commonly. Cooperation and concentration become self-conscious and willed rather than unconscious and determined. Collective desire for collectivity becomes stronger than the individual preferences determined by capitalism. As the movement which abolishes the present state of affairs, communism expands collective voluntary cooperation, the power of many exerted back upon itself. As an organization premised on solidarity, the party holds open a political space for the production of a common political will, a will irreducible to the capitalist conditions in which the majority of people find themselves forced to sell their labor power. Where work is obligatory, membership in the party (like participation in the movement) is voluntary, the willed formation of united power. Among its members, the party *replaces* competition with solidarity.

In a 2006 interview, Alain Badiou notes how, for Marx, "proletariat" is an identity that is a non-identity or an identity beyond all identities. In this sense, "proletariat" is "generic" rather than particular. Today, neither "proletariat" nor "working class" functions in the way that it did for Marx. "Proletariat" is less open to multiple particular contents. It doesn't feel generic. Political struggles fought along raced and sexed axes of domination have made the liberation of the working class no longer appear as the liberation of humanity as such. Badiou concludes that the generic function of the working class is likely "saturated." Moreover, he writes, "We cannot substitute a mere collection of identities for the saturated generic identity of the working class. I think we have to find the political determination that integrates the identities, the principles of which are beyond identity. The great difficulty is to do that without something like the working class."[3]

In the course of working-class political struggles in the twentieth century, such a generic identity did already appear: the people. Georg Lukács credits Lenin's characterization of the Russian Revolution for transforming the idea of the people into a generic revolutionary identity: "The vague and abstract concept of 'the people' had to be rejected, but only so that a revolutionary, discriminating concept of 'the people'—*the revolutionary alliance of the oppressed*—could develop from a concrete understanding of the conditions of proletarian revolution."[4] Mao and Third World people's struggles further this characterization of the generic

---

3   Alain Badiou, "The Saturated Generic Identity of the Working Class," interview, *Chto Delat* 15, chtodelat.org.

4   Georg Lukács, *Lenin: A Study on the Unity of His Thought*, trans. Nicholas Jacobs, London: Verso, 2009, 22–3.

subject of communism. The "people" thus has a powerful legacy as a name for that political subject which strives for emancipatory egalitarianism.

Nevertheless, various ideologies speak in the people's name. Constituting a subject in whose name it can speak is ideology's primary function. Like communism, populism and democracy—sometimes filling themselves in as nations or races—claim the people as their subject. Communism is therefore not unique in its claim of the people as its subject. Its uniqueness consists in its presentation of the people as a divided subject. In contrast with populist emphases on the imaginary unity of the people and democratic reductions of the people to the ways in which they are given (outcomes of elections and polls, categories of demographic identity, media expressions of public and audience), communism presumes that the people are split—bourgeoisie and proletariat, oppressors and oppressed, few and many. Rather than some kind of organic community, society arises around a fundamental antagonism. "Class conflict" is the Marxist name for this antagonism. Lenin's "revolutionary, discriminating concept of 'the people'" asserts this division within the people. Communists recognize the people in and as that division. Instead of asserting unity, communists assert the gap.

The party is a form for this assertion. As Badiou emphasizes, Marx's rendering of the proletariat as that generic group the liberation of which is a universal liberation is an "extraordinary invention." Badiou notes that the history of this invention "was not so much the history of the generic group, of the working class as such, but rather the history of the representation of this generic group in a political organization: it was the history of the party."[5] The problem today is thus not only the inability of "working class" to name a generic identity. It is also and relatedly a collapse of confidence in the party as a political organization capable of representing this identity.

---

5   Badiou interview.

The saturation of the generic political identity of the working class became manifest in the multiplication of political identities. From 1968's intoxication with the politics of the beautiful moment, through the eighties' embrace of civil society and the politics of society's own self-targeting, into the "activistism" and "movementism" of the alter-globalization movement, the Left has claimed as a victory the symptom of its defeat: the erosion of working-class political power and the accompanying decay of its political parties. Defeated on the political plane—the name of this defeat is "neoliberalism"—the Left shifted to the social and cultural terrain. It fragmented into issues and identities. On some issues and with respect to some identities, there were political advances. At the same time, in jettisoning the struggle for political power, the Left lost the capacity to defend and advance the interests of the people. Economic inequality increased. Commitment to social provisioning—education, public housing, welfare, social services—collapsed.

Identity as an operator for a politics is now itself fully saturated. Symptoms of this saturation include the reduction of the space of change to the individual, the circulation of the momentary outrage in the affective networks of communicative capitalism, the practices of calling out and shaming that undermine solidarity, and the contradictory and destructive attachment to national and ethnic specificity. They include as well the complex mutual policing of who can claim what identity under what conditions and what authorizes such a claim.

When identity is all that is left, hanging on to it makes a kind of sense. The reality of the struggle to survive becomes the basis of an identity imagined as dignified because it has to produce itself from itself. Attachment to identity is pathological, nevertheless. It enchains us to collective failure, turning us ever inward as it holds back the advance of a politics capable of abolishing the current system and producing another one. Unfettered capitalism and the repressive state constitute real limits to cultural critique and social experimentation: exploitation, dispossession, incapacitation, incarceration, proletarianization, extermination. Perhaps the most striking symptom of the saturation of identity is thus the economic rupturing of identity categories, that is to say, the emergence of identities as themselves sites of class struggle. In 2014 and 2015, riots in Ferguson, Missouri and Baltimore, Maryland pushed this struggle into mainstream discussions in the US.

Since Badiou's 2006 interview, there has been renewed left interest in the party form. This interest results from the impasses encountered by the crowds and riots in the latter half of the decade. In cities all over the world, hundreds and thousands of people took to the streets and parks in a resounding "no" to the array of policies installed by the capitalist class to protect its interests. These protests signaled a new militancy and determination on behalf of opponents of austerity, precarity, state violence, and the neoliberal mantra of cuts, cuts, cuts. Then the protests ended. The crowds went home. Sometimes they made no demands. Other times they made impossible demands. And still other times they asserted truths both obvious and painful in the urgency of their assertion: Black Lives Matter.

The press of these crowds presents an alternative to Badiou's "identity that is beyond identity." The alternative is movement itself, the force of many where they don't belong, the intensity of the egalitarian discharge. Marx and Engels link socialism not simply to the identity of the working class. They link it to working-class *movement*. In the nineteenth century, worker uprisings were pushing forward, coming together, and breaking out, disrupting capital processes of value extraction. This active movement incited Marx and Engels (and other nineteenth-century socialists and anarchists) to see in proletarian struggle more than demands for shorter working days, safer working conditions, and higher wages. They saw these struggles as the political process of the subject of communism. We can repeat their innovation not by looking for a generic identity (a search that already preoccupied Marcuse and returns in another form in Hardt's and Negri's multitude) but by emphasizing movement. In place of the saturation of identity, we should turn to the process of movement, recognizing the people as the subject of that process. The very fact of the active aggregation of crowds, the rise of political opposition and militancy, directs us to a collective desire for collectivity.

The crowds and riots of the last decade have shown us the many coming to sense their collective power, the capacity of number to inscribe a gap in the expected. Debt, immiseration, policing, and dispossession have incited those proletarianized under communicative capitalism to revolt. Global demonstrations have also brought to the fore the crowd's limitation. Its powers are destructive, creative, unpredictable, contagious, and temporary. The strength that comes with the indeterminacy of the crowd's message is a weakness when the crowd disperses. The crowd lacks capacities of endurance, implementation, and execution. Without mediation, that is to say, absent a transferential relation to another space, it doesn't know what it desires. The crowd doesn't have a politics. It is the opportunity for a politics.

Some on the Left like to repeat Trotsky's warning about substitutionism: the party substitutes itself for the class, the party organization substitutes itself for the party, the central committee substitutes itself for the party organization, and the leader substitutes him or herself for the central committee. They present horizontalism as an alternative that can avoid these problems. Over the past few decades, we've encountered the limits of horizontalism as it fails to scale, endure, or replace capitalist state power. Far from solving a problem of left political organization, horizontalism is the name of a problem. Substitutionism, though, is not. The gaps substitutionism flags are the space of the subject. Neither the crowd nor the party is the people. The people is the gap between them. Political capacity always involves delegation, transfer, and division of labor. Not everyone can do everything.

The very idea of a politics of everyone is a debilitating fantasy that denies the constitutive feature of the political: division goes all the way down.

The crowd enables us to build a theory of the communist party as a synthesis or movement party. Such a party is neither the movements' vanguard nor instrument. It is a form of organized political association that holds open the space from which the crowd can see itself (and be seen) as the people. The communist party is the party faithful to the crowd's egalitarian discharge. It doesn't represent the movements. It transfers their egalitarian intensity from the particular to the universal. The communist party finds the people in the crowd.

Badiou treats the subject-effect as a knot of four concepts: anxiety, courage, justice, and superego.[6] Canetti renders the crowd as a knot of four elements: growth, direction, equality, and density. In the party, the two knots intertwine as concentration, endurance, fidelity, and transference. The party does not represent the people as a collective subject. The party responds to this subject. Hence, it concentrates the subject-effects of anxiety, courage, justice, and superego into a transferential site from which they can work back on the collectivity. The party thus responds to the subject by recognizing it in the crowd and thereby making the crowd into something more than it is. It gives the crowd a history, letting its egalitarian moment endure in the subjective process of people's struggle.

The party occupies the place of division opened up by the crowd. It minds the breach, maintaining it as the gap of desire of the people as a collective political subject. Without the perspective of the party, multiple resistances blur into the menu of choices offered up by capitalism, so many lifestyle opportunities available for individual diversion and satisfaction. The legacy of people's struggle and crowd event are then carried only by university, culture, and

---

6 Alain Badiou, *Theory of the Subject*, trans. Bruno Bosteels, London: Continuum, 2009, 278.

momentary organizations, subjected to the demands of capitalism and deactivated as living resource. The gap of desire is sublimated into the circuit of drive. Without the party, there is no body capable of remembering, learning, and responding. Instead, dispersed individuals, absorbed in communicative capitalism and buffeted by competition, offer multitudes of opinions, suggestions, strategies, and critiques, the collective capable of response present only as an absent addressee. Providing the perspective from which the people can be seen and the space of its desire maintained, the party enables the people to appear in the rupture of the crowd event.

The need for the party stems from the fact that the people are split between the ways we are given, positioned, within capitalism. We are situated within a field that tells us who we are and what we can be, that establishes the matrix of our desire (Žižek's definition of ideology), but that represses the truth of this field in class struggle. Capitalism strives to separate and individuate us, to instill in us the conviction that self-interest matters above all else, that freedom results from individual choices made for individual goals. It blocks from view the systemic determination of choices and outcomes, not to mention the power of collectives in rupturing these systems. When leftists assume the individualism of the dominant ideology, reiterating its emphases on uniqueness and trying to cultivate a politics out of individuated decisions, we undermine our own best impulses to collectivity and egalitarianism. The party asserts the truth of our division. It speaks from the position of this truth and offers another field of possibilities.[7] In opposition to capitalist desire, it opens up a terrain for the desire of a collective political subject. The party doesn't know everything. It provides a form for the knowledge we gain through experience and analyze with our eyes on the communist horizon. Such a party works to extend the collective desire for collectivity after the crowds go home. When it enables the crowd to endure as a rupture

---

7   Slavoj Žižek, *Revolution at the Gates*, London: Verso, 2002, 185–89.

with capitalism (rather than a continuation of or contribution to it) and when it directs the crowd-feeling toward its own constitutive equality, the communist party can hold open the gap for the people as the collective subject of politics.

At different points over the past hundred years, the party has attempted to abolish capitalism and usher in communism in various ways—revolutionary seizure of the state, participation in parliamentary processes, training of cadres and education of masses in order to be prepared when the time comes, support and development of people's cultures and capacities. The communist party has never been simply an organization aimed at achieving a set of economic reforms aimed at restraining capitalism's extremes and providing workers with welfare guarantees. That this is the case is clear when we note the justified sense of betrayal voiced by communists when their parties compromise and retreat. They feel betrayed because the party gave way on communist desire, the very desire its wide array of organizations hold open, the desire underpinning solidarity and comradeship.

The array of classic party organizations—newspapers, literary magazines, clubs, trade associations, sports teams, schools, theater troupes, women's groups, industry-focused councils, to mention but a few—reminds us that communist parties have always exceeded the binary of state and factory, actively engaging on multiple social, cultural, and economic fronts as elements of one struggle. As a red thread throughout the movements of the oppressed, communists connected divergent issues and experiences, enlarging them into a common world and mobilizing the collective desire for collectivity. Unlike standard parliamentary parties claiming representative authority, the work of the communist party involves substantialization, concentration, extension, and transference. Hence communist values of comradeship, solidarity, enthusiasm, and courage support the building of a political organization capable of responding in a revolutionary situation and enduring in less propitious times. Through the party, members push each other into modes of being and acting that appeared impossible before, when they were alone against capital and its state.

The problem the Left encounters today is less a matter of organizational details than it is of solidary political will. As the will emerges, people will figure out the structure in light of the challenges we face in specific contexts, challenges such as expanding militant pressure in ways that inspire and educate cadres while at the same time straining the resources of the state and breaking the confidence of the financial sector; abolishing private property and the capitalist banking system while advancing international coordination in an uneven environment; and increasing popular support of and developing a program for common management of production, health, transportation, communication, food, housing, and education all in the setting of a changing climate, to mention but a few. Responding to these variable challenges generates new knowledge that can be integrated and shared. There is no reason to assume that every component of the party must have the same structure. A global alliance of the radical Left, or, better, a new party of communists, can be knit together from the concentrated forces of already existing groups: militants skilled at direct action, artists adept with symbols and slogans, parties experienced at organizing, issue groups knowledgeable about specific areas of concern, mutual aid networks addressing basic needs. Such a concentration would let people who want to be engaged in radical politics but aren't sure what to do have a place to go, a place to start.

More importantly, such a concentration would amplify specific and local achievements as collective victories in the broader struggle for communism. At the most minimal level, if we are to have a chance of reformatting the basic conditions under which we live and work, we have to share a name in common as a fundamental marker of division. If not, our names will be given to us by capital, which will seek to fragment and distract us. In the movements of the last few years, we've seen growing recognition of the power and need for a name in common as a marker of division—We Are All Khaled Said, Occupy, We Are Seneca Lake. A frustrating dimension of localized political work is the way that it seems not to register (particularly if it occurs outside of major metropolitan areas). When local and issue politics are connected via a common name, however, successes in one area advance the struggle as a whole. Separate actions become themselves plus all the others. They instill enthusiasm and inspire imitation. They provide a sense of directionality and movement: which way is the struggle going? Simply multiplying fragmented, local actions isn't enough—they have to be felt as more than what any one of them can be in isolation, indications of the enduring struggle of the people.

In addition to a common name, we have to build solidarity, to extend the bonds of commitment beyond local ties and small networks. Without solidarity, a common will cannot emerge. Immiseration, precarity, defeat, and betrayal as well as ongoing patterns of sexism, racism, and homophobia have made us deeply suspicious. One way a party helps deal with this is with explicit criteria for membership and expectations for members. It supplements personal relations with relations to an organization, holding members accountable to expectations. Relations between comrades overlay and replace particularized relations anchored in individual preference. Practices of regular reporting help install these expectations. Another way a party builds solidarity is by acknowledging different skills and expertise, providing training and education, and delegating tasks. Developing and respecting one another's skills and knowledge is essential if we are to form ourselves into a political force capable of taking on and replacing global capitalism. In practice, this suggests the utility of working groups in multiple locales and issue areas, groups with enough autonomy to be responsive and enough integration via practices of reporting to formulate and carry out a common purpose. It points as well to the active development of the organizational and political capacities crucial to multi-scalar communist self-governance.

Left anti-party dogma mobilizes anti-authoritarian convictions. Yet this mobilization has resulted in the intensified authoritarianism of global capitalism. Today authoritarianism is less that of centralized state power than it is of power decentralized, dispersed, and extended via private contracts, interbank and interagency cooperation, and the extensive network of treaties, agreements, and provisions enabling capital flow and global trade. National states act as the police force protecting the global capitalist class. We encounter the fragmentation, dissolution, and decomposition of some elements of the state, and the concentration and intermeshing of other elements of states and markets, as in finance, security, and media. Capital as a class has worked to smash the bureaucratic state machine for us, to convince us that it is useless, even as it strengthens parts of it for its own ends. For too long, left politics in the US, UK, and EU has mirrored neoliberal economics, urging decentralization, flexibility, and innovation. Even the neoliberal push to privatize is reflected in left politics: not only do we hear ad infinitum that the personal is political, but the micro-politics of self-transformation and DIY takes the place of building and occupying institutions with duration. In this vein, some on the Left have abandoned social change entirely. Wary of "totalizing visions," they cede society and the state to a capitalist class that acts as a global political class intent on extending its reach into and strengthening its hold over our lives and futures.

The crowd has pushed this Left aside. Rising up in opposition to the decentralized authoritarianisms of interconnected states and markets, it has occupied, blockaded, and rioted. And it has come up against the limits of its capacity to give social struggles political form. The challenge we face is becoming the Left the crowd deserves, a Left that, faithful to the crowd's egalitarian discharge, works to make it endure. A Left that speaks the language of radical change but refuses its forms is no Left at all. It's the means by which political energy and conviction is displaced into styles and practices that make us feel good by making us feel radical. To advance, we need to organize. We need to be a party for the people in the crowd.

Index